Essays in Economic Management

Essays in Economic Management

SIR ALEC CAIRNCROSS

London · George Allen & Unwin Ltd

RUSKIN HOUSE   MUSEUM STREET

© George Allen & Unwin Ltd 1971

ISBN 0 04 330177 0 Cased
     0 04 330178 9 Paper

Printed in Great Britain
in 10 point Times Roman
by Billing & Sons Limited
Guildford and London

Contents

Preface

The papers included in this volume, with the exception of the last, were prepared as addresses for delivery to widely different audiences over the past few years. They were meant to be heard rather than read and to be immediately intelligible by non-specialists rather than studied at leisure by professional economists. From the layman's point of view this may be a positive advantage. I hope that it does not also destroy their claim on the attention of economists even when, as with the Wicksell Lectures of 1960, they have been washed over and partly submerged by later floods of controversy. In preparing the text for publication I have limited myself to a few cuts and additions so as to avoid unnecessary repetition and preserve coherence of argument.

The papers largely reflect my activities (more perhaps than my interests) in Whitehall and the continuous education that I received, first on the Radcliffe Committee and later from my colleagues in the Treasury. Among the latter I am especially indebted to Sir Bryan Hopkin, Mr. Atkinson and Mr. Godley. I have also had the advantage of a number of valuable suggestions from Dr. John Corina.

But since few things are more destructive of leisure and private life than the preparation of addresses my major obligation is to my wife, who has had to suffer the consequences.

A.C.

1. Government and Industry[1]

In May 1962 John F. Kennedy had a talk with André Malraux. 'In the nineteenth century,' Malraux said, 'the ostensible issue within the European states was the monarchy versus the republic. But the real issue was capitalism versus the proletariat. In the twentieth century the ostensible issue is capitalism versus the proletariat. But the world has moved on. What is the real issue now?' 'The real issue today,' Kennedy replied, 'is the management of industrial society – a problem not of ideology but of administration.'[2]

The Management of Industrial Society

The phrase 'the management of industrial society' summarizes a comparatively new conception of the functions of government and of the relationship between government and industry. It is not so long ago that people thought economic management unnecessary and saw little scope for government intervention of any kind. The economic system was thought to be largely self-regulating and more likely to prosper under free competition than through the exertions of government departments. The state was neither a large employer nor a large spender (except in war-time) nor did it feel obliged to raise large sums of taxation. Within living memory the rate of income tax was a shilling or less and the total amount of government revenue including local rates was under £200 million.

Since these happy far-off days (from the taxpayer's point of view at least) the role of the government has steadily expanded as it has assumed more and more control, taken an increasing proportion of the working population on its pay-roll, and enormously extended the range of its current spending and capital investment. At the height of the Second World War the government absorbed half the annual output of this country and regulated with the utmost

[1] Dallas Lecture to the Glasgow Chamber of Commerce, 23 March, 1970.
[2] A. M. Schlesinger Jr, *A Thousand Days: John F. Kennedy in the White House* (Boston, 1965), p. 644 quoted by Herbert Stein, *The Fiscal Revolution in America*, p. 506.

9

stringency the freedom of individual consumers and producers. No one could spend as he chose or work as he chose. That was twenty-five years ago. But even today the state employs one man in four, accounts for half the total capital investment and exercises very wide powers over the whole economic life of the country.

It is natural in these circumstances for the average business man to ask himself where the process will stop and what place there will eventually be for private industry as he understands it. It is also natural for him to ask for some *rationale* of government intervention when he is not conscious as he was in war-time of any over-riding purpose to justify it. If he was reared on the social philosophy of the nineteenth century he may also ask whether there are not certain dangers to individual liberty in the growing power of the state and whether, even if the economic objectives involved in the management of industrial society are altogether admirable, it is not permissible to cherish some continuing suspicion of the political power exercised by the management. He may be less ready than John F. Kennedy to regard the problem as one of administration to the exclusion of ideology.

Political Dangers of Government Control

Some of you may remember, for example, the qualms expressed in a famous passage by John Stuart Mill, himself a professed socialist:

'If the roads, the railways, the banks, the insurance offices, the great joint stock companies, the universities, and the public charities, were all of them branches of the government; if, in addition, the municipal corporations and local boards, with all that now devolves on them, became departments of the central administration; if the employees of all these different enterprises were appointed and paid by the government, and looked to the government for every rise in life; not all the freedom of the press and popular constitution of the legislature would make this or any other country free otherwise than in name. And the evil would be greater, the more efficiently and scientifically the administrative machinery was constructed – the more skilful the arrangements for obtaining the best qualified hands and heads with which to work it.'[1]

There is a curiously old-fashioned ring about that passage, whatever one thinks of the fears of a new despotism which it expresses. I shall not be much concerned with those fears, which the experience

[1] J. S. Mill, *On Liberty* (London 1859), pp. 198–9, quoted by Lord Robbins, *The Evolution of Modern Economic Theory*, pp. 161–2.

of the past twenty years has not so far borne out. My theme must be a more limited one for reasons of time and professional competence. But I cannot, of course, overlook the political aspects of economic management any more than the manager of a large industrial concern can overlook the political aspects of his own powers and responsibilities.

What makes the passage that I have quoted so old-fashioned is that government control over the private sector is now far more complex than Mill and his contemporaries (including Karl Marx) could have imagined. What alarmed Mill – just as it may still alarm some of you – was the threat of a major extension of the public sector through nationalization. But nationalization has long ceased to be a live issue, whatever the outcome of the controversy over Clause 4. You all remember the battle over steel during the post-war years. Some of you may even recall Mr Cube. But what in fact has happened? With very minor reservations the nationalized sector is no bigger than it was twenty years ago. The steel industry has been nationalized, de-nationalized and re-nationalized. There is now to be a National Ports Authority. Some individual firms like Fairfields have come under public ownership. But no new major industry has been nationalized since 1950 and the only candidate in the Labour Party's programme a few years ago was water supply.

It is also increasingly difficult to tell the difference between a large undertaking in the private sector and a large undertaking in the public sector. The same kind of speeches are made by Lord Stokes as by Lord Robens – perhaps Lord Robens is rather more forceful in his criticisms of government policy. The same kind of pronouncements on pricing and investment policy are made by the National Board for Prices and Incomes, when it is called upon to make pronouncements, whatever the status of the industry concerned. Much the same regard to commercial advantage and much the same technique of investment appraisal are held up to approval in the government White Papers on the nationalized industries as in Neddy's reports or in the textbooks used by the business schools.

Semi-Nationalization

The real issue, in fact, is not nationalization but semi-nationalization: not whether there should be a private sector but how private the private sector can hope to be. The issue of ownership has been largely superseded by the much more subtle issue of control. Why should the government bother about ownership when it already

11

gets half the profits in corporation tax and most of the other half in income tax and surtax on dividends? The government may have good reasons for wanting control but for this purpose ownership is not indispensable. Indeed, governments have sometimes found that ownership may diminish, not increase control (you may re-member the dictum: 'if you want freedom from government control, get yourself nationalized'). But the government does not need un-limited control and there are good reasons why it should have no more than is necessary. There is a limit to the advantage that central control confers on a Government and this is as true in economics as in politics. Beyond that limit control is self-defeating because it squeezes out initiative and discretion and all the scope for the incessant urge to innovate that lies behind economic growth and development.

I doubt whether there is anything to be gained by discussing the relations between government and industry in terms of a sharp antithesis between the public and the private sector. It is more fruitful to ask what forms of government intervention are involved in managing the whole economy and what types and degrees of control this may require. In pursuing this question I propose to leave almost entirely on one side those aspects of government intervention which are summed up in the phrase 'the welfare state'. I shall not be much concerned with what is done by the state to promote greater equality, to ensure a minimum standard of living for all, or to improve the quality of life by providing health, educa-tion and other services. My concern will be rather with those forms of intervention that are prompted by dissatisfaction with the out-come of market forces, and may involve limitations on the discretion of individual enterprises in their dealings with one another, with their customers, or with their workers.

Government Intervention and the Limitations of Market Forces

Economists have been very much alive for at least two centuries to the virtues of market forces in bringing about an allocation of resources in keeping with consumer preferences and in maintaining a competitive drive towards greater efficiency. But they have also been diligent in cataloguing the weaknesses of these forces and the ways in which administrative action might be used to supplement or short-circuit them. They have sometimes been so carried away by the scope for improving the price mechanism by administrative measures that they have hardly stopped to look at things the other

12

way round, and ask whether the use of administrative devices is not also subject to inescapable weaknesses.

The Aims of Economic Management

The inadequacies of market forces can be said from one point of view to provide the main justification for government intervention. For example, it can be argued that without such intervention the economy might be subject to an intolerable or unnecessary degree of inequality; the level of activity might be too low or too unstable; the distribution of economic activity between different parts of the country (or between different industries) might be unsatisfactory; and the rate of economic growth might be too low. But one might well ask: Why put things so negatively? Once it is accepted that the government's job is one of economic management is it not sufficient to ask to what ends the economy is to be managed? The answer can then be put in positive terms: to reduce inequality within acceptable limits: to maintain a high and stable level of activity: to pursue an active regional policy: and to seek to accelerate economic growth.

Put this way round there is no reference to market forces: no presumption that government action should be stigmatized as 'interference' and kept to a minimum. The emphasis is on management, government behaviour being looked at through the rosier spectacles with which managerial activities in business and business-like forms of organization are normally viewed.

Merely to list some of the objectives of economic management does not justify government intervention in pursuit of those objectives. Justification must depend on how things work out in practice. Governments constantly profess what they cannot perform; and it does not make it easier to bear the whips and scorns of bureaucracy if all that is offered in justification is an incantation to the purposes of economic management. We should never hesitate to ask what evidence there is that the activities of government *do* reduce inequality, maintain full employment, improve the location of industry and increase the rate of economic growth. It is by no means self-evident that the greater the state's involvement in economic life the more it succeeds in all its various aims.

FULL EMPLOYMENT AND GOVERNMENT CONTROL

Any doubts of this kind are probably least valid in relation to full employment, strange as that conclusion would have seemed a generation ago. It has been the success of governments in avoiding unem-

13

ployment since the War that has done most to establish the idea of a managed economy. I suspect that governments deserve less of the credit for this than they are given; that some at least of the improvement reflects good luck rather than good guidance; and that we are too apt to draw comparisons with the inter-war years without recalling the period before the First World War when there was little unemployment and no one imagined that this was the government's doing. However that may be, the acceptance of full employment as an aim of policy is enough to justify a much higher degree of central control over the economy.

As originally conceived by Keynes this control did not extend beyond general measures designed to stabilize demand and purchasing power without detailed interference by the government in industry. In its most primitive form, going back before the First World War, the idea of demand management involved no more than efforts by the government to defer public works in times of boom and accelerate them in times of slump. Later, emphasis was put to monetary policy and gradually shifted in the course of the 1930s to fiscal policy.

No one nowadays would question the importance of greater economic stability or the use of monetary and fiscal policy for this purpose. But as time has gone on it has become increasingly clear that there is a lot more to demand management than was once imagined. It is all very well to think of it in terms of pulling this lever or that – increasing the budget surplus or the money supply, for example – with no intention of helping one firm or industry more than another. But all government action is directional in practice however non-discriminatory in intention.

Demand Management is Necessarily Directional

Take, for example, monetary policy. Limiting bank credit is bound to have more drastic effects on small firms than large if only because small firms have fewer alternative sources of finance. A restrictive monetary policy will also hit the building industry harder than others – especially those parts of it that are engaged in erecting dwelling-houses. There is no escape from these consequences of tight money, as a glance at the British or US figures of bankruptcies and housing starts will show. Similarly, if hire-purchase measures are taken, the industries supplying consumer durables like cars or television sets are bound to suffer.

But, of course, monetary policy is itself an increasingly complex thing that can have different effects depending on the instruments

14

that are brought into play. Import deposits, for example, are essentially a monetary device and have marked characteristics of their own in their impact on industry. There is also a whole range of interest rates, some of which are directly under the government's control, while for others pressure can be brought to delay an increase or make it smaller.

Precisely because any particular business is affected by monetary measures, firms have to keep asking themselves not just whether the government will act and whether it will use monetary measures but *what* monetary measures it will take. It becomes more difficult as time goes on to draw a clear line between broad measures operating on the level of purchasing power and specific interventions affecting an identifiable group of firms. The professedly unintentional outcome of demand management may come very close to direct discrimination against particular businesses.

All this applies with even more force to fiscal measures. Manipulating the size of the budget surplus so as to withdraw or add to total purchasing power sounds splendidly impersonal. But it must involve changes in specific tax rates or in specific items of expenditure; and these are inevitably far from neutral in their industrial impact. Few firms are likely to be indifferent whether an extra £100 million is raised by increasing SET or corporation tax or, alternatively, by cutting expenditure on roads or investment grants.

Demand management itself has also become less general with the passage of time. There is now a greater effort to adapt the pattern of demand to local variations in pressure, so that demand is restrained where there are labour shortages or bottle necks in capacity and expanded where there is unemployed labour and surplus capacity. I do not say that these efforts are conspicuously successful but only that the objectives of policy are now, in this respect, a little more ambitious and call for policy instruments with a narrower and more precise impact. For example, if the building industry is working flat out when other industries are not, it may be legitimate to use building licensing or take action to delay the placing of contracts for public building. Quite independently of this consideration demand management implies that public expenditure should be controlled with an eye to the total load on resources over time.

The Balance of Payments, Inflation and Government Intervention

Full employment can be jeopardized by balance of payments difficulties on the one hand and the threat of inflation on the other. These

15

are so often cited in justification of government measures that one might suppose that the whole purpose of economic management was to preserve external balance and avoid inflation. But referring to a deficit in the balance of payments is just another way of saying 'borrowing' or 'becoming less liquid'; and what is undesirable about borrowing is simply that it can't go on indefinitely. The danger is of an abrupt stop when finance runs out and of a consequent loss of control over the domestic level of activity. In other words, the objective that is threatened or prejudiced is full employment. Action taken to protect or improve the balance of payments has to be justified, therefore, primarily in terms of an expected gain in economic stability. The fact that the action in question is nearly always calculated to produce *in*stability, in the short run at least, may explain why it has been customary to justify it in less paradoxical terms.

Similarly, fear of inflation may be the immediate cause of government action but is not really by itself the ultimate justification. After all, some countries have lived with inflation for the past hundred years and survived; and in some the rate has far exceeded anything experienced in this country. But we all know that inflation affects different groups of people very unequally and that any useful effects it may have on production tend to be short-lived. It is primarily this unequal incidence on the aged and the poor, unredeemed by positive advantages to economic growth, that makes inflation undesirable.

Balance of payments difficulties may force the government into all kinds of policy contortions in order to avoid or delay a change in the exchange rate; or, if the rate is allowed to float, business will have to adapt its behaviour to the fluctuations in the exchange market as well as to the vagaries of government policy – for the government is most unlikely to stay out of the market or refrain from devising policies to take some of the strain off the rate.

We have had plenty of experience in this country of the variety of ways in which governments struggle with an obstinate balance of payments deficit and in the process submit industry to one shock after another. We have seen an import surcharge imposed and removed, an export rebate imposed and removed, and import deposits imposed and belatedly removed. There have been times when one needed only to suggest that this or that industry would save imports for the government to come forward with assistance which it would never have been willing to offer to an industry less ingenious in its pretexts. This kind of behaviour is not peculiar to

16

the British government; but we might at least hope to learn from experience. Apart from comparatively straightforward methods of protection, like higher duties on fuel oil or bans on the import of coal, we have had more complex methods involving support for agriculture at the taxpayer's expense or doctoring the price of electricity to make aluminium-smelting more competitive. Efforts to improve the capital account have also led to increasingly severe restrictions on foreign investment, first outside then inside the sterling area, sometimes by statutory control, sometimes by so-called voluntary agreement, sometimes by varying the tax system.

I say nothing in criticism of measures of this kind. They all seem to me legitimate devices of a kind that other countries may yet use in similar straits. I merely draw attention to the inconvenience common to such expedients, that they make it difficult for industry to know what will happen next. They also make it difficult for any government falling back on them to win popularity (or even, perhaps, influence people). But essentially this arises not out of the expedients used so much as from the policies giving rise to the deficit in the balance of payments.

Then there are the forms of intervention prompted by fear of inflation. This has led in recent years to efforts to stabilize prices through direct action on individual price and wage settlements. We all know that, like the balance of payments, inflation presents a real problem and that it is no good pretending that there is some simple solution to it, such as throwing more people out of work. We also know that an excessive pressure of demand makes inflation inevitable. Whether it does any good to admonish everybody who charges a higher price or demands a higher wage is doubtful even if legal backing is given to the admonition. Talk will not keep prices and wages from rising. But nobody quite knows what, if anything, *would* do the trick. So one ought not to make too much fun of the efforts that have been made in the past. What *is* a legitimate source of grievance is to be picked on and put in the stocks for doing what others do with impunity; or, still more, to be ordered to do two mutually inconsistent things by different public authorities and reduced to the frame of mind of the father in Aesop who ended up carrying his ass.

The kinds of intervention which I have been discussing so far have been motivated by concern for economic stability or, if you prefer, full employment. They add up to a pretty imposing list, and so long as governments are dedicated to full employment I doubt whether the list will get shorter. It is true that there are some wild men from Chicago who regard much of the paraphernalia of state control as superfluous. They think that floating rates of exchange, control over the supply of money, and some other fairly limited regulatory devices would allow governments to dispense with the kind of intervention which I have been describing. In my judgment they are mistaken. I am inclined to murmur with Hilaire Belloc's doctors:

'There is no cure for this disease'.

ECONOMIC GROWTH AND GOVERNMENT CONTROL

But even if I am wrong, the second main objective of post-war economic policy – the desire to accelerate growth – makes just as strongly for extensive intervention in industry. Governments have always flattered themselves that they were in a position to speed up economic development. Sometimes, as in new countries, they have done so by borrowing extensively for the purpose of opening up new territory, building railways and providing facilities necessary for industrial growth. Sometimes they have made use of tariffs and subsidies to assist particular industries or to accelerate the whole process of industrialization. There is nothing new about the state's participation in economic life to help this industry or that, either on a long-term footing or to overcome short-term difficulties. The Victorians were sceptical whether this kind of activity on the part of the state did any good; but even they never wholly abandoned it. Nowadays, much of it takes place under the banner of the balance of payments and will no doubt continue to do so even if the balance of payments remains in substantial surplus. Much of it also takes place in response to pressure from the industries seeking protection or in financial difficulties. When there is money to be had there is rarely any question of governments forcing their attention on un-willing clients.

The Pervasive Influence of the State

The new feature of the situation in Britain is that the state is no longer content to limit its participation to the offer of assistance on an industry-wide basis, but has become increasingly involved in the affairs of nearly all the major industries and often of the larger under-takings within them. In addition to the £600 million which it pays out in investment grants, and the hundreds of millions which it expends in other forms of industrial assistance, it is in contact with industry from day to day over a very wide front.

18

There are, for example, all the contacts between the nationalized industries and the industries in the private sector, whether as customers or suppliers, collaborators or competitors. There are all the contacts between the central government and major industries like agriculture, computers, machine tools, aircraft manufacture, ship-building, and so on, where the industry, although not nominally under government control, is very much at the mercy of government decisions. Then there are the host of government agencies, using up most of the letters of the alphabet, from which comes a never-ending flow of rhetoric, recommendations and rulings of all kinds on the affairs of private industry.

If there is a *rationale* for all this I suppose that most of it has to be explained in terms other than enthusiasm for growth, since it is by no means easy to see in what way it is calculated to accelerate growth, still less how it actually contributes to growth. There was a time when it would have been possible to argue that at least the anti-monopoly activities of government were calculated to promote economic growth, since they were intended to encourage competition and competition was traditionally the agency through which more rapid growth was attained. But with the superior wisdom of the twentieth century we have been taught to look on economic growth as the outcome of technological development, and on large industrial units with monopolistic powers as an indispensable prerequisite to rapid technological change. So it is no longer fashionable to plead for more competition. The new fashion is to call for re-structuring, which being interpreted seems to mean mergers. This has taken the place of the old battle-cry of rationalization and the still older one of nationalization.

Unfortunately, the new fashion seems to rest largely on assertion. There is no inevitable virtue in size, however it is brought about and for whatever purposes. The evidence that mergers increase industrial efficiency or that the major innovations come from the biggest firms is far from convincing; the need to bring into existence larger business units in order to withstand foreign competition also needs more demonstration than it has had.

There has always been a strong case for industrial reorganization, however described, where production was divided between a number of relatively weak units, none of them sufficiently specialized and yet none of them carrying a full enough range to dominate the market. Even in such circumstances reorganization has frequently been accomplished without government encouragement or participation. As a rule, governments have to ask what they can contribute that

19

would be beyond the reach of any large holding company. Very often, if existing units are not sufficiently large it may be because there is nothing except the government itself standing in the way of a merger between them. Presumably it was not altogether accident that led to such a flood of mergers as soon as the government made it clear that it was prepared to acquiesce in a process of 're-structuring'. In spite of the frequency with which the Industrial Reorganization Corporation is brought into discussion of mergers, only a minute fraction of the total number of mergers taking place can be attributed to the activities of the IRC.

Similarly, it is open to any large undertaking (in the public sector as well as in the private sector) to back its own opinion whenever it thinks that additional expenditure would allow it to market remunerative new developments. It is natural to ask why the state has to come in at all. Is it that it judges that there is insufficient capital in the enterprises seeking to expand? Is it that it thinks poorly of British industrial management and wants to make up for this by taking action from the outside? Is it that it wishes to re-deploy the excessive number of scientists and technologists working in government research establishments without actually dismissing them?

The State and Technological Innovation

These questions bring me to the role of government in technological development. Let me emphasize that I am talking about technological development and not about science, which is a very different thing. Governments like to picture themselves as the patrons of science and as the sponsors of technological development. The first of these roles is one that they cannot escape under conditions in which science teaching and research is paid for almost exclusively by the government. They are also bound to take an interest in technological development for their own purposes, often regardless of cost. But the problems faced by private businesses in a commercial environment are very different from the problems faced in government research establishments. That such establishments have made important discoveries no one would deny. But these discoveries have rarely been of immediate economic significance except perhaps where there is a commercial background (as in the GPO) to the research work.

Neither government research establishments nor the public sector as a whole can take much of the credit for the technological improvements upon which the rise in living standards over the past half century rests. The attempt of governments to pose as the promoters of technological advance or as the architects of a technological community is largely spoof. Their repeated efforts to associate themselves with growth industries or with the most advanced industrial projects have nearly always proved disastrous. They take it far too easily for granted that they can speed up innovation by the provision of additional funds and manpower.

It is important to appreciate that there is no accepted theory of economic growth such as guides the state in its efforts to secure and maintain full employment. It is possible to devise a single strategy for stabilizing the economy because there is sufficient agreement among economists about the lines of action that would be conducive to this end. But it is doubtful whether this applies to economic growth. There are a great many things that could be listed about which there would be unlikely to be any disagreement. But when it comes to devising a strategy some people are inclined to lay emphasis on investment, some on education and training, some on incentives of various kinds, some on social attitudes, and so on.

Over-eagerness to Grow

It is inevitable, therefore, that the state should present the impression, in the present state of knowledge, of feeling its way, following different fashions at different times, and entertaining an exaggerated idea of its own importance. The public has been taught to think that the rate of economic growth is within the discretion of the government, and that if it is less in this country than it is in France, Germany or Japan this reflects some failing on the part of the government. I believe that the direct influence of governments on economic growth is relatively modest and that the common belief to the contrary in this country has been actually pernicious, tempting governments into policies which had the very reverse of the effects for which they were designed. It has been the eagerness to grow through expansionist policies that has too often been the undoing of the British economy. We have suffered on the national scale from a 'get-rich-quick' mentality that is still with us.

If the objects of government policy are as I have described them, what then ought to be the relationship between industry and government? It cannot be a simple one-way relationship in which all the powers are enjoyed by the government and industry is merely expected to conform to government intentions.

21

THE GOVERNMENT-INDUSTRY RELATIONSHIP

First of all, there is no escape from the facts of life of a mixed economy. It is an illusion to suppose that governments can somehow tread so gently that their elephantine pressure on the economy will injure nobody's corns. It is equally an illusion to think that everything can be left to anonymous market forces. Government policy is part of the environment within which business is carried on. It is an environment in which acts of government and market forces have no separate existence since the market is itself shaped by government policy and expectations of government policy, while government action is based on the calculated strength of market forces. In such an environment there can be no anonymity or neutrality in government intervention: whatever form intervention takes some firms will be affected more than others and, given the weight of the government in the economy, all will be affected in one way or another.

But this does not justify capricious interference in the affairs of individual businesses where no general interest is at stake. Nor does it justify an extension of government control in every instance where a good case can be made for it. We have to weigh on the other side the narrowing of the scope for individual initiative and choice that such an extension is only too likely to involve. Even at the level of economics, the size of the government machine is not a matter of indifference. Economic progress does not usually derive from government regulation, however necessary some forms of regulation may be. Wherever there is a choice to be made, the government should seek to exercise control in ways that do least damage to individual freedom, making use of mechanisms that operate *predominantly* to the public advantage, and seeking to improve the ways in which these mechanisms function rather than to replace them by a heavier layer of bureaucracy.

It was (and perhaps still is) the virtue of competition that it acts simultaneously as an engine of economic progress and efficiency, an ally of the small and the young, and a protector of freedom of choice. It does not always act that way. But that is not a reason for seeking to supersede it. On the contrary, it is a reason for investigating whether the imperfections could be overcome in a different framework or whether it would be better to endure them in preference to, say, outright nationalization. Similarly, it is obviously better to have a mechanism such as budget surpluses and deficits that can be used to put pressure on business as a whole, rather than rely on a

22

series of ineffective edicts prescribing the action to be taken by a long list of individual firms.

Secondly, government policy must be clearly laid down and open to debate. It would be disastrous if intervention were allowed to become arbitrary, casual, unpredictable, even unannounced, leaving no firm framework for business decisions. Whatever the policy, business has a right to know what the government is trying to do and why.

Private industry should be told what is expected of it. No doubt it is hard enough for the government to work out what it wants the public sector to do. It is no less hard to lay down ground rules for the behaviour expected in the private sector. But some attempt ought to be made. We are likely to have a private sector for a very long time and the rules ought to recognize that fact. I am thinking of rules about pricing, profits and investment behaviour such as have been considered in the past by the Monopolies Commission and the National Board for Prices and Incomes, or have found expression in some of the White Papers on Incomes Policy.

Next, there is a question of exchange of information. The government is keenly interested in what private industry intends to do and industry is anxious that the government should come clean on its own plans. This is not as easy for either party as it sounds (or was made to sound when everybody was talking about planning). Governments have usually good reasons for keeping quiet about what they are thinking of doing or are just about to do, or may have to do if things take an unexpected turn. The same is true also of individual business enterprises which equally may profess to be about to do one thing and turn out afterwards to have done another.

For this reason it is a mistake to start out with naive expectations about what national planning will accomplish. The days when the FBI agitated for national planning so as to put an end to stop-go have been almost forgotten; but the lesson that national planning may bring on a crisis instead of averting it has not, I hope, been lost on its industrial advocates.

We ought surely to aim at something more modest. So long as it is not petrified by fears of devaluation or default, the government should be able to indicate in broad terms the changes which it foresees over the next few years in the public sector, and the implications that this is likely to have for the private sector. From this, industry could make its own deductions and might at the same time supply tentative indications of its own intentions or expectations. This would not add up to a plan but to an exchange of information,

23

where that information was not just guess-work but rested on commitments of varying lengths and varying degrees of firmness.

The Private Sector is the Private Sector

Finally, it should be accepted that the private sector is the private sector and for that reason cannot be expected to behave as if it were simultaneously part of the public sector. Private undertakings may be invited by the government to have regard to the public interest but they cannot be dragooned into doing so; and although most large firms are anxious to be thought public-spirited they will not submit themselves indefinitely to a code of conduct that is not accepted by their competitors. It is a mistake to pretend that it is the business of private industry to interpret the government's mind for it. The government must lay down the rules by reference to which it proposes to exercise control and leave private industry to get on with the job, unless it thinks that it can achieve better results through outright state ownership.

It is precisely because it usually does not think so that a large part of the economy remains, and is likely to continue to remain, in private hands. Some decentralization of control is inevitable because control becomes progressively more imperfect the more it is centralized. The importance of this proposition is increasingly appreciated within the public sector. But it is the same proposition which in the last resort justifies the continued existence of the private sector. To seek to improve the management of the economy by first accepting the decentralization implicit in the existence of the private sector, and then seeking to lay down rules that extinguish every undesirable feature in the behaviour of independent business units, is to try to embrace simultaneously the two opposite principles of decentralization and centralization. Where you allow discretion you must be prepared to swallow the consequences even if they include mistakes, waste, restrictive practices and other forms of economic sin. As every large firm knows, the great difficulty is to find the point beyond which a further centralization of control is counter-productive. No one can lay down from first principles exactly where that point will be found. But it is everyday experience that there is such a point; and the great secret of efficient management of a national economy as of an industrial concern is to recognise that fact.

CONCLUSION

I close with two concluding reflections.

24

The involvement of the state in industrial affairs is now too complex to be reducible to a few general principles: there are usually too many principles on either side of the question to yield an unambiguous answer. This is, of course, not unusual in a managerial situation. Managing the economy means taking decisions that are rarely simple matters of right or wrong: they are far more often matters of right *and* wrong, more or less, excess of benefit over cost. The most one can usually hope for is to choose the lesser evil and acquiesce in the expedient.

Individual businesses can never hope for complete freedom of action (if such a thing is conceivable). They are bound to be subject to pressure from many directions: competitors, customers, workers, the press, the public. Their relationship with the state seems destined to become increasingly like that of a branch factory in a large conglomerate business. Competition may still go on: interventions from above may be limited and erratic. But all the time business becomes more public and less private. If any of you think that you can work out for yourselves how a conglomerate ought to be organized and what future there is for freedom of initiative within it I wish you joy. You are braver than I have been.

2. The Managed Economy[1]

If not Capitalism, What?

Some years after the war I had a discussion with a young Russian in Moscow about the capitalist system and the changes it was undergoing. I dwelt on the inadequacy of a term like 'capitalism' as a description of the many different economic systems in Western countries, on the high proportion of profits in Britain that went to the government in tax, on the controls imposed on private industry and its dependence on government policy, on the growth of the public sector and a number of other developments in the role of the state since the days of Marx. My friend was unimpressed. If 'capitalism' was not an adequate description of the British economic system, perhaps I could suggest an alternative label? I must not jib at labels since one word was enough to describe all mankind, *viz.* humanity. In desperation I suggested 'the welfare state'. This was unconvincing for a different reason – my inability to think of an adequate translation into French, the language in which our discussion took place.

If a similar challenge were issued to me now, I should probably take refuge in a different label – 'the managed economy' – and feel the same sense of discomfort derived in equal measure from the inadequacy of the phrase and from the lack of a satisfactory French equivalent. But it is, I suppose, the fashionable answer to the question: 'What have we got in place of capitalism?' just as the fashionable answer used to be: 'the welfare state'. Of course, there remains a school of thought which is not content with either label and is dedicated to economic planning. My Russian friend, for example, would still be likely to argue that 'the planned economy', however it may be evolving, is fundamentally different from anything that we have ever had here.

It is worth reflecting a little on these labels and what they signify. The welfare state is fundamentally egalitarian in concept. It grew out of the emergence to political power of the working class, the

[1] Presidential Address delivered to Section F (Economics) at the Exeter Meeting of the British Association, on 4 September, 1969.

26

idea of a common minimum below which living standards should not be allowed to fall, and the need to make collective provision for health, education and old age. It rested heavily on taxation as an instrument for the finance of such collective provision as well as for the redistribution of income or at least for the concentration of fiscal burdens on the broadest shoulders. But it did not, as such, imply any particular system of state control or ownership of industry.

The first objective of a managed economy, on the other hand, was originally stability. It grew out of the heavy unemployment experienced between the wars, the ideas associated with the name of Keynes, and the greater weight of government activity in relation to the size of economy. In course of time other objectives have been brought under the heading of management, notably faster growth, a more even distribution of income, and a wider diffusion of economic development over the country. But the initial emphasis was on the need to maintain uninterrupted full employment.

Management and Planning

It is possible to argue that there is no essential difference between a managed economy and a planned economy, and that planning is simply a rather inflexible form of management. This would mean that we now live in a planned economy without the courage to describe it correctly. But there are, I believe, important differences in emphasis which amount to a difference in principle.

For example, the keynote of planning is certainly not stabilization. There may have been Keynesian overtones to planning even in the thirties but historically it was associated with war-time control or with the efforts of the USSR to industrialize her economy – the antithesis, surely, of stabilization and for that matter a better example of an economy out of control than of one in course of planned development. Nobody would pretend today that those who decided on the first Five-Year Plan foresaw all its consequences and deliberately accepted the sacrifices involved. As so often in later years 'planning' was little more than camouflage for an investment boom and the inflation and controls that went with it.

It is arguable that the difference between planning and management lies in concern for growth rather than stability. Even this is not quite true, or at least not in Britain. For example, in three early and influential discussions of planning by British economists, Professor Meade's 'Planning and the Price Mechanism', Sir Arthur Lewis's 'Principles of Economic Planning' and Evan Durbin's 'The

27

Politics of Democratic Socialism', there is either no mention of economic growth or it is largely disregarded or thought to be not particularly affected by planning.[1] But none of these writers was a believer in long-term planning *à la russe* and they could more accurately be listed as supporters of economic management. Where the argument for planning is in dynamic terms it generally does rest explicitly or implicitly on the view that growth will benefit.

The fact is that those who think of planning as something different from management usually have a longer time-dimension in mind. They are thinking not of what can be done to influence economic activity or the distribution of income over the next year or two but how to bring about a transformation of the economy either in the form of industrialization or of some drastic structural change that would have continuing effects on efficiency and output. Second, they are thinking more of direct intervention to influence production than of attempts to manage demand without detailed intervention. And finally, they usually have in mind a system of tighter central control or at least a closer linkage between the plans of individual enterprises and the plans of central government.

Broadly speaking, therefore, the situation in Britain is that management is linked with the ideas of stabilization, the short-run and control of aggregate demand, while planning is associated with growth, the long-run and structural change in industry and elsewhere.

The Origins of Management

A generation or so ago no one would have claimed that the economy was managed. Public debate hardly touched on the question how the economy should be run even when the existing system was being denounced root and branch. The defenders of the system, although willing to consider detailed improvements calling for government intervention, regarded it as fundamentally self-regulating. The more radical critics, attacking the private ownership of the means of production, gave little thought to the organization of the economy under socialism: what was to follow capitalism could be worked out after it had disappeared. Within the government it is hardly too much to say that economic policy in its modern sense of 'policy towards the economy as a whole' did not exist. There was little or no discussion of measures to promote economic stability or growth;

[1] Devons, E. (1965): 'Planning and Economic Growth', *Scott. J. polit. Econ.*, 12, p. 105.

most of the Budget – in the first two decades of this century at least – went in paying for wars – past, present and future; and the major issues of a macro-economic character tended to centre round the distribution of income.

The term 'management' came in with the ideas of Keynes for currency management. It was already in common use in this context in the early twenties and when the *Treatise on Money* appeared in 1930 it not only featured in the heading of Book VII – 'The Management of Money' – but in the title to each of the eight ensuing chapters. When pre-war economists spoke of 'management' they were thinking almost exclusively of monetary policy and of the greater stability of prices and activity that might follow the sagacious use of monetary policy. When the argument broadened to include the use of budgetary measures for the same purpose, it tended to be conducted in terms of 'management of demand'. The emphasis was essentially on the regulation of demand, and on the elimination of cyclical fluctuations. Management was thus seen as concerned primarily with stabilization policy and with the short-run, since stability is by definition a short-term affair. The management of the economy in this sense inevitably rested with the Treasury because the Budget, monetary policy and other instruments of demand management were already the responsibility of the Treasury.

The Growth of the Public Sector

But management, as now practised, had other and quite different origins. The emergence of the welfare state enormously extended the scope of government and brought about not only a large increase in public expenditure on health, education and housing, but also an equally formidable increase in social security benefits, pensions, family allowances, grants and transfer payments of all kinds. At the same time, the nationalization of a large sector of industry brought formally under public control what previously had been part of the private sector in form if rarely in substance.

The growth of the public sector in these various ways posed problems of management of a more immediate kind. In a country where one man in four is employed by a public authority, public investment exceeds private investment, and the combined expenditure of all public authorities (including the capital expenditure of the nationalized industries) is over half the size of the national income, there are plenty of management problems to be faced that are at least akin to those facing private industry, although there are also

29

many important differences. Apart from this, the total impact of public authorities on the economy is now too compelling to be neglected in the calculations of private industry and must itself be the subject of management.

Indeed, we have moved from a world in which the government played a very subordinate part in economic life to one in which the pronouncements and actions of government are of overwhelming importance to a large sector of industry. The government is expected to take responsibility for almost everything – particularly if things go wrong – and to be correspondingly ready with statements of policy and well-conceived measures on every imaginable occasion.

There is a further reason for the emergence of the managed economy: the growth of big business. The bigger the average size of business unit the more is organized and planned rather than left to the operation of market forces. The possibility of a parallel growth in government planning is suggested almost inevitably by successful business planning; and co-ordination of the activities of large businesses becomes itself an object of government policy.

Management and Control

In considering the problems of a managed economy it is well to begin by recognizing that management is by no means the same as control. In the strict sense of the term no economy is or can be controlled. This is true even of a command economy just as it is true also of an army; once instructions issued at the centre filter down the line they have to be reinterpreted in the face of local circumstances. In a system like ours where the government has to rely heavily on persuasion, co-operation, and incentives of all kinds it does not even have the illusion of control: the system is specifically devised to respond to pressure from below.

Every economic system is, therefore, a mixture of organization and free enterprise. All that is open to debate is the strength of the mixture; the optimum degree of organization and centralized control. At one extreme is complete *laissez-faire* with no one taking conscious thought for the operation of the system and the price mechanism operating as a co-ordinating agency to link together the plans of individual producers and consumers. At the opposite extreme is a war economy, organized for one purpose and one only – to win the war; or a planned economy of the Eastern European type where organization for purposes determined by government requires individual preferences to be subordinated although not, of course, ignored.

30

The system that we now have lies between these extremes. It is not a planned economy in the sense that it sets out to supersede the planning of privately organized firms by obliging them to conform to aims of policy arrived at independently by the state. But neither is it one in which the activities of firms are left to be dictated exclusively by market forces reflecting the preferences of individual producers and consumers without regard to wider social purposes and longer-term goals. Business has to keep one eye on the government and what it will do next. The government sets the framework within which businesses operate; but it still leaves consumer demand as the principal motor force governing economic activity.

The Consumer in a Managed Economy

The market forces that operate have to be rigged by the government since it cannot afford to allow the workings of the economic system to reflect exclusively – and imperfectly – the spending habits of individuals in their private capacity, with all the instability, inequality and short-sightedness that this would imply. But the government cannot carry the process too far without making the system insensitive to consumer preferences and wasteful in its use of the resources necessary to meet these preferences. It cannot set itself up as the sole judge of what should eventually reach the market or of the terms on which consumers should be asked to choose between conflicting products. Management does not mean control over the consumer and an end to uncertainty about what he will want: it does not make foresight redundant or extinguish the risk of error. On the contrary, it means a greater alertness both to immediate wants as well as long-run needs, an acceptance of the fact of change from whatever source it springs, and an effort to turn change to advantage by preparing for it in advance.

It is not true, therefore – as has sometimes been argued – that management means giving the consumer an anaesthetic to prevent him from upsetting somebody's apple-cart. Organizations, large and small, at the national level and at the level of the individual firm, have to reckon with market forces that are only partially under control. Moreover, the kind of business organization that ultimately triumphs is not settled by direct government action but is also shaped by market forces through a competitive struggle between alternative structures. The more the government is willing to let the consumer influence what is produced, the more it must devolve on business units capable of translating market demand,

31

actual or potential, into effective supply. Where buying decisions are dispersed and independent a greater degree of discretion must be allowed to those in touch with the buyers, and a correspondingly looser degree of control and organization is appropriate. Except to the extent that monopolistic influences operate in the opposite direction, market forces are a powerful decentralizing agency.

At the same time, there are many important needs that cannot be satisfied through the market and positively require centralized decisions, as well as other needs that can be met more cheaply or effectively by collective effort than by private initiative. The margin between collective provision and reliance on the free operation of the market is necessarily a shifting one, depending on the willingness of the public to be taxed, the efficiency of public authorities, the threat to the welfare of others in what one man does or neglects to do, and so on. The balance depends also on popular aspirations since the more firmly the government is expected to promote greater equality, faster growth, a more stable economy, and so on, the more centralized the control necessary to secure those objectives.

The Degree of Control

The degree of control exerted in the management of the economy is also affected by international factors. We are all familiar with the tendency for balance of payments difficulties to dictate the way in which the economy is managed. These difficulties are the more likely to arise, the more dependent a country is on foreign trade and finance. The greater is that dependence, the stronger is the compulsion to accept less ambitious policy objectives, to give priority to the accumulation of adequate reserves of liquid assets and to working for more effective management of the international economy.

Management does not imply an equal degree of control over decisions of all kinds. There are some matters where a few key decisions have to be taken centrally while in many others it is plainly impossible to do more than influence decisions taken farther down. This is as true of management of the economy as of other kinds of management. For example, the level of aggregate demand depends closely on governmental decisions while the level of demand for individual products (or, still more, individual brands of the same product) is not so easily controlled; and as a rule it is less neccesary – indeed less desirable – that the government should seek to control it. Similarly, the government has a greater stake in the division of output between consumption and investment than in the balance

32

between different constituents of the two; and the first lends itself more readily than the second to a decision at the centre.

This reflection brings us back to the link between management and stabilization policy. The objective of economic stability is one which can normally be secured by a comparatively small number of far-reaching decisions by a central authority, all of them within the competence of the authority and calculated to leave subordinate authorities and enterprises free of detailed control. For this purpose it is enough to have a limited staff of economists, furnished with general indices of economic activity and performance, and to operate through budgetary and monetary controls supplemented from time to time by intervention of a more direct kind. On the other hand, the object of more rapid economic growth normally requires a very large number of decisions by the enterprises within which growth takes place and may not easily be influenced for the better by decisions lying within the competence of a central authority. The links between centrally-taken decisions and economic growth are not fully understood by economists or anyone else, and are certainly open to dispute. At the same time, the links between decisions at the point of production or sale and economic growth are usually very obvious if by economic growth is meant an improvement in efficiency and productivity. It may be possible to influence these decisions from the centre only by a series of specific measures involving step-by-step negotiations and consultations on an extensive scale; and in the process some of the thrust that normal competitive processes would provide may be sacrificed so that the net gain in productivity is minimal. Some aims of policy, therefore, lend themselves less readily to centralized decision-taking than others; or, to put it more bluntly, are less likely to be achieved by government action.

Organizational factors in Management

I turn next to consider some of the problems posed for economic analysis by management of the economy. I propose to concentrate on some of the facts of life about management which economists too often overlook and to leave on one side those mysteries about the economy and how it really works which are – or should be – the main preoccupation of economists. In making this distinction, however, I should like to emphasize that the activities of government are themselves part of what we call 'the economy' and that it is increasingly difficult to offer useful explanations of the working of the economy without simultaneously trying to explain the working of its management.

C

First of all, I should like to stress the importance of purely organizational factors which are common to management at the national level and at the level of the individual enterprise. Thereafter I shall turn to other aspects of management where the similarity is either less striking or non-existent.

Organizational factors are rarely analysed in economic theory, which developed largely in terms of an analysis of market forces generated by bargains between individual consumers and producers. For this purpose consumers and producers alike were treated as independent, self-consistent units and their behaviour was studied almost entirely from outside, apart from assumptions about motivation derived from introspection. Even the theory of the firm, which might be expected to consider what goes on inside business enterprises, was often developed as a series of mathematical theorems with only the most perfunctory references to management. Organization, if mentioned at all, tended to be confined to those parts of economic theory which dealt with cartels and monopolistic influences reflecting the links between one firm and another; that is, the external, not the internal, relations of the firm.

It was only when economists had to face such questions as: 'What sets a limit to the growth of the firm?' that they found themselves obliged to stress organizational factors. As a rule this question was raised in discussion of the relative merits and survival value of big and small firms. But it is obviously a question that goes to the roots of the whole economic system. For if economists are unable to find in their own discipline of thought any reason why firms cease to grow or any grounds for expecting efficiency to suffer when firms unite, they equally lose the power to find economic arguments against the unification of each industry in turn under public ownership and so in the end unification of the entire industry of the country.

In recent years economists have found themselves taking an increasing interest in management and the domestic problems of running a business and have become more conscious of elements in decision-taking that were previously neglected. Although decision-taking in industry is by no means the same as in government, there are common elements and so far as this is so economists have already begun to address themselves to the problems of the managed economy that flow from the organizational side of management.

Management and Change

Both in industry and in government, management is largely pre-
34

occupied with change: sometimes of its own making, more often arising elsewhere. It is the principal function of management to control and direct change and to develop instruments for this purpose. Whether in reacting to change or in promoting it, however, management has to contend with its own human limitations, notably ignorance, uncertainty and shortage of time.

Limitations to Management

Any manager finds himself obliged to take decisions on the basis of limited information and in a state of uncertainty about most of the relevant variables. He has a great many decisions to take, often at short notice and under considerable pressure of time. He has also to overcome human friction of all kinds: to consult and inform his colleagues, maintain morale among his subordinates, and keep under review the existing arrangements by which his work is linked with that of others. If any economist proposes to analyse his business and put forward useful theories on the basis of this analysis, he cannot disregard these facts even if he finds it necessary, for some purposes, to abstract from them. Similarly, any economist analysing the management of the economy cannot disregard the simple facts of government decision-taking. Decisions do not exist in abstraction from the machinery by which they are arrived at: the machinery imposes its own limitations on the decisions.

(a) *Ignorance* Take, for example, the fact of ignorance. No management or government could ever imagine what it would be like to be in a state of perfect information. When a government acts it cannot possibly know with any real confidence what the situation is. It is bound to be out-of-date. Probably it has to rely on second-hand information. This is particularly true of a government using general economic information made up mainly of aggregates and averages compiled at one remove from the primary data. Once quantitative information has been boiled down into statistical indices there is no possibility of verifying it by direct enquiry, and random checks not only take time but may be highly unreliable. It is one of the inescapable facts of life that the more highly centralized the management the more remote are those who have to assess what is happening from first-hand contact with events. Even if the statistics are completely accurate and the best possible measure that could be devised, they do not carry the hints and overtones of what lies behind them that comes from direct communication with individual businesses.

35

It is common both in business and in government to blame a bad decision on an unnecessary degree of ignorance. This may be entirely justified. But it does not follow that everything would be changed by speeding up the flow of information to the centre. No doubt this would help. But the information available would still be out-of-date; the process of speeding up its collection might be very costly; and very often the trouble lies in the inconsistency of different pieces of information rather than in avoidable lags in collection so that it would still be possible to offer different interpretations of what was really happening, however quickly each item of information came in. Every economic historian knows that long after all the statistics have been published there is plenty of room for debate about the story they tell.

In this respect governments are probably a good deal worse off than individual businesses which have less reason to be in doubt about what is going on under their noses. But I wonder whether large businesses, however efficient, are sure that they know at any point in time just how their capital development is going or how they should weigh a rising trend in some branches against a falling trend in others. The British government's experience at any rate is that it is often hardest to find out what is happening in the public sector – in the nationalized industries or among the local authorities – over which its control (nominally at least) is more direct.

Knowledge of what is happening does not take the government very far in deciding what to do in framing an economic policy unless it can make use of some framework into which the facts can be fitted, i.e. unless it has a theory round which to organize the facts. But very often economic theory indicates only the direction that action should take, not the magnitude of the action that is called for. I am told that President Truman expressed disappointment in the post-war years with the advice that he received from economists because he thought that he could decide without their help in what direction he should move and they could proffer no advice on the one thing on which he needed guidance, i.e. by how much to move.

(b) *Uncertainty* Coupled with outright ignorance is uncertainty. Managerial decisions are almost always taken in uncertainty not only as to the facts but as to the right interpretation to put on them. 'Everything is uncertain, most of all the future' as Per Jacobsson was fond of saying. Theories of managerial behaviour which assume that managers have access to all the relevant facts and are maximizing measurable quantities by reference to known relationships are

36

therefore highly misleading. Any decision that is taken involves the risk of error and the main problem is to decide how to run one's risks. Even if a judgment can be shown to have been 'right' in some sense at the time it was taken, it may prove in retrospect to have been wrong because of events that could not have been foreseen or adequately allowed for. It is often more important to be alive to the real range of contingencies and to have that feel for anything that may upset existing trends which we call 'hunch' than to be able to marshal the known variables in the light of established theory. For this purpose it is invaluable to be able to see economic problems in historical perspective or bring to bear on them a long and varied experience of similar past situations.

It seems to me to follow from what I have said that there are severe limits to the value of economic theory to the policy-maker in a managed economy. The main function of theory is to direct attention to the relevant variables, but this does not take us very far if there is no reliable information about the variables (i.e. if we are ignorant) or if the uncertainties governing decision-taking lie outside economics altogether (e.g. in the political field). Economic theory may help us to see what additional information ought to be collected or what information is really material to any specific problem. So far as it throws light on how the economic system really works it greatly reduces the uncertainty involved in government intervention in the working of the system. But once governments themselves are one of the main elements in the system, their behaviour has itself to be encompassed by the theory. This cannot be done by simply adding another variable to existing models and treating governments as if they were no more than the point at which the second differential crossed the x-axis. Indeed it cannot be done by mathematical methods at all since governments do not conform to mathematical rules.

The plain fact is that ignorance, uncertainty and inconsistency make it correspondingly difficult to devise and apply any logical system of wide generality such as can be based on the simple axioms of economic behaviour. We are driven to rely on limited applications to specific situations except where it is possible to arrive at satisfactory explanations that apply in their most general form in the face of human irrationality (e.g. in explaining economic fluctuations).

(c) *Time*   Next, I would stress the importance of time in economic management. This enters in a number of different ways.

First of all there is the familiar distinction between the short-run

37

and the long. Any act of management has a series of effects over time, some of them quickly apparent, others delayed. It is necessary to visualize all these effects and if, as often happens, some are favourable and others unfavourable, to balance them against one another. The conflict between long-run and short-run considerations is a large subject on which I have little new to say.

It is, however, necessary to emphasize that this conflict is complicated by political and administrative considerations, In democratic society governments have an uncertain length of life and hesitate to curtail it deliberately by giving precedence to long-run gains at the cost of short-term unpopularity. They are to some extent in the same situation as companies exposed to the threat of a takeover in that there is a premium on action conferring clear and immediate benefits.

Economic myopia of this kind does not, however, deter governments from taking large risks with considerable light-heartedness. For they may enter into commitments involving heavy eventual outlays so long as they either win immediate credit or escape from awkward political dilemmas or gratify some critical section of opinion. They may, in other words, accept economic risks for largely non-economic reasons and be tempted to exaggerate the long-term economic benefits or minimize the outlays which they require.

The balancing of short and long-term gains is further complicated by the need to devolve responsibility on subordinate authorities within the public sector. Such devolution may involve laying down criteria for public investment based on success in meeting market requirements. The nationalized industries, for example, may find their performances judged in terms of the profits they earn and may be led to neglect forms of expenditure which, although debited as current costs, are justified mainly by their long-run consequences: for example, expenditure on training, development of new products, improvements in quality, and so on. The solution to this dilemma may lie not, as some economists would instinctively suppose, in refining the criteria laid down from above, but in devising different structures of responsibility so as to leave greater freedom of action coupled with different incentives and a different training for those to whom it is granted.

The Need for Speed

Time has another and quite different significance in management. It shapes decisions by determining the speed with which they are arrived at. Governments, no less than managements, have to make up their minds quickly on most things. They are expected to comment as soon as a problem becomes apparent to the public and that comment may be expected to foreshadow a policy which in turn commits them to action. They are under constant pressure to provide a full explanation of things only dimly appreciated and say at once what they propose to do as soon as questions are asked. Unlike academic and other commentators, governments cannot usually plead lack of time or the need for prior research before coming to a decision. They may set up a Royal Commission here and there but they cannot put policy-making into commission. They may be reminded of earlier pronouncements, and indeed of their party programme before taking office, but once in power they cannot treat earlier views and promises as holy writ or they might as well hand over to the civil servants. They have still to work their policies out in the face of new circumstances, changing opinions and un-suspected objections – always under pressure of time.

It is indeed a frequent source of misunderstanding in public affairs that ministers and senior officials never have unlimited time. They are, in fact, harassed men. A minister's time may be largely hypothe-cated to trivialities – inescapable engagements and urgent matters of detail – so that high policy has to be squeezed into odd intervals and the small hours; there are always strong temptations merely to react to events without trying to be ahead of them. Yet in government as in business, management practice increasingly involves organization for the purpose of getting ahead of events. In a sense this is what planning is all about.

Forecasting

An outstanding illustration of this is the preparation of economic forecasts. These are the basis on which business programmes are drawn up and these programmes – of production, sales, invest-ments, etc. – are effectively summaries of the policies of the enter-prises concerned. Similarly, in government, the forecasts of GNP and the balance of payments, once they are accepted and provided no fresh action seems called for, are tantamount to plans and can be regarded as embodying government policy. Of course, govern-ments may disregard forecasts or abandon forecasting altogether, particularly if they are conscious that there is a risk of crisis for which forecasts cannot allow and to which improvization is the only possible response. But so far as the machinery of forecasting is highly developed it provides the most convenient way of exploring contingencies and the best starting-point for fresh policy decisions. It helps to turn these decisions into amendments to existing plans and ensures that they are forward-looking and geared to a conscious review of future prospects.

While governments may decide to work on the basis of systematic forecasts they have to face the uncertainties of the immediate future and recognize that these uncertainties tend to multiply the longer the time horizon. It is bad enough not to know the outcome of events already in the offing – whether the Suez Canal will open next year, whether negotiations for joining the Common Market will be successful, whether there will be an exchange crisis, and so on. But in addition there are all the possible events not yet on the horizon – assassination, war, major strikes, etc – for which it is impossible to provide on any rational basis. Hence, although decision-taking may be organized around some form of forecasting, the forecasts will always be taken with a pinch of salt and no amount of economic or any other kind of theory tells us how much salt to add. All that one can say is that economic forecasts extending over a period of several years are necessarily very uncertain and may amount to little more than guesses.

There is also a danger that where policy is arrived at by progressive modification of existing plans, the mechanism of policy-making may become too inflexible. The system of forecasting provides coherence and continuity and makes for timely consideration by everybody concerned since they can see and comment on the outcome expected before anything happens. But the machinery may impose its own rhythm on decision-taking and cause delay or reluctance to take fresh decisions, especially if the forecasts are allowed to exercise a mesmeric effect and are taken seriously in their own right as the shape of things to come instead of as a scaffolding for decision-taking.

Overload and Devolution

The fact that time is not unlimited has other consequences for managerial behaviour. It imposes devolution by busy ministers (whose tenure of office is typically short) just as much as by busy managing directors (who enjoy on the average a much longer tenure). Ministers can take only a limited number of decisions so that others, less politically significant, must be taken by officials. There is a limit to what they can find time to read or (still more) to write; and this means that submissions are usually made to them only when officials feel that they have the whole story or all the arguments to put before them. Ministers run the risk, therefore, that an issue which they might have settled one way has to be settled another because delay has put the first solution out of their power. If they ask: 'Why wasn't I told earlier?' they may find that the answer lies in the large number of other matters that are similarly held up for fear of over-filling their in-trays.

Much the same applies to officials, including those dealing with economic affairs, who are responsible for the continuity of policy. They frequently live in a state of perpetual overload from which there is no obvious escape. Take for example the problem of assimilating information about current economic trends. Anyone seeking to be thoroughly posted on the state of the economy does not lack for material and there is no limit to the amount of time that can be devoted to studying it. It is simply not possible, given the limitations of the human mind, to take on board *all* the known facts, and simultaneously to attend all the committees at which an understanding of the facts may be important, still less to combine these activities with working out in time to influence policy what should be done in the light of such an assessment. There has to be a division of labour with all the limitations as well as the advantages that this involves.

Finally, there is the all-important issue of the timing of managerial action. It is never enough to decide what to do and how much: it is also necessary to decide *when* to act. It may well be right to do nothing for the time being and to postpone action, recognizing that the need for action may pass or that in due course the right course may be one that is currently inappropriate. It may equally be right to act hastily and without full consideration of the consequences, lest worse befall.

(d) *Other limitations on managerial action* Even when the government knows exactly what it wants to do it may be unable to act for purely practical reasons: for example, the limited range of weapons that it can employ or the limited ways in which they can be used. In this country the government has to rely heavily on persuasion, co-operation and adequate incentives without any assurance as to the degree to which these will be forthcoming. It has no direct control, in the absence of rationing or licensing, over the evolution of consumer demand or over private saving, although it can exercise a powerful indirect influence through the tax system or through

41

varying social service benefits. It has very limited power over the behaviour of wages and prices, especially in the longer run. Its success in meeting foreign competition abroad or even in the home market is necessarily doubtful. Its access to international credit is limited and the willingness of foreigners to go on holding sterling is liable to fluctuate. Investment plans, even when within the public domain, may not work out as expected or intended.

ECONOMIC MANAGEMENT AND BUSINESS MANAGEMENT

So far I have dwelt almost exclusively on aspects of management common to business and government. But the management of the economy is in many ways fundamentally different from the running of a large firm; and I should like to conclude by underlining some of these differences.

One important difference is related to the accountancy of decision-taking. A single business can usually do its sums in money and may have no need to reflect on what lies behind the money-veil. But governments do feel such a need. They have to look beyond the immediate impact of monetary transactions to the ultimate effects on the economy as a whole, including multiplier and accelerator effects and the repercussions on the balance of payments. They have also to think consistently in real terms and ask of alternative money expenditures not merely whether they will bring different benefits or earlier benefits but whether they will make equal claims on real resources. Rules of conduct and systems of accountancy that are the height of wisdom for a private individual or a public company may be the height of folly when practised by governments.

The truth of this has long been recognized in relation to saving and spending. But it is a truth of far wider application since it means adopting a different approach to all forms of government revenue and expenditure from that appropriate to private income and outlay. No government has as yet succeeded in making all the necessary changes in its system of accountancy (although the British government is as far advanced as any); and every government is bound to be conscious of the confusion and misunderstanding that a dual standard of accountancy must generate in Parliamentary debate and public comment.

This dual standard reflects, secondly, a difference in policy objectives and in the criteria by which policies are judged. The objectives of a single enterprise are different in character from those of a

42

government managing an entire economy, however much both may strive after stability, growth and an acceptable distribution of income. The individual enterprise usually judges its success in terms of its own prosperity whether or not this marches with the prosperity of the economy while the government is obliged to take a wider view.

This brings us to a third and major difference. One cannot equate the management of the economy with business management because decision-taking by government is always and everywhere a political activity. Decisions are not taken on the basis of some simple calculus of economic gain or loss but have to embrace political consideration as well.

Policy is a Seamless Web

Economic policy does not exist in isolation from other aspects of policy. Although young economists are often taught economics as if one could carve up policy and call this part economic, that part military and that other part cultural, the fact is that policy is a seamless web and any particular decision must have different elements in it, some of an economic character and some non-economic. The idea, for example, that because devaluation represents operation through an economic variable it should be governed purely by economic considerations is highly naive. It is equally naive to think that a Chancellor should frame his Budget without first asking himself whether it would commend itself to the Cabinet, to his Party, or to the House of Commons as currently constituted.

The aims of policy are generally obscure, in conflict, and inconsistent. The weight attached to these aims by different people even within the same party are bound to differ. Some people are inclined to take short views where others are more anxious about the long run. The process by which policy is formed cannot, therefore, be a particularly scientific one or take place with the smoothness so frequently associated in people's minds with the term 'planning'. It must inevitably involve group pressures, heated arguments, intrigues, jockeying for position and all that we associate with politics. This is not because politicians are different from other men, but because the resolution of human conflict in a peaceful way inevitably involves struggle at the highest level, not only between parties but within them.

It is not possible, therefore, to proceed in the way so often assumed by economists and start from given value judgments already laid

43

down in working out what should be done. *Whose* value judgments? Is it to be supposed that Cabinets never disagree? Ot that they never reverse previous decisions, or never yield to pressure, or, for that matter, never give way to other Cabinets? It seems to me a travesty to take for granted that value judgments are more certain and calculable than economic trends.

Economic Psychiatry

The fact of political conflict means that what at first sight seem purely technical issues become the subject of party debate. Governments may be inhibited from using particular instruments of policy such as bank rate by ideological considerations or by the force of popular feeling which they have stirred up earlier when in opposition. They may commit themselves publicly to doctrines about how the economy should be run that rest on little more than assertion and then find it impossible to retract when the doctrines are put to the test. Persuasion becomes not merely an act of political leadership but an economic weapon; and skill in managing the economy begins to rest more heavily on proficiency in economic psychiatry than on insight into econometric relationships. One need only look at the gyrations of exchange markets over the past few years to see how political and psychological factors have interacted to complicate the tasks of economic management.

What is new in all this is not the emergence of political and psychological influences in economic affairs – they have always been present – but the pervasiveness of these influences. The expansion of management means simultaneously an increased dependence on government decisions and an increase in the consultations and negotiations preceding these decisions. All this extends the area of psychological warfare. Bluff, rumour, the contrived leak, and other devices come into play. Decisions of policy are influenced more by considerations of prestige, loss of face, announcement effects, immediate negotiability, and so on, and less by ultimate economic advantage. Policy is less flexible and more irreversible.

A democratic government must always be highly dependent on persuasion, most of all when other weapons of policy are inadequate. But this dependence tends to make the government less than frank and assume an air of being in control of events that frequently has little justification. It is not easy for a government to go to the public to ventilate its doubts when everyone expects it to give a lead. This means that there is bound to be some public suspicion of the government and that it is peculiarly difficult to predict in advance how the public will react. The government may over-play its hand and expose itself to criticisms of cocksureness when in fact it is saturated with private doubts. The uncertainties generated by change itself can easily be multiplied by misunderstandings of this kind.

There is here a difference between the normal situation in government and in business. Government decisions are subject to intense public scrutiny and continuous inquest, or at least the outcomes of decisions are scrutinized and criticized, whereas most business management decisions are secrets unto themselves, mediocre outcomes being more easily attributed to the play of factors outside the scope of the organization. This makes economic policy decisions, unlike the decentralized mass of business decisions, more subject to misinterpretation and distortion. Indeed, the mass media which have to reach their public by over-simplifying and dramatizing economic issues, can generate or magnify uncertainty, and unduly hasten or retard the public expectations of timing and outcomes in a way which is not experienced by business.

The Theory of Economic Management

What morals can one draw from all this as to the direction that economic analysis should take? If a subject which we may call 'managerial economics' or 'economic administration' is to be developed it will have to blend economic theory and decision theory with realistic analysis of the way in which organizations behave and administrative structures become adapted to the pressures on them. It will need to start from the fact that ignorance is real, prejudice powerful and uncertainty inescapable and consider a wide range of time horizons. For this purpose historical perspective is at least as important as mathematical subtlety. The theory will have to do justice to recorded experience and lend itself to application by busy men impatient of logical refinement (particularly if coupled with footnotes in small print). It will also have to make provision for the weaving together of economic and non-economic considerations: for it is a truth too often ignored that there is no such thing as economic policy in isolation from other aspects of policy – there is only policy.

3. How Can the Economy be Controlled?[1]

Scientists take readily to the idea of a control – so long, at least, as they are in charge. They start out in search of knowledge of the external world. But it is a short step from trying to understand the world as it is to trying to change it in the light of that understanding and mould it closer to the heart's desire.

Control of the Economy is Government Control

Somebody has to do the moulding and it is here that doubts begin to creep in. Who is to exercise control and for whose benefit? These are questions that can be put on one side in most of the day-to-day work of natural scientists and technologists but they can hardly be disregarded by social scientists. Economists in particular have to recognize that control over the economy is exercised by governments and that the public have a rather ambivalent attitude towards government control. Anything that goes wrong will provoke a public clamour that something should be done, presumably by the government; on the other hand whatever is done is liable to be denounced as government interference. However well meant, government control of any kind is an exercise of power and power is apt to attract suspicion and distrust. In times of war or national emergency comprehensive measures of control over the economy may be accepted as indispensable; but at all other times they have to be justified in terms of clear and demonstrable benefits.

Coupled with this distrust of governmental power goes scepticism about the motives and competence of those who hold office. Only too often there is a wide gap between professions and performance. The government may claim to be able to manage the economy: but to many people this is like claiming to be able to manage the

[1] Based on a paper given at the Boston Meeting of the American Association for the Advancement of Science on 30 December, 1969.

weather. Even if economics were an exact science such a claim would always be subject to the reservation that managing an economy is not a scientific experiment but an act of political leadership. It need hardly be said that economics is not an exact science. When it yields propositions of great logical rigour they generally turn out to be platitudes. (No harm in that. If only people would give platitudes their due, the world would be a better place.) When applied to real problems it rarely points decisively to a particular solution. The guidance that it can give to those in control of the economy must therefore be limited and ambiguous. And just when it is most valuable, the instruments at the government's disposal may be too limited to allow it to be applied with success.

The Idea of a Self-regulating System

It was partly for reasons of this kind that the early economists reacted against efforts to control the economy. They developed the conception of an economic system akin to the natural order to demonstrate that government control was largely superfluous and certainly misconceived. Understanding of the system seemed to them to make it less not more desirable to exercise control over it. Governments, being what they were, were unlikely to be aware of the subtle interactions that held the system together without their intervention.

Even the revolutionary writers of the nineteenth century did not envisage the present economic responsibilities of modern government. Marx, for example, may have looked forward to the dictatorship of the proletariat; but he regarded it as a temporary phase without much interest from the economic point of view, to be succeeded as soon as possible by the withering away of the state. The utopias of the period up to 1914 sketch many changes in the civilization of the future, but none of them pay much regard to the economic fuctions of government or introduce the idea of comprehensive government control.

The Economic System out of Control

All this changed after the First World War and it did so for a simple reason: that in all industrial countries the national economy was clearly out of control. Where instability had previously been a minor blemish of the system, hardly noticed for lack of adequate statistics, it was now on a scale involving a tremendous waste of resources

47

through unemployment of men and machines. In the United States GNP in money terms fell by nearly 50 per cent in three years between 1929 and 1932; in Germany, at the worst point of the slump, one man in three was unemployed. In the less industrialized countries instability took a different form and enormously depressed agricultural prices and so the incomes of the rural population. No one living through those years could fail to absorb the lesson that the economy was not self-regulating. But if it was not, no agency other than the government could regulate it and undertake the responsibility of maintaining continuous full employment.

Curiously enough, the onset of the slump in 1929 coincided with the introduction of the first five-year plan in Russia. The ambition of the Russians to plan their economy was in striking contrast to the absence of any effort at economic planning in the West. It is true that the Russian plan just did not work and that the upheaval in Russia after 1929 was far more terrible than in any western country. But western enthusiasts for planning, taking the intention for the deed, could dismiss this as irrelevant or (more commonly) shut their eyes to the facts. As so often happens, what commanded attention was not actual events but ideological claims. The view took hold in the West that planning in some form was desirable in the interests of economic control. It was not generally appreciated that whereas the Russians had a long-term object in mind in the form of rapid industrialization (even at the cost of greater instability) the need of the West was for short-term measures to raise the level of economic activity and restore prosperity.

Thus it was the extraordinary instability of the economy in the USA and elsewhere between the wars that threw into prominence the need for strong central direction. The experience of two world wars told in the same direction since the resources of a country at war cannot be mobilized to the greatest advantage without some form of central planning and control. The difference is, of course, that in war-time there is a simple over-riding and unifying objective: to win the war. Then, as in a slump, the consumer is relegated to a subordinate position and superseded by planners who claim to know what is wanted if war and slump are to be brought to an end.

Apart from wars and slumps which extended the range of government action there were ideological forces at work, notably the spread of socialism as a political philosophy, which made for the acceptance of wider governmental responsibilities. But although the long-term trend towards an extension of the economic functions of government would certainly have continued, it is doubtful whether

48

the idea of *controlling* the economy (at least in the sense of putting an end to unnecessary instability) would have caught hold without simultaneous developments in economic theory. Up to fifty years or so ago the facts of economic instability had not been intensively studied and there was no really adequate theory of economic fluctuations. Thanks to the work of economists between the wars, a great advance was made at the theoretical level. This advance is usually now associated with the name of John Maynard Keynes.

Demand Management as the Key to Control

The simple point on which Keynes and others fastened attention was that the fluctuations that took place in the economy were primarily fluctuations in demand and purchasing power. Stabilization meant, therefore, efforts to stabilize demand and did not necessarily call for extensive detailed interference by the government in the economy. No one, of course, would deny that there are factors on the supply side such as harvest fluctuations calculated to inject additional instability. Nor would it be denied that there may be difficulties unconnected with demand that make it difficult to run the economy under full pressure without undesirable consequences. For example, there may be what are now usually referred to as structural problems, such as a shortage of one kind of labour and a surplus of other kinds, over-employment in some areas of the country with under-employment in others, bottle-necks in capacity in the industries to which demand is most strongly directed, and so on. In an open economy a substantial part of the demand for the output that is produced arises in export markets over which little or no control can be exercised. For a country heavily dependent on foreign trade, therefore, or affected by large movements of capital in and out, it is bound to be a more difficult task to secure effective control of the economy. But with these reservations the important point remains: controlling the economy with a view to making the maximum continuous use of its resources may not call for detailed planning by the government but does call for management of the aggregate demand on available resources. The management of demand is the key to successful control over the level of economic activity.

There are, of course, many other reasons, with which I cannot hope to deal in this paper, for seeking to control the economy. Economic stability is a theme more than large enough to occupy us. But it is a comparative newcomer to the objectives of government. One need only think of tariffs, minimum wage legislation, progressive taxation, and so on, to see that there has always been an effort by governments to use control for many different purposes. Today we should say that most of these devices were designed to promote more rapid growth or to secure greater equality and protect the weak. Stability has to be reconciled with these other objects of policy: economic development and growth; a better distribution of income; industrial and regional policy aimed at encouraging economic activity of particular types or in particular places. These objectives are not necessarily compatible with greater stability of indeed with one another.

The fact that there are these other objectives which have somehow to be reconciled with greater stability implies that control can never be a purely technical matter. It may be true that the management of demand has become so complex that it must be left largely to experts. But the experts have a choice of instruments and the methods which they elect to use have different effects on particular outputs, the distribution of income, economic growth and so on. Even if it were not necessary to secure public support for the policies adopted, any group of experts entrusted with the job of managing demand would soon find themselves involved in bitter political controversy unless they were themselves very astute politicians.

What it Takes to Manage Demand

Leaving aside this inevitable immersion of demand management in politics, let me now turn to my main theme and start by asking what it takes to manage demand. I shall begin by assuming that the government has all the powers that it requires and that it knows exactly what is going to happen if it takes no action. All it has to do is to make up its mind and act accordingly. Of course, no government is ever in this position: to a far greater extent than is generally realized governments are impotent and ignorant. But let us grant them omnipotence and omniscience. What do they actually do to regulate demand? What instruments are at their disposal? Broadly speaking, they can make use of the budget, monetary policy and a variety of administrative controls either separately or in combination.

The Budget

Take first the budget. Until a generation ago, it was almost universally held that the budget ought to be kept in balance in all circumstances and that unbalanced budgets were inherently wrong. In view of the proneness of governments to over-spend, this may have been no bad rule in ordinary circumstances especially at a time when the central government was a relatively small element in the economy. So long as the economy was in balance or did not depart far from balance, there was no need to unbalance the budget and indeed to have done so would have been to unbalance the economy. But in conditions of boom or slump, when the economy was out of balance, the budget offered a means of redressing the balance of private spending and saving by an appropriate shift in the balance between public spending and saving. Not that such an idea was in fact advocated at a time when the very existence of the trade cycle had yet to be discovered, and economic fluctuations were still thought of in terms of panics and crises. But, even if fiscal weapons had been employed to stabilize economic activity, they might well have been comparatively ineffective so long as the flow of central government revenue and expenditure remained a very small fraction of GNP, as was true in peace-time in the nineteenth century. The smaller the budget, the bigger must be the variation in the flow of revenue or expenditure to offset a given swing in the pressure on resources generated by private demand (including demand for exports and capital formation as well as for consumer goods).

Whatever may have been true under nineteenth-century conditions when it would have been natural to rely primarily on monetary policy as an economic stabilizer, the expanding role of the government in the twentieth century makes the use of fiscal weapons indispensable since the budget is the natural means for harmonizing the spending plans of public authorities and private households (taking into account fluctuations in business outlays on capital equipment and structures, and any unwelcome gap that is in prospect between imports and exports of goods and services).

Nevertheless, the maxim that the budget ought to be balanced is still widely held, usually because false analogies are drawn with behaviour in private life or in business. In a democratic community this may limit or condition the use of fiscal weapons, since without public understanding and support governments hesitate to act.

On top of this, there is a great deal of confusion as to what precisely is meant by balancing the budget. For example, is a budget only in balance if the government does not have to borrow money? Does this hold even for borrowing to finance the building of power stations? If they are excluded what about roads? Or a war? If the government can borrow for these purposes without giving rise to a

51

deficit is there some other kind of borrowing for other purposes that does correspond to a deficit?

The fact is that budgetary balance is highly ambiguous and depends on the conventions used in presenting the constituent items on both sides. In the United States, for example, there are three quite different ways of measuring a budget deficit that have been given official recognition. First comes the cash deficit – the excess of cash payments to the public, over receipts from the public – irrespective of the way in which the deficit is covered by borrowing. The second definition is in national income terms: it excludes transactions in existing assets (e.g. sales of land) and is on an accrual basis rather than a payment basis (e.g. expenditures are recorded as goods are delivered rather than when they are paid for). Yet a third definition brings in social security and other payments and receipts which do not form part of the administrative budget but lie within the control of the government.

To an economist these alternative measurements are much less important than a calculation of the economic impact of the budget designed to show whether the proposed changes in the flow of government expenditure and revenue over the coming year will be expansionary or contractionary, and if so by how much. An economist would attach even more importance to an assessment of the economic consequences of the *changes of policy* introduced in the budget, and would try to evaluate the net expansionary effect of these changes in, say, six or twelve months time.

Although most economists would agree that these are the material calculations and that the size of the budget surplus or deficit, however measured, is entirely subsidiary, this does not appear to be the view of governments and legislatures to judge from the way in which budgets are currently presented and published. One reason for this is that any calculation of the economic impact of a budget is bound to be open to dispute. Nobody really knows what the full economic effects will be of a given change in taxation, nor how fast these effects will show themselves. Similarly, different ways of spending the same sum have quite different effects on employment and output, but the translation of flows of expenditure into demands on resources is not something that can be done unequivocally and automatically. Assessment of the economic impact of the budget or of budgetary changes is inevitably a rough and ready affair.

Some economists would go further than this and argue that the initial calculations neglect or belittle the monetary consequences of the budget. They would at the same time take issue with the suggestion that the size of the budget surplus or deficit is of quite subsidiary interest, because they would see this as affecting the money supply and hence exerting an indirect influence on spending plans that might be at least as important as the direct effect of increased expenditure. So far as these claims have substance – and I doubt whether they have much – it derives from the impact of the budget on the financial system which depends largely on the way in which the government finances its expenditure. If the government makes use of long-term borrowing in order to finance given expenditure plans the economy will not be affected in quite the same way as it would by government borrowing on credit and the consequent inflation of the money supply. Unfortunately, we have no reliable way of working out what the difference would be and how far, therefore, calculations that take no account of monetary effects must subsequently be modified in order to allow for them.

All this may reasonably suggest to you that those who make use of fiscal weapons are in some doubt as to the outcome of their use. But one should not push scepticism too far. There have been plenty of illustrations over the past few years of the successful use of fiscal policy to stimulate or curb expansion, and governments can usually form a fairly accurate picture of what is called for even if they can never be quite certain how fast the medicine will work or whether the dose will prove excessive.

Fiscal weapons have the advantage of great flexibility since they make it possible to inject additional demand in a wide variety of ways so that the stimulus (or curb) can be applied to different sectors of the economy and so as to take effect quickly or over a considerable period of time. The budget furnishes not just one weapon but a whole armoury of weapons that can be combined to promote several different aims of policy simultaneously.

But it must be admitted that there are also considerable limitations to the use of fiscal weapons. They may, as I have already implied, bring with them large and unwelcome changes in the money supply that complicate the task of the authorities both in the short run and, more obstinately, when the time comes to change direction. There may be long lags between budgetary decisions and the reflection of these decisions in economic activity, so that what seemed sensible at the time proves ill-advised in the event. In many countries there is the further difficulty that tax changes cannot be made between budgets: the most appropriate fiscal weapons may then only be brought into use intermittently and at intervals too long for efficient management of the economy. Then there is the political problem of

53

obtaining parliamentary approval both for what may be called 'the budget judgment' and for each and every element in the budget itself: acceptance first of the net change in economic pressure at which the budget aims and at the same time – what is by no means the same thing – acceptance of the individual tax and expenditure proposals that are designed to produce that change.

When all is said and done, the main limitation to fiscal action lies in the need to mobilize public opinion in support of whatever is proposed. What may seem a highly technical issue to those ruminating on the matter in high quarters may be seen in an entirely different light by a public opinion ill-equipped to understand the nicer points of economic analysis. To a European economist who recognizes that the American economy represents roughly half the industrial world of our time it is more than a little troubling that proposals to vary aggregate demand in the United States through the budget should seem to require a year or more to come to fruition. It may be that the swings of activity in the United States in the post-war period have been comparatively limited and that things would be different if there were any real danger of a major slump. But to a non-American it is astonishing to find the executive in such a position of impotence in a matter of so much importance. Not only is the President unable to take immediate action on the judgment that he forms of the economic outlook, but neither he nor Congress has devised a fiscal regulator such as any modern economy requires; and there is little or no prospect of a short-term regulator in the immediate future.

Monetary Policy

I turn next to monetary policy which has a much longer history as an instrument of economic control. Monetary forces used to come into play almost automatically to check expansion or contraction. Expansion, for example, put increased pressure on the money supply and at the same time helped to throw the balance of payments into deficit and set up a drain on the gold reserves which led to a curtailment of the money supply and increased monetary pressure.

Although monetary forces are not allowed to operate in quite this way nowadays there is a common feeling that there ought to be a more automatic mechanism for checking inflation and deflation; and it is the semi-automatic characteristic of monetary forces that recommends them in some quarters and has given some rise to an agitation for greater reliance on monetary weapons. Sometimes this attitude reflects little more than distrust of governments, but it is usually also associated with disenchantment with the use of fiscal policy or with disbelief in the potency of fiscal measures.

At the purely technical level there is still plenty of controversy about how monetary policy actually operates. Without going too deeply into the technical issues there are one or two points on which there would, I think, be fairly widespread agreement.

First of all, if monetary and fiscal policy are being used in combination with one another they are more likely to be effective if they are pulling in the same direction than if they are pulling in opposite directions. But since the two kinds of policy serve different purposes there are bound to be times when to some extent they pull against one another. For example, monetary conditions abroad may make it desirable to maintain tight money at the same time as slackness in the labour market points to the need for a stimulus administered through the budget.

Secondly, no one familiar with monetary history would ever dispute that monetary policy can be extremely powerful. What is open to dispute is whether the resolute use of monetary policy would have consequences that are both unnecessary and undesirable. For example, pressure on liquidity may conceivably have relatively modest effects on demand until things build up to a liquidity crisis with consequences for economic activity and individual solvency of a quite different order.

Thirdly, monetary policy tends to have strong directional effects. It tends to operate by cutting off or seriously curtailing the flow of credit to particular types of borrower. For example, in 1966 it was very apparent in the United States that private housebuilding was particularly vulnerable to tight money conditions. It has always been accepted that smaller firms, with few alternative sources of finance outside the banking system, are more affected than larger firms with access to a wider range of facilities.

Fourthly, there is no way of avoiding having a monetary policy since monetary conditions are changing all the time and inaction on the part of the monetary authorities is just as much an expression of policy as actual intervention. Money markets are functioning continuously and monetary policy cannot, therefore, be an intermittent affair like fiscal policy with action held up for many months at a time by the need for parliamentary approval. In other words, monetary policy does not lend itself to detailed political control but requires the devolution on the monetary authorities of very wide responsibilities. This does not mean that things are left to the central

55

bank since central banks act in increasingly close conjunction with Ministries of Finance. But it does mean that there is usually more flexibility in the use of monetary weapons than of fiscal.

Administrative Controls

A third means of regulating demand is by adminstrative devices such as licensing, rationing and so on. But these devices are not very useful in checking *total* demand unless they are used on a vast scale: and even then, they are highly inefficient because they give rise to queues, black markets and so on. They can play a useful but modest part in special circumstances when the pressure on the economy is particularly acute at a limited number of points, for example in the building industry. When this happens, the inflation of demand in a single industry may increase costs there in a way that affects the whole of the rest of the economy and leads to a general cost inflation when the economy would otherwise remain in reasonable balance. Experience shows, however, that except in wartime when there may be serious shortages of specific materials, rationing devices are not only clumsy but ineffective. In the case of the building industry, which is perhaps the most obvious candidate, the public sector is itself the source of a large part of the demand on the industry and it should be as easy to exercise control by limiting orders from public authorities as by introducing a system of licensing calculated to bear almost exclusively on the private sector.

There may in addition be various ways in which the government can influence specific forms of activity by tax allowances, subsidies, etc. In principle, for example, it should be possible by varying investment grants or investment credits to influence the level of investment, and various experiments have been conducted, notably in Britain and Sweden, in accordance with this principle. It is not very clear, however, how far the action taken by the government (in Britain, at any rate) has been successful in influencing the volume or timing of investment as part of a general programme designed to stabilize demand.

Deficiencies of Economic Information

Given these instruments, the government next requires to arm itself with the information necessary for their proper use. But here it encounters a problem fundamentally different from that facing anyone seeking to control the natural world. It has to reckon with the fact that it does not know and never can know exactly what is happening either at the moment when it is happening or indeed much later. It can never identify all the economic forces currently at work – only those whose operation is reflected in statistics of the past. In deciding what measures of control to take it is inevitably out-of-date, ignorant and uncertain.

This is so for a number of reasons. First of all, the information available relates to a period which may be several weeks or months or even years back. It takes a long time for these statistics, collected from individual producers or consumers, to be aggregated, processed and fed through a bureaucracy to those on whom rests the responsibility of seeking to manage the economy. For example, they cannot possibly tell until long afterwards what is happening to productivity in the sense at least of the steady improvement from year to year in the average efficiency of industry on which it is possible to reckon in the normal industrial country. It is rare to know with any degree of accuracy the changes taking place in the level of output and employment and still harder to form a judgment of the forces lying behind any apparent change of trend.

Even information that seems at first sight to be entirely reliable may turn out subsequently to be totally misleading because, after fuller consideration, the original figures are substantially altered. This has happened on several occasions in the UK and it happens, too, in the USA as well. One recent example is that of the statistics of British exports which were suddenly increased retrospectively by 2 to 3 per cent because it emerged that exporters were no longer filing returns as faithfully as they had done earlier. An error of 2 to 3 per cent may seem small, but it may make all the difference between a balance of payments surplus and a quite substantial balance of payments deficit.

Moreover, even when the figures undergo no change they may come to have a quite different significance when taken in conjunction with other information. Without any change in the basic information relating to the production of steel, electric power, textiles, etc., the statisticians may suddenly announce that what previously looked like an increase in total production was in fact a decrease because they felt obliged to change the relative weights attached to different outputs or to make different seasonal adjustments to the data, or for some other reason such as fuller information about changes in prices, or a different allowance for the outputs of smaller firms not making returns. The longer one handles economic information the more apparent it becomes that what are at first sight hard facts are not

57

hard at all but of a degree of softness at which one is obliged to guess.

The picture that one forms from the available information has also to take into account inconsistencies in the statistical data where by definition no inconsistencies ought to arise. It is well known that there are three ways of measuring the total volume of economic activity: from the side of output; from the side of income; and from the side of expenditure. In principle these three systems of measurements should yield the same result but they never do. It is quite easy to find a year in which one measure rises, another falls and a third shows little or no change in either direction. The fact that statisticians, faced with this problem, seek to evade it by adding up the three figures and treating their average as their last word on the subject does not make for much confidence in their verdict. There are plenty of other examples of this sort of thing with just as little chance of establishing once and for all which figures are right and which wrong.

Economic Development Complicates Control

All this is very disconcerting to anyone seeking to exercise precise control over the economy because it means that no one can say without fear of contradiction what has been happening, is happening and is likely to happen. Economists are in fact in a position like that of historians rather than in the happier position of natural scientists. Not only are they working with limited data that can be made to support alternative hypotheses but the events which they are seeking to interpret are unique and by their nature non-recurrent. The economic system, unlike the natural order, does not stay still and repeat itself; it changes through time and our awareness of the changes that are taking place necessarily lags behind the event.

Hence it is not possible to work with fixed parameters and identify by a process of closer approximation each of the relationships governing the behaviour of the system as a whole. Even the inclusion of a trend term does not overcome this difficulty since the economic system need not evolve in some inherently predictable way as new elements are introduced into the system by technological development, population changes, political conflict and so on.

The Contribution of Economic Analysis

Against these limitations on our power to control the economy – weaknesses in the instruments of control, deficiencies in the available information, dependence on popular support for the action proposed – must be set the great advances in economic analysis over the past generation. We now have what we did not have in 1929 – an adequate intellectual apparatus with which to face fluctuations in the economy. We are more alive to the questions that need to be asked, the information that needs to be collected and the methods by which statistical information can be made to yield useful results. We know a great deal more about what is going on in the economy and about what to do about it. We have, for the first time, trained staffs of economists whose job it is to help governments to get ahead of events through the preparation of systematic economic forecasts.

The greatest single gain is in the more scientific character of economic analysis. Efforts to regulate activity now rest on unifying concepts which at least provide a calculus of action. By this I mean that one can reduce the forces operating on demand to a common denominator and express their interactions in terms of a series of equations or so-called economic model. Econometrics – an entirely new branch of economics – can be used to assign values to the parameters and enable us to estimate how an initial change in any one element of demand will affect the other elements and in turn the level of demand in the aggregate. Rough calculations can then be made of the probable outcome of particular governmental measures, subject of course to a wide margin of error, both as to the time over which these effects will show themselves, and the degree of reliability of the forecast. We can add up what the government is doing in all kinds of different ways and express the answer in terms of a single variable – the expected net change in pressure on the economy.

Other Sources of Instability

I have been talking so far as if the only source of instability was the behaviour of domestic demand. But this is by no means true.

First of all, fluctuations are often communicated from abroad and are not domestic in origin. Efforts to control a single national economy may be thwarted by the compulsions of the situation in other countries. Export markets, for example, may suddenly fall off or credit restrictions in some important financial centre may set up an outflow of funds and push up interest rates. Those mysterious influences which lie concealed in the balance of payments may swarm out of their bottle like a genie in the Arabian Nights and knock the economy out of balance. It may then be necessary to take steps to *de-stabilize* domestic activity in order to restore external balance.

59

It is when a country is wrestling with a large external deficit – particularly if the deficit is not attributable to its own policies or removable through fairly obvious modifications of these policies – that the inadequacy of relying exclusively on demand management is most apparent. In such circumstances deflation is not the most obvious way of dealing with, say, an outflow of capital. Direct controls over the movement of capital, provided that they can be made effective (a large reservation) may be more appropriate and less wasteful.

In some countries instability associated with foreign trade and payments is not a secondary ailment calling for slightly different treatment but is itself the principal evil. The under-developed countries, for example, are typically dependent on a narrow range of exports, most of them subject to wide variations in price. Not only would the prescription of short-term demand management be inadequate and inappropriate as a remedy for the instability from which their economies suffer but it would be largely irrelevant to the long-term structural changes which must dominate their economic strategy. The argument which I have been developing is not intended to relate to their predicament but concerns only the already developed industrial countries with their diversified trade and fully employed resources.

Cost-inflation

In such countries there is a further source of instability for which no adequate remedy has yet been found. This is the form of instability usually referred to as cost-inflation. This is a rather question-begging phrase since it implies a sharp distinction between two kinds of inflation, one associated with an increasing pressure of demand and one associated with exogenous pressures on the level of costs: usually pressure for higher money wages and salaries exerted by trade unions and professional associations. There *is* no such sharp distinction. If economic activity expands, labour shortages result and these shortages are inevitably reflected in rising labour costs, either because employers offer more pay or because workers take advantage of their greater bargaining power to demand more. Demand-inflation generates cost-inflation if by that term we mean no more than rising costs.

But most people do mean more. They have in mind the pressure that organized labour may exert – and exert successfully – when the symptoms of demand-inflation are lacking. Even when expansion

60

is at or below a sustainable rate, and when unemployment is higher than we should nowadays think consistent with full employment, wages may be pushed up faster than productivity, carrying prices upwards at the same time. Once the process starts it may become self-sustaining for workers can either ask to be compensated for the higher cost of living or ask to be put on a footing of equality with some group to whom employers have just conceded a differential increase. No one need look far in 1970 to recognize a situation of this kind; but no one quite knows how to put a stop to it without undesirable consequences.

In pre-war days, inflation of this kind was rare. It required a powerful consensus of opinion among employers and workers that prices were likely to go on rising at home (and perhaps also abroad), leading one side to yield more readily to wage claims and the other to put them forward more aggressively. But such a consensus could not survive the jolts of prolonged and violent slumps and it was as much as organized labour could do to hold money wages steady. Today things are different. Governments are committed to full employment and both employers and workers are well aware of it. There are often generous redundancy payments and re-training grants for those who lose their jobs and security payments for those who strike. Both unemployment and strikes have lost much of their sting. Employers on the other hand have come to make their plans on the basis of expanding markets and the continuous use of plant and are correspondingly reluctant to face a prolonged strike. Equilibrium in the labour market is, therefore, highly unstable.

The root cause of this instability is the removal of a great deal of the uncertainty about the economic outlook. No doubt complete control ought to mean the disappearance of uncertainty; but in the labour market effective control has yet to be established without some degree of uncertainty and may be impossible without it. As in other human affairs, control may fail if pushed too far.

The fact is that the state is now an invisible third party in all collective bargaining between employers and employed. But in seeking to correct one kind of instability (in employment) it has created another (in incomes and prices). The task of stabilizing demand within fairly narrow limits is a manageable one. But the task of stabilizing costs is a far more complex one and cannot consist in the mere enunciation of guidelines for the benefit of both parties. The state has enormously strengthened the bargaining power of labour through full employment and social insurance. It cannot hope to limit that power effectively by exhortation, expostulation, declarations of intent, and so forth. Nor can it do so by encouraging private employers to resist strikes, nor by seeking to intervene itself in the enormous mass of wage bargains all over the country without far-reaching legal powers. There will have to be some more drastic re-thinking of the responsibilities as well as the rights of labour in a fully employed economy before we see an end to cost-inflation.

CONCLUSIONS

So what are we to conclude? I leave you with six very brief reflections.

(1) First of all, we have clearly no choice between control and no control. We all live in a managed economy and it is inconceivable that management will be discontinued. No one wants to go back to a world in which governments disclaim interest in the level of employment and output and leave them to be determined by blind market forces.

(2) The choice is really between one form of control and another. In the main it is between control over aggregates on the demand side of the market, letting market forces operate freely within the resulting ceiling, and a multiplicity of detailed controls designed to operate from the side of supply. But there are times when administrative controls too are required and these may bite either on consumers or on producers.

(3) The choice can never be between perfect and imperfect control of the economy since, whatever methods are used they are bound to be imperfect for one reason or another. A high degree of centralization may appear to enhance the government's power to control the economy. But it does so only by ensuring that decisions are arrived at in a greater state of ignorance and action is taken with far more friction than would result from a system of decentralized control that made greater use of market forces.

(4) Whatever the imperfections of demand management – and there are many limitations to the available instruments, information and governmental powers – it seems to work, judged by experience since the war. We may have been lucky but it certainly has not been luck alone that has maintained continuous prosperity for so long.

(5) We have been a great deal less successful in maintaining stability of prices. To some extent this is the other side of the medal. Prosperity has meant inflation because it has meant greater pressure on the economy. But another factor at work, and one of increasing

62

importance, has been the changed balance of power in the labour market. There is no obvious technique for preventing this from producing inflation.

(6) Successful management of the economy requires support for the right kind of management or for the right kind of proposals, whatever the management. It can never be a pure matter of technique. The issues are as much political as economic for they are issues of what I was brought up to call Political Economy.

4. Demand Management: the Changing Background to Monetary Policy[1]

To address an audience of Swedish bankers and economists on monetary policy is roughly equivalent, in the international commerce in ideas, to carrying coals to Newcastle. Thanks to the work of Wicksell, to whom we are here to do honour, you have long possessed a great comparative advantage over less sophisticated observers of the monetary system and have strengthened that advantage by the cumulative process of development which Wicksell's successors have analysed to such purpose. I cannot hope to offer you ideas on very advantageous terms and should hesitate to select a subject so familiar to you, but for three reflections.

First of all, as I discovered many years ago from those weekly addresses from the pulpit which have contributed so much to Scottish education, there is a special virtue in a discourse in which the audience can pick plenty of holes. You have much more fun and a stronger incentive to keep awake.

Secondly, it gives me a certain exegetical advantage that until two or three years ago I could reckon myself something of a heathen in these matters. After indoctrination by Cambridge missionaries in the thirties, and study of some of the rival heresies propagated in Stockholm, I lost touch almost completely with the development of monetary thought. Without ever becoming altogether an unbeliever, I found myself not so much lacking in faith as in need to practise it. Thanks to a lucky chance, I have been submitted to a lengthy process of brainwashing from which I am only now recovering. This experience gives me the double advantage of sympathy for the backsliders and familiarity with the ways of the believers and may help me to approach my subject with more detachment than if I were steeped in the finer points of doctrine.

[1] The first of two Wicksell Lectures, delivered in Stockholm, on 3 May, 1960.

64

The lucky chance to which I have referred arose out of the habit of democratic governments in selecting a number of citizens for an intensive education at public expense by appointing them to a committee of enquiry. The British government, although by no means averse to this practice – it has appointed no less than seventy committees on social and economic problems since 1955 – has been sparing in its use of committees covering the whole field of monetary policy; there was only one in the century between 1858 and 1957.[1] The reports issued by such committees, of which the Bullion Committee Report of 1810 and the Macmillan Committee Report of 1931 are the best known, have often proved landmarks in the history of theory, however practical their object, and some of them have aroused keen interest outside the United Kingdom even when their recommendations were set in the context of British institutions and British dilemmas.

The Radcliffe Committee

The appointment of the latest in this line of committees, the Radcliffe Committee, in April 1957 gave rise to high expectations both in Britain and elsewhere, and its Report,[2] issued in August 1959, has set off fresh controversies on the role of monetary policy in the modern world. These controversies do not appear to be confined to the United Kingdom and foreign comment has attached to the views expressed in the Report a wider relevance than may have been intended. While I cannot hope to offer a translation of those views into Esperanto – much less into Swedish – it may be of some service to you if I try to disentangle the central ideas of the Report from the institutional network in which they are entwined. This is my third and principal ground for addressing you on monetary policy.

The members of the Committee were selected on the ancient principle of two by two adopted by Father Noah when faced with an even more difficult problem of excess liquidity. The Committee included two bankers, two industrialists, two trade unionists and two economists, with a lawyer in the solitary role of Noah; even the secretariat of civil servants conformed to the same principle. In due course the Committee issued a unanimous Report. which was in

[1] There was a Select Committee on Banks of Issue in 1875, which dealt with limited questions relating to the note-issue. The Cunliffe Committee on Currency and Foreign Exchanges after the War, which issued reports in 1918 and 1920, also dealt with limited issues.

[2] *Report of the Committee on the Working of the Monetary System* (Cmnd. 827, London, H.M.S.O., 1959).

E

most respects extremely orthodox in its findings. Some passages in the Report, however, gave rise to a good deal of bewilderment in Britain and in some other countries it narrowly escaped burning.

Even the fact that the Committee managed to agree was held against it. No doubt in an age of conformity, unanimity may be considered a blemish; and there may be some who look with nostalgia to the happier days of the Macmillan Committee, no two of whose fourteen members were in entire agreement with one another, the Chairman alone finding it unnecessary to sign a reservation or addendum or to enter a memorandum of dissent. But to those who doubt whether a report of this kind is the proper occasion for a symposium, there is some merit in unanimity, particularly if the signatories of the Report find remarkably little about which to disagree. The fact that monetary policy did not feature as a party issue in the general election fought three months after the Report appeared is perhaps not altogether accidental.

The Reports covers a wide variety of topics some of which, although they may appear of subordinate importance to the theoretical economist, are far from irrelevant to the working of the monetary system and absorbed much of the time of the Committee. These included, for example, agricultural credit, the adequacy of existing facilities for the finance of exports, and the special problems of small firms. At the request of the Chancellor, the Committee gave special attention to the constitutional framework within which the monetary authorities operate, and heard extensive evidence from witnesses who included four ex-Chancellors on the position of the Bank of England and its Court of Directors. All of these were subjects which might have justified a separate enquiry and had to be treated within the compass of a document intended for a wide public and therefore of modest dimensions. In addition, a large part of the Report is given up to a descriptive analysis of the functioning of British monetary institutions and a commentary on the monetary history of the post-war years. The central argument of the Report – the theoretical core—occupies a correspondingly limited space – less, indeed, than some of the lengthier critiques that have since appeared.

The Argument of the Report

This central argument embraced a number of negative propositions which antagonized some readers and a number of positive propositions which others found rather obscure. On the negative side it expressed scepticism about the emphasis customarily laid on the supply of money as the fulcrum of monetary pressure and doubted whether changes in the supply of money were the most satisfactory means of varying the whole complex of interest rates. It was also sceptical about the direct impact of changes in interest rates on the level of investment and about the wisdom of using abrupt changes in interest rates to check short-term fluctuations in investment. There was at least a hint that action to limit investment was unlikely to prove the best way of tackling sustained inflationary pressure. On the positive side, the Report sought to substitute the structure of interest rates for the supply of money as the centrepiece of monetary operations. It treated money as one liquid asset among many, and changes in the supply of money as more or less incidental to the effects sought in other directions – effects either on interest rates or on liquidity. The effects on interest rates, although of little assistance in the short run as a check on investment, were represented as exerting an increasingly powerful influence in the longer run. Interest rates, therefore, should not be held stable but should be varied, and varied deliberately. Changes in interest rates, particularly long-term rates, were the 'proper method of affecting financial conditions and eventually, through them, the level of demand.'[1]

This argument has important implications. First of all, it clearly implies a refusal to identify monetary policy with banking policy. It says in effect that, however important the commercial banks may be in the financial structure, they are not the sole creators of liquid assets and it is necessary, therefore, to have regard to the operations of other financial institutions that are playing an increasingly important part in determining 'the state of liquidity of the whole economy'. Secondly, it implies that the central bank should pursue an active policy and not remain passive. It is impossible, in any event, not to have a monetary policy and inaction is just as much an expression of policy as action. Nor, thirdly, should the central bank confine its operations to the money market and short rates of interest, over which, in Britain at least, its powers are all but absolute. It must also take a view of long rates and give up any pretence that these rates are unaffected by its own behaviour. This does not mean that it must swing to the other extreme and try to impose long-term rates that are out of touch with the underlying forces of the market; in Wicksellian terms, it should aim to let the market rate move in line with the natural rate. But, fourthly, this is a counsel to be interpreted broadly and over a period of years, not in relation to sudden pressures likely to issue in an investment boom or slump. To deal

[1] *Report*, para. 982.

67

with those pressures, monetary policy is no longer the most effective
instrument and may have to be subordinated to other measures.
But what other measures? If monetary policy will not do the trick,
what will?

On this the Report is not very explicit. It points out that in the
modern world, government influence on demand covers three distinct
types of action: through monetary policy, fiscal measures and administrative controls. It is impossible to prescribe in advance the
proper blend, the right 'package deal', and decisions must be left
to the government of the day. But the plain implication of the Report,
which frowns on administrative controls and is rather Laodicean
about monetary policy, is that the burden should normally rest on
fiscal measures. This is by no means a novel conclusion. It was
already evident nearly thirty years ago that the budget was a far more
powerful instrument for dealing with a prolonged depression than
low rates of interest and excess liquidity. After the war, it was the
budget, coupled with direct controls, that was employed to regulate
demand while monetary policy remained largely passive. It would
have required strong evidence of the effectiveness of monetary policy
in the fifties to have brought about a marked change of emphasis.
This evidence was not, in the Committee's judgment, forthcoming.

Money and Liquidity

The Report has given pain in some quarters because it appears to deny
any importance to the quantity of money and puts in the forefront
the vaguer concept of liquidity. Since money is itself a liquid asset
the change does not drive money off the stage altogether; but it does
leave it with a rather humbler role. The argument for concentrating
on liquidity in one sense or another is that there is no direct link
between the quantity of money and individual decisions governing
expenditure and the level of effective demand; that there is an indirect
link through the rate of interest and the state of liquidity; and that
it is these that matter rather than the particular operations, whether
on the supply of money or on other elements in the situation, by
which the monetary authorities seek to influence the cost and availability of finance. To concentrate exclusively on the supply of money
is to forswear action aimed directly at the complex of interest rates
and to assume that so long as the quantity of money is rigorously
controlled the danger of monetary disturbances will be minimized.
Now there may be economies in which the monetary authorities
can, by exerting leverage on the money supply, do all they want to

do with comparative ease, or in which the state of liquidity is a simple function of the money supply. Whatever may be true of those economies, the United Kingdom cannot be numbered among them.

The Report directs attention to a wide range of liquid assets which, without serving as means of payment, act as near-substitutes for money and are as relevant to decisions to spend or invest as the stock of money itself. So long as these alternative assets are freely convertible into money without capital loss, they can be used with comparatively little trouble to make monetary payments and the fact that they are not immediately acceptable without encashment is largely irrelevant to monetary management. It is the liquidity of an asset, not its acceptability in final payment, that marks it out as a potential source of embarrassment in inflationary conditions.

The more strongly anyone believes that the prime object of monetary policy must be the control of the money supply, the more precisely must he draw the line between money and other things. But in practice the line can never be precise nor can it remain fixed. Are time deposits money? The International Monetary Fund excludes them; but in England the commercial banks are usually prepared to allow their depositors to draw cheques against deposit accounts when their current accounts are exhausted. Similarly, whatever the withdrawal conditions laid down by the building societies, an investor can in practice obtain small sums more or less on demand.

It is more sensible to think of money as lying at one end of the spectrum of liquidity and forming a limited and variable proportion of the community's stock of liquid assets. This stock includes deposit accounts, building societies' shares and deposits, savings certificates, defence bonds, commercial bills, Treasury Bills, tax reserve certificates, deposits with saving banks and many other short-term liabilities which are unlikely to have exact counterparts in other countries. There is no reason why this total need mount at the same rate as bank deposits, or deposits plus notes, and it can in fact be shown that large divergences do occur. Mr Gurley, for example, calculates that in the United States the increase in the money supply formed 45 per cent of the total increase in liquid assets between 1939 and 1946 but only 20 per cent of the increase between 1946 and 1958.[1]

Bank Credit and Commercial Credit

There is nothing particularly new in the Report's insistence on the

[1] J. G. Gurley, *Liquidity and Financial Institutions in the Post-war Economy*, Brookings Institution, Reprint No. 39 (1960), p. 5.

importance of other liquid assets; not is the growth of these assets itself a new phenomenon. But their significance for monetary theory and policy has not been fully realized – at least not in Britain. The stress laid on money has been coupled with a corresponding stress on the commercial banks as if banks were quite different from other financial institutions and unique in their power to generate liquidity or create credit. It is true that bank deposits are more liquid than other liquid assets and have important advantages in acceptability; but this does not make the operations of commercial banks fundamentally different from the operations of other financial institutions. A commercial bank which attracts additional deposits creates liquid assets in the form of bank liabilities and can offer correspondingly greater credit in the form of loans and advances. A building society is in exactly the same position except that its deposits cannot be directly transferred from one depositor to another; and at the same time the Bank of England happens to disinterest itself in the total for building society mortgages. It a public company offers credit to its suppliers it is performing the same function as a bank; and the objection that it must first get hold of the money applies equally to the bank. If banks are able to run down their liquidity ratios in creating credit, so also are public companies.

All this was said forty years ago with much more pungency by Lavington: 'In addition to the various forms of currency manufactured by the specialized institutions of the market is the purchasing power created by manufacturers, merchants and others when they allow their customers to buy goods from them on an implicit promise to pay recorded in the form of a book debt. It may be objected that this system of trade credit does nothing but postpone payment, that it merely defers the use of currency and consequently adds nothing to the average volume of purchasing power. This would be only partially true if the total volume of book debts were always about the same; for although in that case the creation of new book debts would proceed concurrently with the extinction of old book depts by the use of currency, it would still be true that the average volume of purchasing power had been increased by the mere fact that payment was deferred. The average volume of these deferred payments would still constitute a net addition to the total stock of purchasing power, for corresponding to it would be an average volume of goods purchased without the use of currency. The significance of book debts, however, lies less in the addition which they make to the average volume of purchasing power than in the ease with which they are expanded and contracted, and in the fact that these variations are

70

free from any control on the part of the market organizations whose business it is to regulate the supply of purchasing power. If, for example, the immediate outlook is favourable and business men wish to increase largely their stocks of materials and finished goods, their ability to purchase against book entries constitutes a net addition to the total volume of purchasing power in the same way as, in similar circumstances, would an expansion of cheque currency. But while the latter form of expansion is more obvious and can be dealt with by the Bank of England or the banks generally, the former kind of expansion is quite beyond their control.'[1]

Now commercial credit, as any study of balance-sheets will show, is far from negligible in comparison with bank credit. On the contrary, for the larger companies whose shares are quoted on the stock exchange it is four or five times as large. The trade credit received by such companies averages about 15 per cent of their total assets whereas bank credit averages not much above 3 per cent. Similarly, cash in hand and bank balances are small in relation to other current assets including what is due from debtors, tax reserve certificates and so on. No doubt, bank credit and bank balances are the most sensitive indicators of company liquidity; the amount of trade credit that a firm can take or must offer is not always easily controllable by the firm itself, so that no firm could afford to treat a reduction in its bank balance as adequately offset by a corresponding increase under the heading of 'trade debtors'. But given the relative magnitudes, it is hard to see why a small change in bank credit should be of critical importance so long as liquidity is not threatened from some other direction, nor why a small reduction in the supply of money should put it beyond the power of business to maintain its existing commitments.[2]

The Demand for Money

It would be possible to take a different view if the demand for money were highly inelastic so that business sought to maintain a fixed stock of it in real terms and could not easily replenish this

---

[1] F. Lavington, *The English Capital Market* (London, 1921), pp. 39–40.

[2] Compare also R. F. Henderson: 'Between 1949 and 1953 . . . increases in bank credit amounted to only 3·8 per cent of the growth in net assets of all companies in the aggregate. Issues of shares and loan capital for comparison amounted to 26·6 per cent of the growth in net assets. Reliance on control of bank advances seems a case of using a small tail to wag a large dog. *Studies in Company Finance*, ed. by Brian Tew and R. F. Henderson (Cambridge, 1959), p. 78.

stock from the public because it, too, had fixed ideas of its monetary requirements. But the demand for money is rendered elastic by the multiplicity of other liquid assets. If the business outlook is favourable and profits are rising, firms will not be deterred from expanding by regard for their immediate cash position which, in any event, is likely to be strong. When they do begin to feel illiquid, they may have to reconcile themselves to higher rates of interest since they will be bidding for a larger share of the limited stock of liquid assets; and these higher rates of interest may bring other, more restrictive, consequences in their train. But the process may be a protracted one, and over the critical period restriction of the money supply is likely to be ineffective as a brake. Both in the short run and in the long, it is the movement of interest rates, the accompanying fall in asset values, and the caution that these changes may induce that are the crux of the matter.

If we are to make up our minds what reliance to place on this mechanism, we have to be on our guard against assuming that it operates nowadays in the same way as previously, or that it works in the same way in every industrial country. Over the past generation a whole series of changes have transformed the working of the monetary system, particularly in Britain. Some of these changes have been in ideas, some in institutions and some in the economic climate within which the system works.

The Role of the Budget

The most far-reaching change, of which we are not always sufficiently aware, has been the extension of the public sector. We live in a mixed economy to which generalizations derived from the private enterprise system of fifty years ago no longer apply. In 1958, for example, the expenditure of public authorities in Great Britain on current and capital account (including transfer payments) came to 40 per cent of total domestic expenditure; their expenditure on goods and services alone came to nearly 25 per cent. This proportion relates only to direct expenditure and takes no account of the innumerable ways in which expenditure in the private sector is influenced by rates and taxes, subsidies, levies, tariffs and so on. There can be hardly any direction taken by private spending over which the budget does not exercise some influence, however remote. If, therefore, the state wishes to raise or lower the level of demand it has at its command a weapon of tremendous potency. If it adds to its expenditure or remits taxation, it can increase the flow of expenditure in the

72

most direct way. It can do so without being deliberately selective or it can, if it chooses, be selective in the industries, areas and groups whose incomes it wishes to augment. Its indirect influence, through variations in price incentives or through direct controls, can be even more extensive. It can, for example, by taxes or subsidies or in other ways, adjust the pattern of demand when a lack of balance in the economy is threatening inflation at the bottlenecks and leaving resources elsewhere unemployed.

This may seem to you a highly fanciful account of the powers of government in a democratic society. Budgets are not the work of master-minds juggling with figures in a political vacuum. They have to be voted on by people with very decided views. Almost any proposal to vary taxation or expenditure will meet with stiff opposition in some quarter; and if, to use a sporting analogy, the Minister of Finance does succeed in getting the ball out of the political scrum, he is liable to be forced into touch without much chance to take a drop at his goal of stabilizing demand. Nevertheless, he cannot escape the responsibility that falls on him by virtue of the large slice of national resources that he nowadays controls. If he cannot stabilize the expenditure of public authorities by his budget, what possible hope can there be of stabilizing it through monetary policy? If he does succeed in stabilizing it without changing the level of taxation, he will already have made a major contribution towards keeping the economy in balance, both because this will concentrate fluctuations in the private sector of national expenditure and because any surge in that expenditure will automatically be damped down by the need to pay additional taxes on the increment in output.

Public Investment

In addition to the enlargement in central and local budgets, there has been a great expansion in Britain in the spending of public corporations. It was not one of the stated objects of nationalization that it should bring within the direct control of the state a large proportion of the capital investment of the country but this has in fact been its most important outcome. Public investment in fixed assets during the fifties has run sometimes above and sometimes below private investment in fixed assets but at all times has been comparable in size. The scale of public investment does not derive entirely from the post-war nationalization measures since the local authorities have programmes almost as large as those of the public corporations, and the central government has also a fair-sized programme of its own.

But the public corporations alone had become responsible by the middle fifties for one-fifth of the gross capital formation of the country – more than half as much as all non-nationalized companies taken together. Their borrowings on the new issue market were larger than the amount raised by all public companies with a stock exchange quotation.

Public authorities of all kinds, including the nationalized industries, are thus in control of an even larger proportion of capital investment than they are of national expenditure. If investment is the most volatile element in demand, as we used to be taught, half of it can be operated upon directly without recourse to monetary measures. There is, of course, no reason why the transfer of any activity from the private to the public sector should insulate it from the effects of changes in interest rates or give it immunity from a general shortage of capital throughout the economy. The long-run level of public investment has to have regard to the cost of raising the money; and public corporations cannot free themselves from the need to use some rate of interest as a criterion for the worthwhileness of particular projects. But if cuts in public investment have to be made, it is natural to short-circuit monetary policy and decide directly what cuts to make. They can then be made with greater certainty and swiftness and are likely to be better co-ordinated than if made by each public corporation acting independently under financial pressure. It would indeed be strange if, in a fit of schizophrenia, the government were to decide in one capacity to take steps to limit investment and with this in view, put up interest rates, leaving itself in another capacity to decide whether and how to respond to the higher rates.

Insensitivity to Changes in Interest Rates

The transfer of the major public utilities to the public sector has removed from the private sector the very types of activity that were supposed to be most sensitive to changes in interest rates. The average manufacturing firm has never been thought to vary its investment plans much because of changes in long-term rates. It is thirty years since Keynes, expressing the view of most well-informed observers, pointed out in the *Treatise* that:

'Willingness to invest more or less in manufacturing plant is not likely to be very sensitive to small changes in bond-rate. But the quantity of new fixed capital required by industry is relatively trifling even at the best times, and is not a big factor in the situation. Almost

74

the whole of the fixed capital of the world is represented by buildings, transport and public utilities; and the sensitiveness of these activities even to small changes in the long-term rate of interest, though with an appreciable time-lag, is surely considerable.'[1]

'Buildings, transport and public utilities' – most of the first and nearly all of the last two are now in the public sector where their sensitiveness to changes in interest rates is no longer the determining factor.

The insensitivity of private investment has been heightened by other changes. Of these one is the level of taxation. When interest can be debited as a cost and rates of tax run at eight shillings in the pound, it is inevitable that a rise in tax should lose nearly half its force in checking borrowing for productive investment. Of the increase in outgoings in which a firm is involved by higher interest rates, 40 per cent is deductible from tax payments. This circumstance is likely to be of particular importance in small firms which are usually more easily inhibited from investment by financial difficulties.[2]

Full Employment and Investment Plans

A more important factor is the change in the business outlook in conditions of full employment. The government's pledge to maintain full employment does not, of course, guarantee a steady market for each industry, much less for every firm. But it does enable firms – once they trust the government's power to carry out its pledge – to count with more assurance on a growing level of aggregate demand, and to plan their own expansion with corresponding confidence. The larger firms in particular – as was clear from the evidence which a number of them gave to the Radcliffe Committee – draw up their investment programmes on a long-term footing and would not be deflected from carrying them out by a small rise in interest rates. They might hold off the capital market in the hope of better terms later and might trim their programme slightly by cutting out offices and canteens (which British business men obviously regard as dispensable); but they would not abandon them and would rarely

[1] J. M. Keynes, *Treatise on Money* (London, 1930), Vol. II, p. 364.
[2] On the one hand, these firms are likely to have higher debt/equity ratios and on the other hand, they pay rather higher rates on their loans. Thus their capital charges tend to be high and their vulnerability to an increase in interest rates is normally correspondingly great; but they have no more power to recoup the cost of additional interest than larger firms with less indebtedness or lower interest charges.

postpone them. They would be influenced much more by the market outlook than by interest costs and, given the prospect of full employment, would not be panicked by a temporary recession.

It is not easy to decide how far such views reflect expectations not of full employment but of inflation. After nearly thirty years of rising prices it does not require much study of White Papers or Election Manifestos to take a bullish view of the future. Nor does it require much courage to disregard a rise in interest rates from 5 per cent to 6 per cent if money is losing its value at an average rate of 3 or 4 per cent per annum. The real rate of interest has been so near to nil throughout the forties and fifties that it is hardly surprising if it does not enter much into business men's calculations. The only real mystery is why businesses have been so shy of incurring *more* debt, not why they should have been willing to go on borrowing in such favourable circumstances.

It is possible that industrial and commercial investment might become more sensitive to changes in interest rates if prices ceased to rise. Indeed, it is highly likely. But I should still expect a rather limited response; and I should also expect – although this is a large question which I cannot argue here – that once surplus capacity began to emerge, as at a fairly early stage it almost certainly would, private investment would begin to taper off by itself.

The consequences of the expansion in public spending and public investment do not end with their direct impact on the level of demand. The state has to finance its expenditure and it has also to finance public investment. It is already a heavy debtor and its activities oblige it also to be a heavy borrower. The size of the public debt and, still more, the weight of public borrowing, have transformed the capital market and the money market.[1]

Public Debt in the British Capital Market

It is hardly too much to say that the major problem of the British capital market has become the finance of public investment. The government has to advance at least £600 m. a year to the nationalized industries against fresh capital expenditure. The local authorities

[1] I pass by the interesting question of the effect of the expansion in the public sector on money flows within the public sector and between taxpayers and public authorities. The latter are not only a major source of disturbance to the money market but have converted the Inland Revenue into a financial institution in its own right, giving credit to dilatory taxpayers and accepting loans in the form of tax reserve certificates or, on occasion, interest-free advances from taxpayers who are in a hurry to pay their taxes.

have to finance capital projects totalling about £400 m. a year and nearly all of this has to be borrowed on their own credit. If the central government has no budget surplus on which to draw (as, however, it has), this makes a total demand on the market of about £1,000 m. a year – all of it in fixed interest securities. Both the central government and the local authorities have large recurring maturities that keep them constantly in the market, the re-financing operations of the central government alone involving some £600 m. to £1,000 m. annually 'for the foreseeable future' (para. 115). Thus the government is in a very different position from fifty years ago when its debt to the public was firmly held, largely in Consols with no fixed redemption date, and it rarely had any occasion to come to the market either to finance maturing debt or raise fresh money. The size of the public debt, which now exceeds the British national income by about 50 per cent, was at that time about two-thirds of the national income, so that the growth of the debt, although more rapid than the growth in income, is not of an altogether different order. The really important change is not in the size of the debt but in the need to enter the market year in and year out as a borrower.

The debt that was created in the Victorian capital market was largely private debt, much of it in the form of foreign loans; now the leading borrower on fixed interest is the British government. Fifty years ago the loan capital raised in the London market for British and foreign borrowers could reach in a single year a quarter of the national debt while the British government did not need to raise a penny. Today comparatively little private loan capital is raised by British borrowers (and then by the simple process of outbidding the government as price-leader in the bond market); overseas borrowers can make an issue only with government approval; even British local authorities have to queue up; and the new business takes the form of sales of gilt-edged by the Government Broker.[1]

This is a situation from which there is really no escape so long as public investment is half the national total, It is idle to propose, as some economists have done, that the whole of this investment should be financed within the public sector either out of the profits of public corporations or through a larger budget surplus. Some British public corporations cannot finance their investment out of

[1] It is a measure of this predominance of gilt-edged securities in the bond market that British government and government guaranteed securities quoted on the London Stock Exchange at market values, exceed company loan capital in the ratio of over 13 : 1.

profits for the simple reason that they conspicuously fail to earn them; the others could not hope to provide more than a limited proportion of the total. Moreover, if the public sector were wholly and deliberately self-financing, whether through retained profits or a budget surplus, it would be necessary for the private sector to be self-financing too, in the sense that it would have to absorb all private savings. But there is no reason to suppose that this would be possible without disturbance to employment and income. To abjure the use of the budget as a means of balancing savings and investment merely because it is awkward to have to borrow regularly is to jump from the frying-pan into the fire. So long as the public saves more than the private sector can absorb in capital formation, it is the sensible thing to do to offer the public a means of investing their surplus funds, either directly of through intermediaries, and let the outstanding volume of debt rise *pari passu* with the surplus.

Long-term Debt and Short-term Debt

The real issue is a different one: can the public be persuaded to put their money into long-term securities or will they insist on holding cash or short-term debt? If they do the first, it may be relatively easy to stop them from dipping into their savings when demand is already excessive; if they do the second there will be a corresponding stock of ready money and short-term assets forming a pool of excess liquidity and threatening to break through at any moment in a flood of purchasing power. Thus it is not the fact of a growing debt that is disturbing; it is the loss of control over the maturity distribution of the debt.

The British government has in fact had great difficulty in preventing a rapid accumulation of short-term debt. Before the war, in 1935, nearly the whole of the gilt-edged securities held by the market – to be exact, 86 per cent – were due for repayment in fifteen years or more.[1] By 1952 the proportion had fallen to 63 per cent and six years later in 1958 it was below 50 per cent. If Treasury Bills were to be included, the fall would, of course, be still steeper – from 80 per cent in 1935 to 40 per cent in 1958. Gilt-edged securities and Treasury Bills do not by any means make up the whole of the public sector – in fact only about three-fifths – but the remaining items, of which so-called 'small-savings', local authority debt and foreign debt are the largest, do not alter the general picture.

---

[1] *Report*, page 194. The proportion relates to a total which excludes local authority debt.

78

This increase in short-term government debt introduced into the monetary system a large volume of additional liquid assets with obvious inflationary consequences. But it also served to some extent to make good the relative decline in commercial paper which has been in progress for many years. In 1914 the market held £5 m. in Treasury Bills and £500 m. in commercial bills. In 1957 the market held £3,000 m. in Treasury Bills and £650 m. in commercial bills. Thus the ratio has changed from 1 : 100 to nearly 5 : 1.

The change in the money market has transformed the process of credit creation in the United Kingdom. Up to the First World War, the liquid assets that formed the base of the pyramid of credit were almost entirely private debts in the form of bills of exchange. These bills were particularly abundant in London because of the use of sterling bills as an instrument of international finance. The market was largely engaged in accepting and discounting bills to finance the movement of goods between Britain and foreign countries or between third countries, and there were in addition many finance bills in circulation divorced from commodity transactions. For many reasons – the rise of other financial centres, the relative decline in Britain's trade, the increasing proportion of her exports that consists of capital goods and is financed in other ways, the growing preference for bank advances as a source of short-term finance – the supply of bills has failed to keep pace with the growth of financial institutions. It is now so low in relation to the total volume of credit that unless the banking system were prepared to modify its liquidity ratios very considerably or to make use of alternative liquid assets, it could not support the present stock of bank money. The contraction in the supply of commercial paper left a gap in the monetary system which could most readily be filled, and has only too readily been filled, by Treasury Bills and short-term government paper.

Monetization of Debt

The first consequence of this change has been to turn bank-money more and more into a form of public debt. The process has not gone as far as it has with bank notes, which have departed so far from their original character of private liabilities that they are now a form of interest-free government debt. But if bank advances are held constant, an increase in bank deposits means a corresponding enlargement in the banks' portfolio of government paper. Changes in the money supply are, therefore, inextricably bound up with changes in government debt.

79

The second consequence is implicit in the first. If the lending policies of the banks are governed by a regard for their liquidity, so that the fixed point in those policies is an unwillingness to allow their net liquid assets to fall below a certain proportion of their liabilities, then the supply of money will be controlled by the availability of Treasury Bills. The monetary authorities can bring pressure on the money supply only by limiting the issue of Treasury Bills, and since the government's borrowing requirements are highly inelastic, this limitation in practice obliges the monetary authorities to sell longer-dated securities to the public so as to be able to reduce their current borrowing on short term. If they can carry out funding operations, they can issue fewer bills, curtail the liquid assets in the hands of the banks and force on them a contraction of credit. If they are unsuccessful in selling their bonds, they have no option, short of redrafting the budget, but to offer an unchanged supply of bills which will provide the banks with the liquid assets they need in order to maintain their current ratios.

This is to put the matter in rather too unqualified a manner. It leaves out of account any other liquid assets in the hands of the banks and assumes also that the monetary authorities are powerless to redistribute the supply of Treasury Bills between the banks and other holders. But in the United Kingdom neither qualification is now overriding. There was a time when an increase in bank rate could reduce the credit supplied by the London market to the rest of the world and by limiting the whole of commercial bills discounted in London could deprive the banks and the discount market of a source of liquid assets. At the end of 1958, however, the London clearing banks held Treasury Bills to a value ten times as great as their holdings of other bills and in the discount market the ratio was not much lower. There are countries where the banks hold only a limited proportion of market Treasury Bills and the distribution can be varied by credit policy; in March 1957, for example, the US banking system held only one-eighth of the privately held Bills issued by the Treasury. But at the same date the corresponding proportion for the British banking system was one-half and most of the other half was held, comparatively firmly, by overseas holders.

A third consequences, in Britain at all events, is that cash reserve ratios have ceased to be the pivot of the monetary system. A bank which is short of cash can replenish its stock automatically by allowing Treasury Bills to mature or by reducing its bid at the tender. Nor can the monetary authorities deprive it of access to cash so long as their borrowing requirements are inelastic. From their point

80

of view a high cash reserve ratio means little more than a saving in the interest they would otherwise pay on Treasury Bills. From the point of view of the banks a reserve ratio appreciably above the minimum dictated by operating requirements would only be justifiable if Treasury Bills were liable to become suddenly illiquid or convertible into cash only on penalty terms. But the Bank of England cannot refuse to make cash available when Treasury Bills are maturing at the rate of over £60 m. a week and when instead it has to be at hand to ensure that the weekly tender is covered. It is not surprising, therefore, that the cash reserves of the British banks are a resultant of the level of their deposits and have no real influence on the process by which that level is arrived at.

Operations in the Gilt-edged Market

Operations on the money-supply are now indistinguishable, therefore, from operations in gilt-edged. These operations are not so intermittent in the United Kingdom as they are in most other countries; the authorities are continuously in the gilt-edged market. A new issue of government bonds, for example, is not privately underwritten or sold outright to dealers: what the public does not subscribe for on the day of issue is taken up into the portfolio of the Bank of England's Issue Department (which in effect acts as the underwriter) and peddled out over the following months. Although new issues are made at intervals, there are always supplies of fresh stock 'on tap' and it is indeed the need to replenish the 'tap' that is 'the main consideration in the minds of the authorities in determining the timing of new issues'.[1] These tap stocks always include at least one medium and one long-dated stock and the prices at which they are on offer is an important influence on yields and prices in the gilt-edged market and so on the general structure of interest rates. Apart from these transactions in tap stocks, the Issue Department is habitually a buyer of stocks nearing maturity with the object of reducing the amount of stock that will fall to be converted or repaid. Just as the sale of tap stocks spreads the process of issuing stock to the public over a longer period, so the purchase of maturing stock extends the period of refinancing and enables the authorities and the market to make more gradual adjustment to large issues instead of concentrating them, at irregular intervals, within a few days.

But this is not all. For the authorities have an interest in maintaining an orderly market and this disposes them to offer support to the

[1] *Report*, para. 111.

F

market in the face of heavy selling pressure or in order to facilitate exceptionally large transactions. The dealers in the gilt-edged market are not able to absorb a large volume of sales out of their own resources and at the short end of the gilt-edged market there is an almost total absence of dealers who will undertake the function of the jobber and set themselves against the market trend. Mr A. W. Trinder, of the Union Discount Co., was able to tell the Tribunal which was investigating an alleged leakage of information about the change in bank rate in 1957: 'I am the market in . . . short bonds'. It is not surprising, therefore, that there were complaints before the Radcliffe Committee of difficulty in making large sales of such bonds or that it should be common practice to ask the Government Broker to quote a price on such occasions. It is also known that, in spite of their professed policy of 'continuous funding' there have been periods when the authorities were substantial net buyers of their own securities. It has been estimated that last February, when the authorities suddenly lowered their support price, to the consternation of the market and the general public, they did so after the banks had thrown on the market no less than £80 m. in government securities within a single week.[1]

Thus, although the authorities still claim to follow the market and never to press sales at prices below current levels, their operations are an indispensable part of the market mechanism and allow them to influence long-term rates in ways that were not previously part of the armoury of central banks. It is not possible for the Bank of England, as it is for the Federal Reserve Bank, to limit its intervention to the money market and leave this intervention to work its way through to the longer end of the market. It is already, and cannot help but remain, an integral part of the gilt-edged market.

Debt Management and Monetary Policy

This circumstance helps to account for the concern shown by the Radcliffe Committee, not only for a more deliberate policy towards longer rates of interest, but also for the closest possible co-operation between the Bank of England and the Treasury. If it were possible to separate debt management from monetary policy, there might be something to be said for regarding the first as the affair of the Treasury and the second as the affair of the Bank. Some witnesses before the Radcliffe Committee did in fact attempt just such a judgment of Solomon. But if there is really only one baby, it must be treated as indi-

[1] *The Times*, 23 March, 1960.

visible. It is not possible to let the Bank of England make the running in matters of bank rate while the Treasury decides the terms on which it will borrow. A decision to suspend funding operations affects the money market just as directly as a change in liquidity ratios. Action on the short end and action on the long end of the market are complementary weapons and cannot be allowed to run counter to one another without destroying their effectiveness.

Finance Ministers and Central Banks

In the same way, it would be impossible to allow monetary policy to be governed by criteria different from those shaping budgetary policy, since both are intended to tell on the level of demand and must be co-ordinated with that object. No doubt there are grounds for fearing that Finance Ministers will court popularity more freely than Governors of Central Banks and for making it at least a little awkward for the Governor to be overridden by his Finance Minister. But given the prestige attaching to his office, and the shock to public opinion that would follow his resignation – all the greater because unprecedented – it is doubtful whether any Governor need fear that his advice will be given insufficient weight. The greater danger is that in seeking to reinforce his title to an independently-formed view, he may hold aloof from the policy-forming departments of government and inhibit a free interchange of ideas at staff level. In a community that trusts its Finance Minister to frame a budget, there is something a little archaic in the notion that he can be rescued from his errors by the Central Bank: not indeed by the overt pursuit of a monetary policy inconsistent with the government's intentions but by obstruction and delay, as if the bank were a kind of House of Lords, wiser and more mature than the Lower House.

The changes that I have described all tell in one direction: against relying heavily on monetary policy. Either they provide alternative weapons or they weaken the effectiveness of monetary measures. But are the alternatives adequate and is monetary policy altogether ineffective? What scope is left for its use in a mixed economy such as I have described? It is to this question that I turn in my next chapter.

5. Demand Management: the Scope for Monetary Policy in a Mixed Economy[1]

The question we have to consider is how the growth of a mixed economy, with all the changes that it involves, affects the choice of regulatory instrument. Does the contraction of the private sector enfeeble monetary policy by limiting the area within which it takes effect and does the extension of the public sector arm the government with powers to secure directly what monetary policy aims to do indirectly? What should be the monetary component, in modern circumstances, of economic policy?

What I have to say on this subject will be largely, although not entirely, an echo of the Radcliffe Report, and will relate, therefore, to the situation in my own country. My knowledge of other economies, including your own, is much too limited to allow me to judge whether conclusions based on British experience are applicable.

The Aims of Monetary Policy

If we are to form any judgment of the scope for monetary policy, we have first to lay down what we should like it to do. Now there are many objectives to which most people are ready to subscribe – the Radcliffe Report lists five – although nobody has much confidence that they are all mutually consistent. It is perhaps better to talk of the *ambition* of the authorities than of the objectives of policy: and this ambition appears to be to achieve rapid economic growth, keeping demand on a steady path of expansion, so that, on the one hand, full use is made of available resources and, on the other, internal and external balance is preserved. Just what is to be understood by 'steady', 'full' and 'balance' it is not polite to enquire too closely. Can there be internal balance if money is losing its value,

[1] The second of two Wicksell Lectures, delivered in Stockholm on 5 May, 1960.

84

and if so, for how long? What changes in reserves or in capital movements are compatible with external balance? An economy can make fuller use of resources when it is run at such pressure that prices are sure to rise; external balance is easier to maintain if internal balance is not a prior aim; the quickest way to grow may not be along a path of steady expansion. When there are conflicts such as these, which is to take precedence: full employment or price stability; internal or external balance; stability or growth?

These are familiar conundrums to which different countries return different answers. Some elect to hazard a little unemployment in the hope of rather less inflation while others run greater risks of inflation for the sake of a higher level of employment. The way in which a country takes its risks affects the scope for the use of monetary measures. If it seeks to maintain so great a pressure of demand that costs cannot help but respond, it is idle to look to monetary measures to put things right: that would be to pour water on a fire as soon as it had been carefully stoked with petrol. If it is intended to keep demand rather lower, and within the limits where the movement of costs and prices is somewhat indeterminate, monetary measures may help; but they may be relatively ineffective unless other action is taken to bring the movement of costs under firmer control. It is only too easy to set monetary policy tasks that are mutually inconsistent or for which it is obviously unsuited and then complain that it does not work.

Given the general purposes which monetary measures are intended to serve, there are three principal ways in which they may be used. First of all, they may be directed towards regulating the pressure of demand by acting on the cost or availability of credit. This is essentially a short-term aim, calling for early diagnosis of changes in pressure and a fairly quick response to the measures adopted. Secondly, monetary policy is capable of influencing the rate of capital accumulation through its effects on the incentive to create new physical assets. It can, moreover, alter the balance between saving and consumption and between investment at home and overseas. While some of these effects may show themselves quickly, they do not all exhaust themselves in the short-term; there are longer-term effects on the growth of the economy, distinct from the shorter-term effects on its stability. Thirdly, monetary policy has external effects and can be used in various ways to alter the balance of payments or the rate of exchange.

I cannot hope to deal in any detail with these various roles of monetary policy. I propose to concentrate on the first (regulation of

85

the pressure of demand), leave the second entirely on one side (ignoring effects on growth as distinct from stability) and pass briefly over the third (the regulation of external transactions). I shall also, in dealing with this third, and least controversial role, confine myself to a single type of monetary measure – the use of interest differentials as a means of influencing the flow of international capital.

Interest Differentials and Capital Flows

This flow is undoubtedly the most volatile element in the balance of payments and is peculiarly difficult to control. Under gold standard conditions, it could be made to respond to changes in interest rates: a great part of banking policy has traditionally been aimed at just such a response in order to maintain convertibility at the existing parity.[1] It is, indeed, this response that has made the average central bank so preoccupied with the money market and short rates of interest. In present circumstances, so long as there is no fear of restrictions on the international flow of credit or of changes in parities of exchange, higher rates of interest can still check international borrowing in a particular centre and increase the flow of funds to that centre. But in the 1950s, at least, these conditions were rarely fulfilled. The British authorities were faced with lack of confidence in their power and determination to maintain the external value of sterling and fears that forward contracts in sterling might be overridden by fresh restrictions on the withdrawal of funds. Small changes in the return on sterling balances were much less influential, therefore, than action to remove distrust in the authorities' intentions; and it was as an ingredient in such action that they saw the principal justification for the use of bank rate. In their evidence to the Radcliffe Committee, they argued that changes in short-term interest rates, unsupported by other measures, would be unlikely to bring about any large-scale transference of funds to London, though they still attributed some importance to the effect of higher rates in strengthening sterling through a shift of short-term and commercial borrowing to other centres.

These views did not prevent the authorities from using bank rate in a foreign exchange crisis: nearly every increase in bank rate in the fifties coincided with a drain on the reserves. But the authorities

[1] See, for example, the study of the working of the gold standard by A. I. Bloomfield, *Monetary Policy under the International Gold Standard, 1880–1914.* (Federal Reserve Bank of New York, 1959.)

were relying not so much on the direct effect of higher rates as on what might be called their advertising value. A foreign banker might be in doubt what interpretation to put on changes in the budget or on new administrative measures designed to improve the balance of payments; he would have less difficulty in interpreting a change in bank rate as a signal, if not as an instrument, of dearer money. This may seem to imply a rather poor opinion of the sophistication of foreign bankers. But it is not, after all, only banking opinion that has to be influenced when there is speculative pressure against a currency, and leads and lags in payment begin to show themselves. At such times, as a rule, it is commercial credits quite as much as banking funds that are in flight. Even if bankers are unmoved by changes in bank rate, it is unlikely that the business community will be, provided it takes these changes as reliable indications of a definite shift in policy, likely to be reinforced by other government measures.

It would be reasonable to suppose that in the circumstances of the sixties, interest differentials will have more influence on the flow of international capital, both short term and long. The final evidence given by the Bank of England to the Radcliffe Committee a year ago laid more stress on this influence than earlier evidence, but implied that transfers in response to interest differentials were still limited in amount.[1] Within the past few months the Governor has expressed confidence in his power to keep short rates below the level in other centres without inviting a large drain on the reserves. The attitude of the authorities is thus that while there is more fluidity of international capital so that higher rates can be used with effect in a crisis, this fluidity is not powerful enough to require any rigorous alignment of rates in the leading centres.

IMF Loans

There are, moreover, other ways of achieving what variations in interest rates have traditionally been used to achieve. First of all, when the currency of a well-managed country is under temporary pressure which its reserves are inadequate to withstand, it seems more sensible to make use of international financial institutions rather than rely on private capital to provide relief. Loans and standby credits from the IMF can do all that higher interest rates can do to buttress a country's external position; no doubt such credits are unlikely to be granted without restrictive conditions but these conditions need

[1] Q. 13434 *et seq.*

not impose the attendant costs and harmful side-effects of higher interest rates. This is a line of thought strongly endorsed by the Radcliffe Report which recommends both a strengthening of the IMF and its transformation in the long run into 'an international central bank with its own unit of account, free to accept deposit liabilities or external overdraft facilities to the central banks of member countries'.[1]

A Wider Band in Exchange Rates

In the second place it is possible through control over forward exchange rates, as Keynes pointed out in the twenties, to offset interest differentials if international transfers of capital are becoming embarrassing. In normal circumstances, variations in the forward exchange rate are likely to remain within limits set by permissible departures from parity in spot rates, and it is arguable that those limits are too narrow. In the case of sterling, the range of variations in dollar rates lies between 2.78 and 2.82, which is well within the limit of 1 per cent in either direction permitted under the Articles of Agreement of the IMF. A slightly wider range – say, between 2.76 and 2.84 – would make it easier to use the forward exchange market in order to shelter the domestic economy from the pressure of changes in interest rates abroad. The Radcliffe Committee made no recommendation of this kind but it saw an important place for operations in the forward market in conditions in which there was confidence in the pound.

Capital Controls

Thirdly, there are various controls that can be used to strengthen the currency and improve the short-run balance of payments: exchange control over dealings in foreign exchange; control over capital movements, including restrictions on capital issues for foreign borrowers: and administrative measures designed to restrict imports or encourage exports. As the Radcliffe Report points out, for the ten years prior to 1949 'these controls were the sole means in use, other than fiscal measures, for checking any loss of reserves and maintaining equilibrium in the balance of payments';[2] and in the ten years since 1949 they have continued to provide an important instrument for this purpose. That they have serious limitations is by now well understood and there should be no need to emphasize

[1] *Report*, para. 678.   [2] *Report*, para. 723.

the fact. What is more likely to be forgotten, as the world moves towards full convertibility of currencies, is that controls also have their uses and are by no means completely ineffective. Even Switzerland, for example, has had occasion within the past few years to close her capital market to foreign borrowers; and many countries with strong currencies use quantitative limitations on imports for balance of payments reasons.

The Domestic Effects of Monetary Measures

When we turn to the domestic effects of monetary measures we are faced at once with the difficulty of establishing what those effects really are. If we look for evidence of them in the statistical record of the British economy since the war, we find remarkably little. There were no violent oscillations in economic activity in which the restrictive effects of monetary policy might become visible. The gross national product (at constant prices) was higher in each year than in the preceding one with only two exceptions, in 1952 and 1958, when the fall was well under 1 per cent. Although long-term interest rates doubled and short-term rates fluctuated between ½ per cent and nearly 7 per cent, fixed capital investment, in real terms, increased in every year without exception, apart from short periods of less than a year when the trend was interrupted. It is difficult to find corroboration here for the speculations of those economists who attribute to British monetary policy damaging effects on investment and growth. There is no easily interpreted lag of one variable behind another from which the operation of monetary measures can be clearly traced, and the causal sequence is obscured by the simultaneous operation of other measures and other forces. The one clear exception is the marked reduction in sales of consumers' durable goods that followed the imposition of hire purchase restrictions and the sharp increase that succeeded the removal of those restrictions.

If we dig further back into the past, we have to jump over the inter-war period to get to a world faced with similar inflationary pressures and it is doubtful how far we can make use of evidence from that far-away time. That monetary policy had real effects there can be no question; but they were often slow or violent. It is easy to be fascinated by cyclical rhythm of interest rates in the Victorian era and attribute a corresponding modulation to monetary policy. May this not be an illusion? Was the trade cycle much affected by anything that was done by the central bank or is its hand visible more as the hour-hand of a clock than as the hand that holds the

89

reins of finance? The operations of the Bank of England look in retrospect a little like the elaborate procession of legendary figures pursued by Father Time that emerges with the striking of a medieval clock. Our attention is riveted to the procession and we have no patience with onlookers who insist that there must be some other, and hidden, mechanism that causes the clock to strike. But may it not have been so? If there had been no central bank at all, would the fluctuations of the nineteenth century have looked so very different? Can we be confident that the banking system did much more than add a little elasticity?

Let us leave aside the past, which does not tell a conclusive story, and look at the way in which monetary measures are supposed to work. And here let me explain that under monetary measures I include for the present only the classical instruments of discount policy and open market operations. There is no need for me to remind you that central banks have never limited themselves to these measures, do not all use them in the same way, and have in the recent past used much more peremptory and selective methods of control over the availability of finance. All these complications I shall, for the present, ignore.

As I have already explained, the first of the classical instruments, open market operations, can nowadays be broadly identified with what in Britain is called 'funding' – the sale of bonds in substitution for bills. These operations are not necessarily promoted by the simultaneous use of the second of the classical instruments, a higher bank rate. The immediate effect of an increase in bank rate is to raise the whole range of short-term rates, including the rate on time deposits, and to make short-term assets more attractive relatively to long-term. For this and other reasons it may cause some weakness in the bond market and obstruct the efforts of the authorities to increase their sales in that market. Far from discount policy and open market operations pulling in the same direction, as we are often assured they must, it is easy to imagine conditions in which they pull quite strongly against one another.

The Modus Operandi of Bank Rate

What then does a higher bank rate do to check an inflation of demand? If it hinders rather than promotes funding operations – and I do not suggest that this is always so – it does nothing to contract the credit base, so that, whatever else happens, there is none of that elimination of 'idle money' to which some economists appear to attach primary importance. There are, however, other effects that may operate to restrict credit and investment.

First of all, in the British system, there is a strong customary connection between bank rate and most other rates for short-term funds. When bank rate is put up, these rates move up more or less automatically and, as a rule, to a corresponding extent. One of the most important of such rates is that on bank advances which for most customers is fixed at 1 per cent over bank rate, with a minimum of 5 per cent. It is possible that an increase in the cost of bank credit might be sufficient by itself to induce merchants and others to reduce the level of their stocks and that such acts of disinvestment would provide an effective check on business expansion. Given the importance of the banks as lenders, there is no doubt *some* rate at which this effect would show itself. But there are reasons for expecting quicker reactions to higher interest rates in other directions; and whatever may become true in the 1960s, the demand for bank credit has until recently been so much restricted by other factors that its cost can have exercised little influence on the level of advances. Even if we broaden the argument to take account of other sources of short-term credit, and assume that the banks act as price leaders in the credit market, it is doubtful whather such elasticity as shows itself on the side of demand is large enough to allow bank rate a decisive influence on stockbuilding. The Radcliffe Committee heard evidence to show that stocks of some commodities such as wine and timber, were affected by the cost of financing them, but it remained unconvinced that this effect was sufficiently large or widespread to give changes in bank rate the required 'bite' or purchase on the level of demand.

A second effect, on which Keynes in particular used to insist, involves tighter credit rationing by the banks. In normal circumstances there is an unsatisfied fringe of borrowers, which can be contracted or enlarged by varying the banks' standards of eligibility, with effects on private investment out of proportion to any that might result from the simultaneous changes in short-term interest rates. But as Keynes recognized, this process ceases to be effective if first-class borrowers are denied bank credit and thrust into the queue: for they are bound in the end, to find ways round, even if at somewhat higher cost.[1] Moreover, if a credit squeeze is to be inaugurated by a change in bank rate rather than by quantitative limitations on

[1] 'The existence of this unsatisfied fringe and of a variability in the banks' standards of eligibility of borrowers in respects other than the rate of interest, allows the Banking System a means of influencing the rate of investment supple-

advances, the banks must already be lent up to their limits; and this was far from the situation in Britain over the past thirty years.

Although the Radcliffe Committee found no reason to take account of this effect, given the asset ratios of the banks, they gave a more general version of it, applicable to a wider range of financial institutions, in their discussion of the liquidity effect of changes in interest rates. They suggested, following a line of argument made familiar by Mr Roosa, that lenders as a group might ration credit more severely if bank rate were increased. Some commentators have been puzzled by this suggestion. In the case of the banks, credit rationing is forced on them not by the rise in bank rate in itself but by the contraction in their holdings of liquid assets, and so in their liquidity ratio, which is presumed to accompany the rise in rates. Other financial institutions are under no such obvious compulsion. If they must offer higher rates in order to retain their funds, they are also in a position to recoup these higher costs by raising their own lending rates. It is only, so it is argued, if the rates offered and charged by lenders are 'sticky' that it is possible to set much store by the so-called Roosa effect.[1]

This is a highly complex issue into which I cannot enter fully. I should be inclined to argue that the effect of a change in bank rate resides more in the fact of change, with all the uncertainty that this arouses, than in the precise level established by the change. If all that happened were that one continuing rate was replaced by a higher continuing rate, the liquidity effect might well be minimal. It would be governed largely by the consequential fall in asset values and show itself in a disclination of borrowers to realize those assets and a desire on their part to restore their liquidity, quite as much as in the anxiety of lenders to strengthen their reserves. But if the change in bank rate also gives rise, as in practice it must, to speculation about the period for which it will continue, the possibility of a

---

mentary to mere changes in the short-term rate of interest. The process of stimulating investment in this way cannot be continued beyond the point at which there is no longer any unsatisfied fringe; nor can the reverse process be continued beyond the point at which the unsatisfied fringe begins to include borrowers so influential that they can find ways around, e.g. by creating bills of first-class quality or by borrowing direct from the banks' depositors. But within these limits the banks can produce effects on the rate of investment out of proportion to what properly corresponds to the changes, if any, in the short-term rate of interest which are taking place at the same time.' J. M. Keynes, *Treatise on Money* (London, 1930) Vol. II p. 365.

[1] See, for example, J. Spraos, 'Control by Stickiness of Rates', *Banker's Magazine*, November 1959.

further change in the same direction, the pressures in the economy that have forced the authorities to act, the additional measures that their action may portend, and so on, the effect on liquidity may be of a different order. It is not so much that financial institutions will seek to hold more cash as that they will be likely to restrict their new investments to more liquid assets and to stiffen the terms on which they will lend to the private sector.

It is a profound mistake to think of finance for the private sector as capable of analysis in exactly the same terms as finance for the public sector and to treat the finance available to a single enterprise as a simple function of its price. The average private borrower has to think of the possibility of failure or of the capital losses that he may sustain if forced to realize his assets at an awkward time; this makes him discount his prospective earnings at a much higher rate when he is threatened with illiquidity than when he is not. At the same time, if money becomes tighter, he may obtain less finance through his normal channels, whatever the rate he is paying, because lenders are unwilling to maintain their existing commitments in any single direction; and he may be obliged to seek extra credit from sources unfamiliar with his standing and reluctant to extend themselves in his favour. The marginal cost of finance to any except the largest borrowers tends to slope upwards relatively fast and rises discontinuously whenever fears of illiquidity are aroused. A rise in bank rate, if it provokes such fears however mildly, can have a quite disproportionate effect on the readiness of borrowers to proceed with their investment plans and on the terms on which they can finance those plans without at least some marginal retrenchment.[1]

Yet even this mechanism works more feebly nowadays. It relies on pricking the confidence of the business community in sustained expansion, on alarms and jolts, not on a cumulative and controllable response to a tightening of credit. It relies also on memories of the liquidity crises of the past, when bank rate climbed to 10 per cent and additional credit was not to be had at any price. But in a world where inflation is almost taken for granted and where governments are pledged to full employment, the danger of capital losses in a crisis is greatly diminished. Private borrowers can raise money even when the government cannot sell its bonds. A large part of the business of the country is in the hands of firms with relatively easy

[1] For a development of this line of argument see C. Segré: 'The Supply of Finance and the Theory of Investment in the Firm', *Quarterly Review of the Banca Nazionale del Lavoro*, November 1957, and B. Tew, 'A Case for Financial Controls', *The Banker*, January 1960.

access to additional finance and the differential between the terms on which they can borrow and the return on gilt-edged is narrower and less responsive to monetary pressure than it used to be. Thus while there is no doubt that a change in bank rate, particularly if it is thought to herald other measures with a more direct impact on demand, can have real and powerful effects, the change has to be one of great and unexpected violence if it is to do what much smaller changes formerly did; and governments may reasonably hesitate to resort to such violence in the interests of greater economic stability.

Reacting on Long-term Rates

A third possible *modus operandi* is through long-term rates. A change in bank rate, and the accompanying changes in other short rates, has effects in the gilt-edged market, sought or unsought. If the connection is a close one, it can be argued that changes in bank rate will sooner or later work through to the long end of the market and check or encourage interest-sensitive forms of investment. The Macmillan Committee, which developed this line of argument, drew attention to the role of the banks in mediating between the two parts of the market. If a fall in bank rate were backed up by open market operations, this would enlarge the credit base and put the banks in a position to buy government securities. Their purchases, together with those made by the central bank in carrying out open market operations, would give a lift to the gilt-edged market and thus would encourage other buying. The movement would spread to other parts of the market and improve the cost of long-term borrowing by other first-class borrowers until, with the revival of the new issue market, real investment also recovered.[1]

This is in fact an almost exact description of the course of events after 1931; the Macmillan Committee scored a bull's eye. There is not much room for doubt as to the working of the mechanism in the conditions of the thirties; but do these conditions still obtain? Leaving aside the interesting question whether the mechanism works in the same way in periods of credit restriction as in periods of credit expansion, the answer is plainly that conditions are by no means the same. Public utilities and housing which the Committee singled out as the most interest-sensitive types of investment, are now largely in the public sector and can be restricted or expanded by other methods. The responsiveness of private investment to changes in long-term interest rates is much slower and smaller than it used to be.

[1] *Report of the Committee on Finance and Industry* (Cmnd. 3897, 1931), paras 231–9.

But there are in addition, difficulties in the use of banking policy in order to change long-term rates. In the 1930s these difficulties lay mainly in the need to persuade the public that cheap money had come to stay; the authorities had no reason to be inhibited in buying securities and forcing up their price. They had, moreover, the great advantage of starting with very little short-term debt and the power to convert at short notice the great mass of high-yielding bonds. In the fifties the object of the authorities was to sell securities, not to buy them, and selling in a market congested with government paper is far more difficult than buying for cash which no one has learned to distrust. The authorities, moreover, were attempting in the fifties the still more difficult task of selling without forcing prices down instead of, as in the thirties, buying with the object of forcing prices up.

Selling Gilt-edged

Herein lay the paradox of British monetary policy. The authorities were not prepared to take the necessary steps to raise long-term rates while the logic of all their other actions implied higher rates. On the one hand, they sought to reduce the size of the Treasury Bill issue, to limit the liquidity of the banks, to extend the maturity of the debt, to find a market for the securities of the public corporations, to make room for issues by local authorities and Commonwealth borrowers. On the other hand, they hesitated to offer bonds on terms that would have brought willing buyers. They preferred to follow the market and make sales whenever it was rising, whatever the price, rather than find bottom at a price that would assure them of a market.

The explanation of this paradox lies in the view taken by the authorities of operations in the gilt-edged market. They do not appear to have seen any particular virtue in high long-term rates in their own right (e.g. as a check on investment) and regarded such rates as a reflection of the government's credit. If they had to choose between high rates and sales of bonds they preferred to sell bonds, no doubt because this restored their grip on the money market. But they were not prepared to cut prices in order to sell bonds because they thought that such action would spoil the market and add to their difficulties in finding buyers rather than make it easier to sell. They insisted that sales could only be made on a rising market and that they had been trying hard to make sales all along.

As a matter of market tactics it may well be easier to find buyers on a rising market; that this was the Bank of England's experience is not in question. But it would be absurd to rest policy on such a maxim, without first ensuring that the point of departure for the rising market was itself well-chosen. We need not stay to ask whether the maxim implies that the more you have to sell the more you must concentrate on making the price rise; if this were true, the management of the national debt could be undertaken at negligible cost by letting bond prices rise steadily towards infinity. The fact is that while buyers ask themselves whether they will regret their bargain tomorrow, and hasten to buy before prices become still higher, they have first to make up their mind to buy at all and before doing so want to satisfy themselves that the level of prices is advantageous. If they are already loaded up with depreciated government securities, they will want to make sure that bonds are really cheap, not just that they are becoming dearer, before they buy any more.

Their reluctance to press sales left the authorities with one principal expedient for operating on gilt-edged prices: they could jab at the market by raising bank rates and then try to make sales in the intervals of recovery. But this was a doubly expensive process. In the first place the use of high short-term rates was costly in itself and cut right across the policy of funding by making it worth while to remain liquid. The second and more disastrous result was that the market was demoralized by the long decline in gilt-edged prices. As the Radcliffe Committee reported, commenting on this result, 'if the authorities half-heartedly follow trends, gradually and reluctantly raising interest rates, the prolonged downward drag of bond prices will in the end do permanent damage to the market's appetite for government bonds'.[1]

Yet the authorities have a case; and the Committee was not altogether unsympathetic to it. In their Report they held firmly to the view that a more deliberate view should be taken of long-term rates and that they should not be left to such partial and spasmodic influence as could be exerted by money market pressures. But they were also sufficiently impressed by the difficulty of making large bond sales quickly to argue against a suspension of funding and a reduction in rates in times of slackness in production. 'The lower rates and the increased liquidity entailed', they pointed out, 'might well be reached just in time to be a nuisance in the next boom'.[2] If the authorities were to remain habitual net sellers of bonds, they would be unwise to try to concentrate their sales in boom periods when the market was at its weakest and would find it preferable to make steadier sales

[1] *Report*, para. 566.　　　　　　　　[2] *Report*, para. 577.

at steadier prices. To make long rates fluctuate more widely in order to control the less sensitive forms of capital expenditure left within the private sector would also be to raise the minimum below which, on an expansionist tack, interest rates could not be lowered. Bond prices should reflect long-term changes in the shortage of capital, but not necessarily short-term cyclical changes. In the modern world, money might have to remain dear even in a recession and reliance would have to be placed on budgetary policy to restore prosperity.

If one follows this line of thought to the bitter end, it still leaves the authorities in something of a quandary. The downward drift in the gilt-edged market has not been due merely to an exceptional shortage of capital; it has its origins at least as much in fears of inflation. It is one thing to ask the authorities to use more deliberation in their approach to long-term rates and make them reflect the underlying trends in thrift and productivity. It is quite another to ask them to adjust long-term rates so as to reflect a more realistic view of the prospect of inflation; to do so would be to expose their own helplessness. What if the market is weak because it distrusts the power or resolution of the authorities to cope with inflation? Are the authorities to overcome this weakness by lowering their support price for gilt-edged? Such action might do no more than confirm the market's fears and renew the slide. There is, in fact, no way of restoring morale in the gilt-edged market so long as inflation is constantly in the background; and the authorities may well find that their problem in the bond market is less how to use interest rates so as to exert pressure on investment than how to reassure the investor that money will preserve its value.[1]

I turn now to the wider question whether monetary instruments are preferable to fiscal or direct controls in the running of a mixed economy. There are a number of advantages in the use of monetary instruments that are not shared by alternative forms of control.

The Advantages of Monetary Instruments

First, I would place acceptability. A large section of informed opinion is willing to endorse policies of dear money or cheap money in the right set of circumstances when it might hesitate to accept budgetary changes or direct controls. It may be, as Professor Kahn has argued,[2] that dear money is more acceptable than cheap, and

[1] For a similar view see R. F. Henderson, 'Money in Practice', in *Not Unanimous*, ed. by A. Seldon (London, 1960).

[2] *Memorandum of Evidence to the Committee on the Working of the Monetary System*, para. 7. (Memoranda, Vol. 3, p. 139).

that the choice tends to be biased towards monetary measures on the restrictive tack and other measures on the expansionist tack. It is certainly true, as he points out, that there is a greater disposition to persevere with monetary restriction and apply another turn of the screw if the initial effects are disappointing than to continue with monetary expansion and rely exclusively on cheap money when a recovery is slow in coming. But there is nothing sinister about this: it merely reflects the greater power of high interest rates to check investment than of low interest rates to encourage it. We ought perhaps to be thankful, given the bias of governments against the use of any restrictive measures, that there is at least one that popular opinion finds acceptable.

If, secondly, we ask why monetary measures should be more acceptable than others, the answer lies in their anonymity. They operate through market mechanisms on the whole range of borrowing and lending transactions and do not single out some group of individuals or some particular forms of demand for control or regulation. This means that they are, in general, less compulsive and less selective than other measures. It would be wrong, however, to push the contrast too far, since even the classical weapons of monetary policy relied on credit rationing by bank managers and more recent measures have made extensive use of selective credit control; there is, therefore, and always has been, an element of compulsion in the background. It is also wrong to overlook the selective influence of monetary measures on investment; in pre-war theory at least, it was precisely because of its special power to smooth out fluctuations in investment that the use of monetary measures was favoured.

It is a point in favour of monetary measures that they make for a freer economy. But is it so desirable that they should be non-selective? The danger of inflation is greatly aggravated if the pressure of demand is uneven, so that capacity working is reached earlier in some industries and areas than it is reached elsewhere. A general restriction of purchasing power may be ineffective as a means of aligning the pattern of demand with the pattern of economic activity and it may be necessary to impose selective checks where excess demand is greatest. This need will be most evident where industrial mobility is low and where producers are least inhibited in raising their prices when they have full order books. If bottlenecks appear only in isolated industries, they can usually be quickly removed without creating any great strain in the structure of costs or starting off a wage-inflation. But when the bottlenecks are more widespread and intractable, there is a danger that measures intended to restrict demand will reduce output but fail to stop inflation. More selective methods of control would then be preferable.

When we turn to fiscal and administrative measures and consider their *lack* of anonymity, the virtues of monetary measures stand out much more clearly. It may be fairly easy to decide what budget surplus to aim at – in point of fact it is not all easy, and governments are not very good marksmen – but even if we assume that a docile Minister of Finance accepts what his experts tell him, he has still to find a way of satisfying, not a series of Walrasian equations, but large numbers of his less docile supporters. The processes by which budgets are made are unlikely to approximate very closely to those by which changes in bank rate are decided, and in some countries the divergence is obviously a very wide one. Reliance on budgetary control over the pressure of demand runs certain risks, therefore, from which monetary measures are more immune.

It is possible to claim with minor reservations that any private gains or losses resulting from monetary measures are undesigned and can be disregarded. But no such claim can be made for budgetary or administrative measures. The mere fact that such gains and losses will result and are demonstrably the outcome of government action tends to cause delay in coming to a decision and the decision itself is affected by regard for the interests concerned.

A third advantage of monetary policy is its flexibility. No one expects bank rate to stay put for a year at a time or is surprised to find a succession of increases followed by a succession of decreases. This advantage might become a real one; but it was not very apparent in Britain during the fifties. In the eight years following the revival of monetary policy in 1951, bank rate was changed thirteen times, and five of those changes were in a single year, 1958, when the rate was brought down by gradual steps from 7 per cent to 4 per cent. If we exclude 1958, there were eight changes in eight years while over the same period there were nine budgets, including the autumn budget of 1955. Moreover, on almost every occasion on which bank rate was raised, the change was associated with other measures as part of a 'package deal'. These measures included restrictions on bank advances, hire purchase, and capital issues, as well as cuts in public investment; they were not coupled, as a rule, with budgetary changes or with non-financial controls. The authorities were disinclined to make frequent changes in bank rate or to lean very heavily on monetary measures.

If the experience of the past decade is any guide, therefore, the

99

greater freedom with which the bank rate can be changed may be to some extent illusory. If it is to be changed no more frequently than the budget, and if it is to be reinforced by simultaneous restrictions on borrowing and lending, it is not very apparent wherein the advantage exists. So long as nothing catastrophic happens – and monetary policy is certainly not designed to deal with catastrophes – it is doubtful whether the authorities require liberty to alter the pressure of demand more than about once a quarter, although they might want to indicate more frequently how their minds were moving. Given the power to introduce an autumn budget when necessary, and the possibility of altering some of the more important forms of indirect taxation between budgets, they are already equipped to alter pressure at six-monthly intervals or less, so that the added convenience of a freely variable bank rate, unless it is more effective or more quickly effective than fiscal measures, may not in practice greatly fortify the authorities.

To this there is, however, one important reservation. Changes in bank rate may be an effective means of allowing the Chancellor to foreshadow budgetary changes without showing his hand in detail. Bank rate changes are not yet part of the budget – though references to credit policy in the budget are becoming commoner – and they can be made, therefore, 'out of season' partly for their direct effects and partly as a warning of what is in store later.

This advertising power – if I may so describe it – may be regarded as a fourth advantage of monetary measures. I have already emphasized the importance attached to it by the authorities in their efforts to check a drain on the reserves. But it may also be used to influence domestic commitments so long as bank rate changes are treated as a pre-view of other government measures to come. There was a time when an increase in bank rate may have offered a very powerful inducement to caution and the postponement of large commitments: at that time it was likely to trail with it cloudy memories of past liquidity crises. These associations must by now have disappeared and a higher bank rate is by no means the infallible harbinger of a tough budget. I incline, therefore, to some scepticism of the domestic advertising power of bank rate changes in present circumstances.

The Limitations of Monetary Policy

Against these various advantages of monetary policy must be set definite limitations. Firstly, and most obviously, the expansion of the public sector and the contraction of the private sector extend the possibilities of direct action and limit the response to monetary measures. Secondly, the fact that monetary policy operates on a broad front, without regard to bottlenecks or shortages, puts it, in certain circumstances, at a disadvantage. Thirdly, although monetary measures, given time, do exercise an influence on fixed investment, this influence may be harmful rather than helpful if it is used in order to bring about sharp changes in industrial and commercial investment. Finally, if monetary policy is intended to influence long as well as short rates of interest it is bound to develop a certain irreversibility and cannot be used freely to assist recovery without simultaneously jeopardizing its subsequent use to check inflation.

These limitations were particularly evident in the fifties; but none of them are likely to diminish much in the future. Other limitations may operate less strongly from now on. The supply of liquid assets has contracted in relation to the volume of transactions to a point at which it would be easier to make monetary measures bite. The banks, in particular, are no longer seriously under-lent, having increased their advances by 60 per cent within two years. The ever-present fears of inflation domestically and devaluation externally have receded, at least for the time being. Long rates of interest are above rather then below long-term expectations. All these things would lend force to monetary restrictions; but if, by any chance, it were necessary to take the opposite course and follow an expansionary tack, they do not offer much assurance that monetary measures would be quickly effective.

The Radcliffe Committee, pondering these matters, concluded that there was a limited role for for monetary policy in the traditional sense. It had little to say about short-term rates and concentrated its attention on long-term rates. These it thought should not be held stable in face of a major change in the incentive to capital development; neither should they be made to fluctuate widely in order to make them bite more deeply. To follow the first course would be to destroy all control over liquidity in the economy by making government securities as liquid as bank deposits; it would also make for a wasteful use of capital. To follow the second course would be to spoil the market for government paper and embark on sales and purchases that might prove very difficult to carry out or reverse without disastrous side-effects. The Committee preferred an intermediate solution with long rates moving from 'middle' to 'high' gear in periods of sustained pressure on the supply of new capital and from 'middle' to 'low' when the demand for new capital re-

101

mained continuously low. It wanted these changes of gear to be an object of deliberate policy, not accidental by-products of action on discount rates.

If interest rates – or, at least, long rates – have to be kept fairly stable in times of boom or recession, other, more direct, means can still be used to control lending to the private sector. Bank credit has a special importance not only because the banks have larger total assets than any other group of financial institutions but also because the power to obtain bank finance often plays a critical, 'bridging' role in the early stages of business investment. If the government is unable to carry out funding operations on the scale necessary to limit the liquidity of the banks, it may be necessary to apply a brake to bank lending by imposing higher liquidity ratios or by obliging each bank to add to its deposits with the central bank. This form of control does not necessarily force the banks to cut down their loans to the private sector, which is, or should be, the main purpose of the control; on the other hand, it may well push the banks into selling government investments – that is, into the very transactions in the gilt-edged market in which the authorities conceive it to be out of their power to engage. It might be preferable, therefore, assuming that the check on lending was not intended to last for more than a year or so, to make use of the system in use 1957–8 of a ceiling on the absolute total of bank advances: or alternatively of a maximum proportion for each bank of its advances to its deposits.

In certain circumstances it might be necessary to impose comparable restraints on other important financial institutions. The Radcliffe Committee, in making this suggestion, mentioned the 'building societies, hire purchase finance companies and probably the life insurance companies';[1] it also referred rather vaguely to pension funds and investment and unit trusts. It would be a formidable undertaking to try to limit lending by such a large number of heterogeneous institutions and the Committee was careful to disclaim any recommendation in that sense except in a crisis of long duration. But if the restrictions were confined to lending for specific purposes, such as on property mortgages, they might be much simpler to administer.

Leaving this possibility on one side, we can treat bank advances, capital issues and consumer credit as the three main channels of lending to be controlled in emergency. The inconvenience of such controls in ordinary times needs no emphasis but if desperate re-

[1] *Report*, para. 509.

medies were necessary in order to check inflation, such a threefold control would be extremely powerful.

The instruments to be used must clearly depend upon the side from which the stability of the economy is threatened. If the authorities are afraid of a boom in private fixed investment, they may want to check it by putting up interest rates. But if such a boom meant an increase of no more than £200 m. to £300 m. in the output of a wide group of industries – which is a plausible enough assumption in British conditions – it would represent an increase in demand equivalent to only 1 per cent of the national income and about 4 per cent of the national budget. Is it really difficult to make room for such an increase within the normal limits of budgetary action? If it is a stock-building boom that is feared, then the most effective action might be to limit bank advances, as the most elastic source of finance for this purpose. If, on the other hand, it is personal spending on consumers' durables that starts to run away, then it would be reasonable to impose selective controls on consumer credit. The action to be taken has to vary with the threat to be parried.

CONCLUSION

Let me now try to sum up.

1. The government has a duty to stabilize its own spending, or to offset as far as possible changes in either direction in the private sector. If it foresees a need for additional resources at the expense of the private sector it should take steps to reduce the level of private demand. If the pressure of demand in the private sector threatens to increase, the government must either be prepared to provide a cushion by reducing its own spending or find means of drawing off or damming up private purchasing power. In all such efforts to maintain balance in the economy, the first line of action should be through the budget, and this action, if taken in time, based on a sound diagnosis, and proportioned to the threat to stability, should go far to make further action unnecessary.

2. Monetary policy should normally be a second line of defence. It should embrace measures affecting both long and short rates of interest and measures intended to bring about a tighter rationing of credit.

3. Long-term rates of interest have a long-term role. They should be allowed to reflect underlying trends in capital requirements and not made to fluctuate sharply.

4. Short rates may have some effects on economic activity because

103

of their influence on the administered rates that are linked with them. They can be used to improve the balance of payments through their effects on the flow of capital. They also affect to some degree the movement of long rates so that a central bank which is reluctant to intervene directly in the gilt-edged market can make use of changes in short rates (though not always effectively) to bring about changes in the same direction in long rates. Apart from any direct effects, short-term rates can also be used as a signal of the intentions of the authorities.

5. Changes in interest rates may have to be buttressed by other measures of financial control. Among these, some power to vary bank liquidity appears to be indispensable, although it should be used sparingly. Hire purchase controls are likely to be effective in obtaining quick results but they have important limitations and inconveniences. In some circumstances, it may be necessary to use them in conjunction with quantitative limitations on bank advances, new issues on the capital market, and lending on mortgage.

I cannot pretend that these are conclusions to be accepted with any complacency. We are all, I suppose, a little distrustful of governments and would much rather have some automatic device for keeping the economy in balance. But it is time we recognized that automaticity in a mixed economy is a will-o'-the-wisp. The public sector is big enough to wreck any mechanical regulator of the money supply or of demand, and it would be foolish to put the private sector in a strait-jacket while the public sector was left free. We may still try to impose checks on government spending or government borrowing or try to find ways of building stabilizing elements into the economic system so that we do not have to rely too heavily on the perceptiveness and resolution of the Minister of Finance. But in a democratic community the checks, other than informed discussion of economic policy and a free vote in Parliament after full disclosure of the grounds of action, are as likely to become a handicap to a skilful administration as an effective bar to a spend-thrift one; and the built-in stabilizers, however welcome, are usually happy accidents rather than designed for the job. If the economy has to be managed, then we have to reconcile ourselves to the dangers of bad management as well as take comfort from the improvements that good management may effect.

6. Demand Management: Monetary Policy and Fiscal Policy[1]

The main purpose of monetary and fiscal policies, treated as the component parts of what is nowadays called demand management, is to regulate the pressure of demand. Ideally, if one could disregard the balance of payments and external factors, demand management would be designed to operate on the flow of income and expenditure so as to maintain full employment and let demand grow in step with the economic potential of the country. But things are in fact a great deal more complicated. Let me take in turn five of the main complications.

First of all, the authorities can never entirely disregard the balance of payments and it is very often the prime object of their attention. To try to explain the development of monetary and fiscal weapons without bringing in the balance of payments would be a very curious proceeding, and I shall be returning to this point presently.

Secondly, the objectives of demand management – particularly if they embrace the balance of payments – are not necessarily in harmony with one another. There are obvious conflicts between the claims of full employment, the balance of payments and price stability. If full employment is pushed too far the result is apt to be inflation, with the usual consequence of a deficit in the balance of payments and the draining away of liquid external reserves. If the balance of payments is given absolute priority, this may communicate to the economy at a time when it is under-employed strong deflationary pressures originating in other countries.

Conflicting Policy Objectives

Similar conflicts arise, thirdly, with other objects of policy. Demand management is part of general economic policy and has to be

[1] Lecture to the 23rd International Banking Summer School at Christ Church, Oxford, on 21 July, 1970.

105

harmonized with it. The range of economic policy and the objectives to which it is directed have become increasingly comprehensive and ambitious, covering full employment, faster growth, economic equality, a satisfactory balance of economic activity between regions and the encouragement of a satisfactory industrial structure. The effects of monetary and fiscal weapons on all of these objectives and not just on the pressure of demand have to be taken into account and may influence both the decision to use or refrain from using such weapons and the specific way in which monetary and fiscal policy is brought into play. These wider objectives of policy are themselves in conflict: too much concern for economic stability or regional balance, for example, may get in the way of economic growth. There are also conflicts all along the line between short-run and long-run considerations. One of the major problems of economic management is to resolve these conflicts and decide what weight to attach to each of the underlying objectives. But this is essentially a political, not a technical problem. It follows that demand management, however complex, is not something that can be left entirely to experts but has to be handled at the political level. So long as there is a choice between alternative policies with different outcomes for different groups in the community, different effects on particular outputs, individual regions, the level of capital investment, and so on, the choice is not one that can be made on technical grounds.

Selective Measures

This raises a fourth complication. Monetary and fiscal policies necessarily have directional effects. They cannot be devised so as to operate in some neutral way throughout the economy on all the constituents of total demand but inevitably press harder at some points than at others. This may happen as a side effect of a general policy aimed exclusively at reducing the pressure of demand, or it may happen because of the adoption of a selective policy aimed at accelerating or intensifying some specific outcome of more general measures. Governments are often anxious to concentrate deflation on limited sectors of the economy and shelter other sectors from the pressure of restrictive measures. As a result, monetary and fiscal policies have come to include an increasingly wide range of selective measures instead of being limited to the more general form of variations in the credit base and in the size of the budget surplus or deficit.

I shall not attempt to list or even illustrate these selective measures of which you have all had plenty of experience. Not all such measures are effective and many of them weaken the impact of more general measures. Too much concern to screen the victims of restrictive measures may diminish the number of victims but may also frustrate the policy. At the same time any general measures tend to seep round any barriers erected selectively and create fresh difficulties of an unforeseen kind.

Co-ordination is a Political Act

While different monetary and fiscal policies have different effects on demand, they can be regarded as alternatives to one another for the purpose of bringing about a given change in the level of aggregate demand and they cannot sensibly be considered in complete isolation from one another. If follows from this that it would be a mistake to entrust responsibility for monetary policy to one authority while vesting responsibility for fiscal policy in a quite separate authority. At some point, co-ordination becomes more or less indispensable; and, since this co-ordination must be an act of political leadership, it is hard to see how it can proceed anywhere else than within the government. Central banks are bound to retain considerable moral authority and the head of any central bank remains an important figure in his own right, especially since he gives continuity to relations with foreign monetary authorities. But no amount of argument about the wisdom of leaving central banks independent of political influence can in the long run prevent governments from taking steps to ensure that fiscal and monetary policy are used in support of one another and in harmony with general economic policy.

Administrative Controls

The final complication to which I want to draw attention is that the objectives of demand management may sometimes be better achieved by weapons other than monetary and fiscal policies or may be beyond the reach of such policies. There are alternative weapons in the possible use of administrative controls such as were widely introduced in war-time, for the most part progressively abandoned by industrial countries after the war, but still in use all over the world in one form or another, usually for balance of payments reasons. These controls include consumer rationing, building licensing and quantitative limitation of imports. Controls imposed by the government on the financial system, such as exchange control, control over capital issues, or even ceilings on bank credit, might also qualify for inclusion instead of being treated as monetary and fiscal weapons.

There is, of course, no presumption that these controls are more effective or more satisfactory than less peremptory instruments like bank rate. In normal circumstances the presumption is rather the other way round. But governments do opt from time to time for administrative rather than economic regulators and there are obviously circumstances in which they are quite right to do so.

Cost Inflation

Cost inflation provides the most important example of a situation where monetary and fiscal policies are inadequate although by no means altogether ineffective. Even when expansion is at or below a sustainable rate, and when unemployment is higher than we should nowadays think consistent with full employment, wages may be pushed up faster than productivity, carrying prices upwards at the same time. Once the process starts it may become self-sustaining, for workers can either ask to be compensated for the higher cost of living or ask to be put on a footing of equality with some group to whom employers have just conceded a differential increase. Demand management seems powerless to halt the process, although it can check it. What is doubtful is whether governments can hope for any greater success, except for short periods, if they try to tackle cost inflation by other methods.

Whatever form it assumes, management is not a very scientific affair. Management of the economy is no exception. Even at the expert level, economists have a very imperfect understanding of how the economy actually works. They may construct elegant theories and models and advance ingenious hypotheses; but this does not enable them when faced with an actual situation to identify with confidence the forces at work, much less assign to each of these forces a precise measure of its relative importance. However well they can explain the past (after a suitable lapse of time) in terms of the continuous operation of identifiable economic forces, they are bound to hedge forecasts of the future around with reservations, if only because of the erratic influence of the non-economic forces that are simultaneously at work. Not only are governments far from omniscient; they are also very often far more impotent than they think it proper to admit. They may know what is happening but be incap-
108

able of devising in time measures that would significantly change the course of events. They have to operate within the limited range of weapons available to them, often in the face of serious misunderstandings about what is going on or what they propose to do.

External Pressures on Policy

They are, moreover, *national* governments managing economies that are fragments of a much larger world economy and necessarily open to the pressure of events abroad. The degree of openness varies greatly and so does the scope for independent management. But even a country like the United States – so often thought of as almost a closed economy – can disregard neither the external impact of its own policies (which can be very large) nor the impact of other countries' policies on its commodity trade and its financial markets. In all countries, changes in international trade and payments may frustrate domestic policies. The balance of payments may be volatile for reasons unconnected with these policies and may enforce unwelcome and unpopular adjustments in them. This volatility might be dampened by a regime of floating rates of exchange, although this is by no means inevitable and floating rates have other drawbacks. But even if the dilemma were softened it would still remain. A country that is not insulated from dealings with other countries cannot expect policies to be insulated either.

What it can do, however, is to try to preserve as much domestic stability as possible by using weapons that offer a high trade-off between domestic and external impacts: that is, produce a large improvement in the balance of payments for a given sacrifice in domestic activity. In the circumstances of recent years when there have been large disequilibrating flows of capital, it has been natural to look for weapons that could operate directly on these flows, and a great many new devices have been brought into use (without, however, arresting the progressive increase in the scale of international capital flows).

For example, central banks have made increasing use of the forward exchange market in an effort to offset interest differentials and have engaged in swop and re-purchase arrangements with commercial banks in order to channel funds abroad. There have been attempts in several countries to discriminate in the interest paid on foreign- and domestically-owned deposits. In other countries, the fiscal system has been used to produce a similar result in relation to longer-term capital movements, either by taxing outward

109

investment (for example, through an 'interest equalization tax') or by offering less advantageous tax treatment than previously to earnings from foreign investment. In the United Kingdom, portfolio investment outside the sterling area has been tapped for the benefit of the reserves through the surrender for sterling at par of 25 per cent of the value of any sales of foreign securities. Even import deposits can be regarded from one point of view as a means of combating lags in payment.

All these devices are another reminder of the preoccupation of the authorities in almost every country with the balance of payments. But in what follows I wish to concentrate on the more elementary question of how fiscal and monetary policies bite on domestic demand. Let me begin with the less controversial issue of fiscal policies and the budget.

FISCAL POLICY

It needs no very sophisticated training in economics to perceive that if government spending goes up while rates of tax do not, this will expand demand, output and employment. Hence, if the government is prepared to aim at a lower budget surplus or to run a budget deficit, it can exercise an expansionary pressure on the economy. There are many ingenious arguments that can be brought forward to controvert this elementary proposition but they are all more ingenious than valid. The trouble is that people are never entirely rational when they come to discuss matters of this kind, and hold strong opinions that are usually based on false analogies either with domestic housekeeping or with good business behaviour. For example, many people still have a strong prejudice against allowing the budget to get into deficit, particularly if it is likely to stay there for a long period or indefinitely. A budget deficit may tie the hands of the government to some extent later on, especially if it adds to the money supply, and it is certainly not free from inconvenience. But there is nothing inherently wrong about a deficit or a succession of deficits. The wisdom of taking action through the budget must depend on the expected immediate gain in total national production, adjusted for any subsequent damage to production that might conceivably follow in the longer run. Admittedly, if enough people *think* that a budget deficit is bad for the country, their reactions to it may be sufficiently perverse to justify their own belief. What people think of what the government is doing can be just as important as what the government actually does.

Objections of this kind (i.e. that deficits are *ipso facto* bad) to the use of fiscal instruments are now comparatively rare. But other objections are often brought up that rest almost as much on sheer misunderstanding. When a tax cut is proposed, for example, even the Secretary of the US Treasury has been known to explain that he expects tax reductions to work round to output and employment through their effects on incentives to additional effort rather than on demand. By far the biggest and most calculable effect, however, *is* on demand, and this is the effect which tax cuts are designed to produce, especially in the short run. It is only in the long run that the incentive effects on productivity are likely to be substantial, and we know very little about the probable scale of such effects. Very often, too, arguments about the size of the budget surplus get mixed up with non-economic arguments about whether expenditure should be cut or taxation should be increased. It seems to be impossible to divorce a discussion of measures designed to regulate the pressure on the economy from political debates over the entirely different issue of the long-term future of government expenditure.

Does Fiscal Policy Work ?

It has become quite fashionable recently to argue that fiscal policy just does not work. This has been argued from time to time in the United Kingdom, and it now seems to be an extermely popular line of argument in the United States. This is not the time or place for me to enter into detailed rebuttal. But as one who has had to watch year in and year out the reaction of the British economy to frequent changes in taxation and expenditure, I rub my eyes a little when I find views of this kind still expressed. Naturally, there are circumstances in which a rise in taxation may for the time being make relatively little impression on public spending because people have become obsessed with the idea that prices are going to rise still higher. There are also circumstances in which the strength of the forces making for an increase in government expenditure or private investment is miscalculated by those who have to judge what action the government ought to take. But these qualifications amount to little more than saying that in some circumstances control of any kind is difficult and that in the best of circumstances the controllers may misjudge the situation. I do not recall that when a tax cut was made in the United States in 1964 or in the United Kingdom in 1963 anyone alleged that these cuts had no effect on spending. Similarly, although tax increases, *accompanied by devaluation*, did not prevent

111

a surge of consumer spending in Britain in 1967/8, the much larger tax increases in the budget of 1968 checked spending in a very marked way.

Effects of Government Over-spending

It is, of course, true that governments are prone to overspend and that this may have inflationary effects. There are strong forces in nearly every industrial country making for a steady expansion in government expenditure, even under conditions in which defence expenditure may be stationary or declining. This can easily mean, where deficits result and governments try to keep down interest rates from ideological or self-interested motives, that the monetary authorities are left to find the necessary money and feel themselves doomed to connive at inflation. To make matters worse, the public sector tends to be left immune to monetary weapons – although there is nothing inevitable about this – and the use of monetary policy, therefore, comes to be looked upon as a means of throttling down the private sector in order to clear the way for additional government expenditure. Governments are never very skilful at forecasting their own expenditure some time in advance and are liable to make serious errors which can only be compensated by drastic measures, often of a monetary character, falling on the private sector. There have been several examples in industrial countries in recent years of a surge in public expenditure that was largely unforeseen and proved largely uncontrollable, forcing governments to a succession of deflationary packages that were slow to take effect. The control of the public sector is a subject that receives too little attention in western countries.

It was characteristic of the circumstances I have described that the the increase in government expenditure was greater than had been foreseen. Where the increase is foreseen and its impact on demand has been correctly assessed, the fact that it gives rise to government borrowing does not make it inflationary. It will increase demand but only to the extent already taken into account when it was sanctioned. But what if government borrowing has to be financed by the banks? Does it make no difference how much additional bank money is created? On this point economists are divided. One school of thought which comes very close to the old Treasury view derided by Keynes regards additional government expenditure as having a net expansionary effect if and only if it adds to the money supply. Others would argue that additional government expenditure on

112

goods and services will necessarily generate additional income and that the success of the government in selling bonds to the non-bank public to a similar amount may do little or nothing to offset this. This is really the old conundrum – how much does money matter? – to which I will be turning in a moment.

Problems of Timing

Apart from this issue, the use of the budget as a regulator raises plenty of awkward technical problems. There are first of all problems of timing. It is not easy to formulate or win acceptance for cuts in public expenditure at any time, and still more difficult if the cuts are expected to come into operation more or less at once. British experience has often been that cuts in public expenditure made at the height of a boom begin to affect the level of demand just when the economy is moving into a condition of slump. This is particularly likely to happen when the expenditures involved are those of local authorities remote from the central government and with spending programmes that cannot be trimmed back quickly. Changes in taxation are also difficult to implement quickly, especially if, as in the United States, one government proposes and what amounts to another government disposes. Although all that may be sought is a net change in the total, it has to be reached by specific changes in taxation, and any change in taxation is bound to arouse opposition from one quarter or another.

Hence, in addition to the problem of timing, there is an acute political problem in mobilizing support for the package of changes in expenditure and taxation that make up the net change in the pressure of demand at which the government is aiming. A Parliament that might agree without difficulty that a net change in the size of the budget surplus was called for, might take a very different view once it saw that this net change was made up of individual increases and decreases in specific items of public spending or tax revenue.

MONETARY POLICY

I turn next to monetary policy, which happens to be in the forefront at the moment. As is well known, there are considerable differences of opinion among economists as to the usefulness of monetary policy as a stabilizing instrument. There are also important differences of view as to what monetary policy should seek to accomplish.

H   113

On some points, however, there is not likely to be much disagreement. It is common ground that fiscal and monetary policies should usually operate in the same direction; and some might add that monetary policy would not be very effective if fiscal policy were pulling strongly the other way. It is, however, also common ground that the impact of monetary policy is very different from that of fiscal policy, and that this difference is particularly important in relation to the balance of payments. While fiscal policy may affect the current account by operating on the level of domestic demand, it is unlikely in normal circumstances to react directly on the capital balance except in so far as it gives rise to greater confidence or distrust in the government's intentions. Monetary policy, on the other hand, through its effects on financial markets, can have a direct effect on the capital balance, both short term and long.

Blending Fiscal and Monetary Policies

This difference has led some economists to suggest that the blend between fiscal and monetary policies should be varied with the type of threat to equilibrium that has to be met.

The implicit assumption is that fiscal policy is the appropriate instrument for preserving domestic stability if there is no special need to worry about the balance of payments; while monetary policy would be more appropriate as a means of dealing with an external deficit if there were no need for a sharp check to domestic demand. A mixture of fiscal and monetary policies could come into play if the domestic situation pointed one way and the external situation pointed the other; for example, tight money, combined with a budget deficit, might allow a country to cope simultaneously with an external deficit on the one hand and under-employment on the other. The mixture could also pay regard to the impact on other countries: for example, efforts to contain inflation by higher interest rates would be unwelcome to foreign monetary authorities if they were obliged to follow suit when free of any excessive pressure on domestic resources, and in circumstances of this kind it would be right to rely principally on fiscal policy.

All this is much easier to explain than to do. Governments are rarely so placed that they can combine monetary and fiscal expedients at precisely the time and in exactly the proportion that the prescription would imply. The dilemmas of policy are usually complex and not easily resolved even with variable rates of exchange; with fixed rates, the history of the past few years is witness to the apparently

114

endless contortions of policy that may attend a conflict between full employment and the balance of payments.

Let me turn now to some of the points of controversy in recent years over monetary policy. There are, I think, three main points at issue:

1. What should be the focus of interest of the monetary authorities: the complex of interest rates, the supply of money, or some other variable?
2. How effective is monetary policy?
3. How desirable is it to rely on monetary policy?

I doubt whether the answer to these questions can be the same in all countries. Not only are there differences in institutional arrangements and in the relationship between the central bank and the complex of financial institutions affected by its actions, but there are also differences in the range of weapons available to the authorities (not just the monetary authorities) and in the attitudes and responsiveness to official policy of financial and other agencies. It is a mistake to assume that the use of monetary policy in Britain should necessarily resemble its use in Italy or, say, in Ceylon. Similarly, the scope for monetary policy in Hungary or China is bound to be very different from the scope in Japan or Brazil.

For example, I should expect that there would be a big difference between using monetary policy in conditions in which there was a developed capital market and in conditions where such a capital market does not exist. The range of liquid assets in the first case is bound to be much wider than in the second, and the range of alternative sources of funds is correspondingly more limited. In many countries it has been the absence of a capital market independent of the banking system that has enabled monetary policy to be used with outstanding success in checking the boom; but this success has rested on the greater ease with which pressure can be brought to bear on liquidity because of the dependence of the main lending institutions on banking funds.

THE FOCUS OF INTEREST

To go back to the first of the questions which I listed, opinion is now running strongly in favour of the proposition that the natural centre of interest for the monetary authorities should be the money supply, however defined, rather than the complex of interest rates. There are

115

several reasons for this, although I confess that I do not find them altogether convincing.

First of all it has been pointed out that, if the authorities fasten their attention on market rates, they may make insufficient allowance for the extent to which these rates already reflect an expectation of continuing inflation. The authorities may be deceived into thinking that they have tightened credit when in fact an upward movement of interest rates has been insufficient to offset a stronger conviction of continuing inflation or a conviction that inflation will proceed more rapidly. By concentrating on the supply of money the authorities have at least a measure that is independent of inflationary expectations and pressures, so that they will be less readily deceived.

I find this argument unconvincing because the test of inflationary pressure in an economy is not a monetary one, whether it be the movement of interest rates or the changes taking place in the supply of money. The true criterion is the pressure of demand; and this pressure can increase while the supply of money is constant or diminishing, just as it can decrease while the supply of money is constant or increasing. If what is under debate is the criterion by reference to which the monetary authorities should decided in which direction to operate, that criterion should be neither the supply of money nor the complex of interest rates.

Can the Money Supply be Planned?

If the question at issue is what the monetary authorities should be operating on, the answer must in part depend on the normal practices of the authorities and on the instruments at their disposal. It is commonly assumed that the monetary authorities have control over the supply of money or enjoy such control in a way in which they do not enjoy it in relation to interest rates. But there are times when the reserve is true. In Britain, for example, the monetary authorities may start off at the beginning of the year with some view as to the increase in the supply of money which they think to be consistent with the rest of the government's policies, but it is very unlikely that even if everything else goes according to plan they will find the supply of money rising exactly as they foresaw. It would be extremely difficult for the British authorities so to direct their policy over a period of twelve months as to ensure that the increase in the quantity of money (or even domestic credit expansion) was kept within stated limits. If they succeeded, I should maintain that luck played a large part in their success. On the other hand, there are circumstan-

116

ces in which, if they set out to maintain certain rates of interest over the year, they would have every chance of succeeding. The argument here turns on the special difficulties of operating in the British gilt-edged market as well as on the serious inconvenience, given the very large national debt in this country, of bringing about (or even acquiescing in) large and sudden changes in long-term rates of interest. To this point I shall return below because it seems to me the essence of the matter.

The Money Supply and Economic Instability

A second reason for directing attention to the supply of money is that there undoubtedly has been over the long run a close association between variations in the rate of growth in the money supply and variations in the level of prices. It was this association which was enshrined in the original formulation of the quantity theory of money by David Hume, and it has a long and honourable place in the history of monetary doctrine. If we could assume that changes in the money supply were the main source of economic instability and that in the absence of such changes the economy would remain on an even keel, it would be natural to conclude that the right prescription for policy is to require the monetary authorities to let the supply of money expand at an even and predetermined rate. This is a conclusion which is particularly popular among American economists of widely different persuasions. But I see no reason to accept the premiss. It is very far from obvious (in this country at all events) that the main sources of instability now reside in credit policy and that fluctuations in activity would be of minor importance if a decision were taken to allow the supply of money to expand at some planned rate.

Money, Financial Assets and Spending

There is, thirdly, a more technical reason for concentration on the money stock. It is agreed that money is simply one financial asset among many and that monetary policy operates on portfolios (whether private or institutional) by altering relative prices and preferences. If this were all, one could confine attention to the complex of interest rates and go on to ask what effects on the real economy a change in the structure of interest rates would be likely to have. But those who approach the matter in terms of the quantity of money argue that, whatever juggling of portfolios takes place, there is a

117

stable demand for real money balances, so that an addition to the stock of money has to be absorbed and can only be absorbed by generating income or raising prices or both. Where one might be tempted to think exclusively in terms of swaps between money and other financial assets without any necessary overflow into real demand, the neo-quantity theorist would argue that an increase in the quantity of money in excess of what had previously been in accordance with consumer demand would give rise to additional spending or investment; and it would be this phenomenon of additional demand against which the monetary authorities should be forewarned.

It would be impossible for me to pursue this argument through all its econometric labyrinths. I will merely register some old-fashioned doubts. It seems to me abundantly clear that it makes all the difference in the world whether the government gets hold of more cash by spending less on the construction of roads or by selling bonds to investors: all the more so if these bond sales reflect, not excess holdings of cash, but a judgment by investors, perhaps quite irrationally, that the prospects for the balance of payments look better, so that the government is less likely to take savage deflationary action. The first type of reduction in the money supply would be accompanied by a sharp contraction in demand and output, while the second, in ordinary circumstances, would leave demand completely unaffected. While the second type of situation may be waived away as a temporary aberration over a span of years, it can certainly not be disregarded by governments interested in what is likely to happen to employment over the next six months – a period in which much that was unforeseen may happen and during which policy cannot be left in abeyance while debatable long-term relationships assert themselves.

THE EFFECTIVENESS OF MONETARY POLICY

The second question which I listed related to the effectiveness of monetary policy. Here the current controversy seems to me to exaggerate needlessly. Just as Milton Friedman, in his presidential address to the American Economic Association in 1968, was at some pains to spell out what monetary policy *cannot* do, so the authors of the Radcliffe Committee Report never pretended that money does not matter. If used with sufficient resolution, monetary policy can undoubtedly be a powerful restrictive influence, although often in rather unwelcome ways. It may be comparatively ineffective under

118

the conditions of the 1930s when confidence has been badly shaken and rates of interest have fallen to a level below which it would be difficult to imagine any appreciable further reduction. But on the opposite tack, when inflation has to be curbed, the monetary authorities can always, if need be, bring on a liquidity crisis. The difference of opinion is much more about the speed with which monetary policy can take effect, about the way in which monetary influences and confidence effects interact on one another and about the desirability of relying on monetary policy rather than resorting to some other action.

These are not matters that I need spell out in detail to you. All of us (or nearly all of us) would recognize that monetary policy affects, and is intended to affect, investment much more than consumption; that within the total of investment it tends to be housing that takes the brunt; and that it is nearly always the smaller firms with limited sources of finance outside the banking system that suffer most, not because the commercial banks discriminate against them but because they are more vulnerable than their large competitors.

We have also to recognize that in the world as we know it – whatever might happen in a different kind of world – monetary policy tends to operate not through a gradual rise in the cost of credit to all borrowers but through a selective exclusion of particular types of borrower from credit facilities. If industrial investment is hit, it is usually because the firms concerned are unable to raise the money; and this in turn arises because the total supply of funds contracts sharply and becomes inelastic to the terms offered by the borrower. The mechanism of credit limitation also involves the injection of additional uncertainty at critical points; and this uncertainty, since it relates not just to immediate market prospects but to the intentions of the monetary authorities and the central government, may be highly intractable to ordinary economic weapons and make the consequences of a particular act of monetary policy highly unpredictable.

THE DESIRABILITY OF USING MONETARY WEAPONS

All this takes us to the third question: the desirability of relying on monetary weapons. I have already drawn attention to the directional effects of monetary policy and to the way in which it impinges directly on investment of all kinds when it might be more appropriate to take action affecting consumption. In its external impact it can react on the flow of funds between countries in ways which may

119

seriously disturb the domestic economic policies of friendly nations. If it takes the form of a credit squeeze, this has serious inconveniences from the point of view of the banks since it makes competitive behaviour more or less impossible and opens the door to the expansion of non-banking intermediaries that are free from the restrictions imposed on the banks. If on the other hand reliance is placed on big swings in interest rates these, too, have considerable disadvantages. They may, for example, threaten the solvency of important groups of domestic institutions, including the banks themselves. They may provoke disequilibrating flows of international capital of a highly dangerous kind. They also give rise to grave problems of debt management, particularly for those governments that have a large outstanding debt and correspondingly large maturities to meet from year to year. It can also be argued that, the more use is made of monetary policy, the higher will be the rate of interest in the long run, since an unstable gilt-edged market is likely to diminish the appetite for gilt-edged and lower its normal price. It is not too difficult to get long-term rates of interest up, but when it comes to getting them down again the memories of investors are apt to get in the way.

There is one outstanding advantage of monetary policy compared with fiscal policy. It is, almost by definition, incapable of being submitted to debate and resolution in parliament. *Someone* has to be entrusted with the executive responsibility for the conduct of monetary policy and, however much *ex post* justification may be sought, action is not usually held up, or held up for long, by congressional or parliamentary pressure. What does tend to happen is that, as governments take more and more responsibility for monetary policy, political considerations enter increasingly into the decisions that are taken.

CONCLUSION

My main conclusions are three.

1. There is no escape from demand management combining the use of fiscal and monetary policies. It may not be very good: forecasting mistakes are inevitable; policies may be misguided; fluctuations may even on occasion be aggravated. But neither has it been very bad: it cannot be just luck that has kept the world in a more continuously prosperous state than ever before.

2. There is certainly no escape by reducing demand management to monetary management in the hope of making it more automatic; or of making it fully automatic by reducing it still further to a for-

mula such as a steady expansion in the money supply. There may be a monetary component to economic instability, but fluctuations in activity are not exclusively a monetary phenomenon. In particular, fiscal policy cannot be dismissed as a kind of tail wagged by a central banking dog. No doubt budget deficits, like the creation of banking credit, tend to increase the quantity of money at the same time as they fuel the engine of inflation. But this does not justify us in implying that central banks have it in their power to put an end to inflation through their control over the money supply.

3. It would be hard to maintain that what the world needs is the still more resolute use of monetary policy. It needs an attack on inflationary tendencies from several sides at once; and in the longer run the weapons that most stand in need of improvement are the non-monetary ones – fiscal regulators on the one side and methods of containing cost inflation on the other.

7. Economic Forecasting: Preliminary Reflections[1]

A forecast is never a statement of fact. We know only what is behind us, never what is in front of us. To pretend to inside information about coming events and treat forecasts as anything better than useful hypotheses is to court ridicule and disillusionment. When the Prophet Jonah rashly cried, 'Yet forty days and Nineveh shall be overthrown', he was asking for trouble. He was not to know that Jehovah would change his mind and spare the city. No wonder when he came a cropper he was 'displeased exceedingly' and 'very angry' and went off to sulk under his gourd.

Or take the case of Montezuma, surrounded by a corps of astrologers, augurs, necromancers and mediums. He, poor fellow, thought he knew exactly what was coming to him and got completely mixed up between Cortés and the god Quetzalcoatl. The fact that everything that Cortés did fitted in with the forecast for Quetzalcoatl and that Montezuma never doubted the forecasts for a moment cost him in turn his treasure, his kingdom and, ultimately, his life. It is best not to be too sure of what is in store.

Yet nobody is quite reconciled to ignorance of the future. We are all planners in our various ways and in order to plan we have to form the best view we can of what is likely to happen. If we know nothing about the future, we at least know something about the past and, by judicious interpretation of the past, have found it possible to make worth-while forecasts of the future: worth while, in the sense that they help us to plan what to do or avoid doing. As I shall have occasion to point put, however, our knowledge of the past is usually a great deal more imperfect than we imagine and the processes by which we construe it so as to yield a forecast are often ramshackle and rule of thumb. This is particularly true when we are dealing with human as distinct from physical events, since human events are by definition unique and unrepeatable and some at least of the many

[1] Based on the Alfred Watson Memorial Lecture, 27 April, 1964.

122

aspects of each event must almost inevitably elude us. Forecasting of human affairs can never be an exact science.

This applies particularly to the kind of forecasting which I propose to discuss: forecasting of the behaviour of economic aggregates such as demand, output and employment, with a view to improving the planning of economic activity as a whole. Very little has been written in the United Kingdom about economic forecasting. So far from being classed as an exact science, I suspect that it is more commonly regarded here as bordering on magic and witchcraft, fitter for discussion by the learned necromancers of Montezuma's court than by the no less learned academic economists of today. In the United States, by contrast, it has become a popular pastime, with thousands of practitioners filling in their coupons and posting them off regularly, much as happens here in a rather different area of forecasting. The process has lost its magic and there are even textbooks about it. In Britain, economic forecasts are still rare, mysterious and potent – and there are no textbooks. But even here, forecasting is increasingly systematic and based on science rather than soothsaying. In the world of the actuary, this has always been so; in the world of business and of government, science can never completely prevail but its domain is steadily expanding.

To an economist it is a little shocking that forecasting should have been so long neglected as a subject of study. The whole purpose of economics is to shed light on how the economic system works and what consequences will follow given actions. We have been taught to identify science with prediction; and anyone who jests at economic forecasting – as everybody does from time to time – is really expressing his scepticism of the scientific foundations of economics. Of course, we all know that there is a large unpredictable element in people's behaviour. This is not, however, the main reason why most of us are hesitant to make claims for economic forecasting. Apart altogether from the practical difficulties, to which I shall come later, economists have always recognized (with some outstanding exceptions) that economic factors do not completely dominate our behaviour, and that it is not possible to follow the main stream of economic causation in complete disregard of the other streams that feed into it from changes of a political, religious, administrative or technological source. However much economists may dam back those streams with the embankment of *ceteris paribus*, in the real world there are all manner of things such as speeches by prominent persons, elections, wars, assassinations and so on, that burst through the embankment. So it comes about that economists

123

can play happily with their models and pursue the full rigour of economic logic without any compulsion to make special claims for their powers of vaticination.

It is also true that, until a few years ago, economists took relatively little interest in short-term economic forecasting and limited themselves almost entirely to making predictions about the long-term or about some limited area of the economy such as the behaviour of individual prices. Some economists, notably Malthus, Ricardo and Marx, made some very bold and stimulating predictions about economic aggregates such as the size of the population, the distribution of the national income, and the degree of concentration of economic power, or, like Jevons, analysed the long-term consequences of localized scarcities such as the tendency for British fuel costs to rise.

The Emergence of Short-term Forecasting

But prediction of the behaviour of the economic system as a whole in the short run remained relatively rare and most of it had to do with the idea of inflation or of a change in exchange parities. It is hardly too much to say that short-term economic forecasting only emerged in the controversies between the two wars, first over the return to the gold standard and subsequently over the Great Slump. The next big forward stride came with the development of national income accounting during the last war.

The emergence of short-term forecasting of economic aggregates seems to have been due to two main factors. The first of these is the great improvement that has taken place in the supply of economic statistics to serve as short-term indicators. The second – and, since it has helped to bring about the first, the more important – is the development of a system of ideas seeking to explain short-term fluctuations in the level of economic activity. This system of ideas centres on what may be called for short 'the management of demand' in the sense that it attributes changes in the level of economic activity to changes in the level of demand and places on the government responsibility for controlling total economic activity by managing the level of effective demand. The instruments at the disposal of the government are frequently slow to act, and there is a series of lags between changes in demand, the receipt of information demonstrating such changes, and the taking of decisions calculated to restore demand to the desired level. This makes it all the more necessary to have some forecasting apparatus for reducing those lags to a mini-

124

mum and for ensuring that corrective action is taken sufficiently early and geared to a proper appreciation of the likely course of events.

The management of demand has assumed mounting importance throughout the post-war period, not as one might imagine because of increasingly violen tfluctuations in activity, but because economists have tended to lay increasing stress on a steady pressure of demand as a factor in economic growth rather than on more obvious factors influencing productivity directly. The economists who incline to this way of thinking would hesitate to argue that the faster growth that other countries have experienced is attributable to a positive act of management; but they do appear to hold that there has been some peculiar failing in the management of demand in the United Kingdom, associated with 'stop-go', that has caused us to make larger mistakes or miss our opportunities more frequently. Whatever one may think of this view, it is a common belief that if growth in the United Kingdom were smoother it would automatically become faster, and that it could be made smoother if the management of demand were more successful. This in turn obviously implies heavy reliance on economic forecasting as a tool in management of the economy.

The forecasts that I am discussing are of two kinds. There are those that relate to the domestic economy and attempt to predict the behaviour of the main components of aggregate demand – exports, fixed investment, stock-building and consumption. Then there are balance of payments forecasts which focus on the external situation. The object of these is to show whether the economy is likely to move into surplus or deficit on external account just as the object of the first type of forecast is to predict the pressure of demand and the strength of the tendencies towards inflation or deflation.

Forecasts of aggregate demand are usually more complex than forecasts of the balance of payments. The items making up the balance of payments are to a great extent independent of one another; their interactions are usually indirect and in the first instance on the domestic economy. For example, imports are likely to reflect changes in domestic purchasing power more than anything else, although they also respond to changes in the level of exports in so far as these add to requirements for imported materials. The connection between capital flows and exports and imports is limited, variable and obscure and consequently very hard to predict. In practice, therefore, forecasts of the balance of payments are to a large extent corollaries of other forecasts – home demand and production on the one side

125

and world demand and production on the other – without much attempt to adjust the constituent items to take account of their possible interactions.

Forecasts of Demand

Forecasts of aggregate demand, by contrast, have to be made internally self-consistent. Each of the four main components not only enters into the total but reacts to it, and some of the four react on one another. If demand and production expand, this adds to consumers' income and expenditure, induces a more expansive attitude to fixed investment and stock-building, and affects exports in some ways favourably and in other ways unfavourably. This means that whilst it is quite possible to make independent estimates for each component of the total, the estimates have to make sense in relation to one another and to the total to which they add up.

Although the forecast is essentially a demand forecast, it is also by implication a forecast of production, unless there are grounds for expecting that some part of total demand will be thwarted by bottlenecks in capacity. But, although the future levels of demand and production are of intrinsic interest, they are not the ultimate object of short-term economic forecasting as conducted by the government since this is directed towards predicting the pressure rather than the level of demand; that is, the extent to which demand is rising faster or slower than the resources available to satisfy it. This requires a separate investigation of the underlying rate of growth in those resources: the rate at which they can be expected to increase in quantity and efficiency. To complicate matters, this underlying rate of growth (of which we have heard so much over the past year) may itself be affected by the pressure of demand: not in the sense that there is normally a sharp improvement in output per head in the course of a cyclical upswing (for this has nothing to do with the true underlying rate of growth), but in the more fundamental sense that growth may be faster when the pressure of demand is sustained at one degree of intensity rather than another.

The limiting factor to the growth of production is usually manpower, and it is in the labour market that changes in the pressure of demand are most clearly registered and most quickly apparent. Thus, although the forecasts are in terms of demand and productive capacity, the nub of the matter is the behaviour of the labour market and the signs that it is easing or tightening. The best single indicator of this is the unemployment percentage and other indicators – employment, overtime, vacancies, immigration, participation rates, the regional dispersion of unemployment rates – all seem to move in a reasonably consistent way with the percentage of workers who are wholly unemployed. In a sense, therefore, the upshot of national income forecasting can be expressed as a prediction of the future level of unemployment.

I do not want to imply that the only way in which to measure changes in the pressure of demand is through the labour market and in the form of an unemployment percentage. Other measures exist and are used. For example, the size of order books in relation to current deliveries is the kind of measure used by individual firms; and a similar measure can be devised for manufacturing industry where fluctuations in demand have a special significance. But for a number of reasons the unemployment figures have proved the most satisfactory general index of the state of the economy and the best summary of short-term forecasts of its behaviour.

THE TIME HORIZON

One of the key problems in forecasting is how far ahead one should look. If one looks very far ahead one can escape all the uncertainties of the immediate future, the known problems with their unknown answers. But other uncertainties multiply to the point at which detailed forecasting becomes absurd. On the other hand, if one looks only a short way ahead the forecast loses interest. It may show the situation over a period too short for government action to have any effect. Or it may cover a period in which conflicting influences are operating and the material question is left unresolved: which influence will gain the upper hand and when? Sometimes the interest of the forecast lies in the predicted order of events: the date at which some things will happen or cease to happen, or the speed with which one thing is likely to follow another. Sometimes the interest is concentrated on the strength rather than in the timing of reactions. Whatever the source of interest, the period covered must be sufficiently long to allow time for the expected reactions to show themselves.

In national income forecasts, the period covered is usually not less than a year and not longer than two years. In some countries – particularly those which have to rely heavily on annual data – the forecasts take the form of year-to-year comparisons. These are of limited interest to anyone seeking to foresee the situation at a point in time. In the management of the economy, it is much more impor-

127

tant to have some idea how things are likely to look next April than how they are likely to have looked in an average month on the way there. For this reason, British forecasts have for many years been expressed in terms of the predicted situation x months away and do not even purport to show the precise path likely to be followed over those months, although quarterly figures are included as a matter of form.

I should not trouble to insist on this point were it not for the extraordinary interest still shown in one form of national economic forecast, namely the budget estimates, in which year-to-year comparisons are made. There is no doubt a certain interest in the light thrown by the estimates on the borrowing requirements of the central government over the next twelve months. But the estimates tell us nothing about the economic situation likely to prevail at the end of the twelve months or about the budgetary action appropriate to it. As for the exchequer out-turn for the past twelve months, I should have thought it superfluous to say that this was, if possible, even less relevant to the current budget judgment if I had not seen the contrary view urged on the Chancellor by at least one distinguished economist as well as by a number of knowledgeable journalists.

Practical Difficulties in Economic Forecasting

I should like next to turn to some of the practical difficulties in economic forecasting in this country. Our power to predict the future always rests first on our understanding of the inner logic of events (i.e. on an adequate theory) and second on our knowledge of what has been going on and is going on now (i.e. on adequate statistics). Without an adequate theory we do not know what statistics matter and where to look for the essential data from which to derive a correct view of the movement of the economy. Without the statistics, there would be nothing for us to look at.

I shall take it for granted that we already possess an adequate theory, although this seems to me to be true only in a very large sense. By this I mean that we know what variables to concentrate on, we have a fair idea of the kind of interactions that take place between them, we have reason to believe that some of the more important functional relationships are comparatively stable, and we have a definite point of view from which to examine what is going on and organize the available information. Of course, this does not take us very far unless we can assign values to the relationships,
128

and move from mathematical functions to specific magnitudes, lags, coefficients and the rest of the apparatus of statistical analysis. A conceptual framework is indispensable; but it only tells us what information we need and a great deal of this information takes the form, not of raw statistical data, but of presumed quantitative relationships that can never be directly observed. The precise character of some of these relationships is also far from clear, and it is in this sense that existing theory can be said to be still not at all satisfactory.

When we turn to the statistical basis for forecasting, the first and most obvious requirement is that the statistics should exist. This is not such a modest assumption as it sounds. We cannot rest content with statistics devised for other purposes but have to ask ourselves what figures we need for the preparation of economic forecasts and then set about collecting them. Just as the deliberate decision to hold a census and the later decisions to make the registration of births and deaths compulsory have been the foundation of modern demography, so it has been necessary to extend the scope of official statistics in many different directions in order to provide a more satisfactory basis for an analysis of economic trends. This has not always been a popular undertaking; and it is still rarely understood that the management of a modern economy is just as dependent as the management of a modern business on a comprehensive set of statistics that make it possible to take stock of what has happened, is happening and is likely to happen. Broadly speaking, these statistics are of three kinds: those corresponding to balance sheets which show quantities at a point in time; those corresponding to profit and loss accounts which show flows over time; and those corresponding to order books which indicate directly what seems to lie ahead.

Leaving aside for the time being the third type of statistical information, I should like to turn to some of the problems that confront the forecaster in using statistics. First of all, there is an inevitable lag between events and statistical knowledge of events. My predecessor, Lord Roberthall, used to say that the hardest thing to forecast is where you are now. This would obviously be much less true if statistics were always bang up-to-date and related to a period ending only a few minutes ago. In practice, however, many of the key figures are bound to be several months out of date, either because the figures are collected and published a fairly long intervals or because they become available only with a considerable lag.

We are, of course, infinitely better off in this respect than we were only a few years ago before the appearance of quarterly national

I   129 accounts and balance of payments estimates. But even quarterly figures, appearing three months or more after the event, do not do more than give us, about the beginning of April, a provisional view of the state of the economy centred on the preceding November and it is June/July before we get the next snapshot.

Fortunately we have other less complete data on a more up-to-date footing. For industrial production, which represents about half total production, figures are published six or seven weeks after the end of the month to which they relate so that at any point in time the average lag is about two months. Retail sales, covering half total consumer spending, are available about a fortnight earlier. By far the most up-to-date – as well as the most reliable – indicator of economic activity is unemployment, figures for which appear monthly little more than a week after the date to which they relate.

But the very frequency with which figures are issued, as we all know from recent observation of the trade returns, makes them more erratic and difficult to interpret. If we use weekly, or even monthly data, we have to reckon with large random fluctuations associated either with the weather, with holidays, with administrative convenience, or with chance factors that cannot be identified. It is not possible to assess the changes that are going on by taking at their face value the variations in the weekly or monthly figures. They have first to be smoothed in order to bring out the underlying trend. But if the raw figures do not tell us what is going on, how can we be sure that the smoothed figures do? For it is of no use to suppose that the process of smoothing is so scientific that it reveals the same underlying trend to everyone. On the contrary, one can rarely tell what is random and what is significant until much later. This does not prevent many skilled commentators from pontificating about the trends at work in the economy on the basis of small variations between one month and the next in, say, the index of industrial production. If we know that the upward trend is of the order of 4 per cent per annum and are uncertain whether it is in fact 3 or 5, what we are trying to isolate in a monthly variation is something that we know to be of the order of one-third of a point with a view to deciding whether it is in fact one-quarter or five-twelfths. Remembering that the index of industrial production is published only to the nearest integer, we can see at once the absurdity of the whole enterprise.

We have also to reckon with the possibility that the published figures may subsequently be amended. This does not apply to the unemployment returns which relate to a count taken on a particular

130

day and, once taken, cannot be changed. The production index, however, when first published, is based on partial information and is subject to revision as more complete data are obtained. Moreover, the seasonal adjustments that are made may be revised when they come to be reassessed. These revisions, indeed, may radically alter the impression conveyed by the original figures. For example, the revised figures for 1962 indicate a relatively slow climb up to the third quarter of the year instead of the much more rapid rise shown at the time.

The difficulty of making seasonal corrections is one which the public seriously underestimates because it is increasingly provided with figures that are nominally purged of seasonal influences. But the seasonal pattern is not something fixed; it alters between one year and the next. It may alter because of exceptional weather conditions; but it may also alter because of changes in the habits of producers or consumers. For example, there was a marked change in the seasonality of motor-car buying once cars became freely available so that the date of purchase was fixed by the consumer and not, as previously, by the manufacturer.

I draw special attention to the importance of seasonal corrections because very much the same logical difficulties underlie the making of such corrections as underlie the construction of index numbers. There is no uniquely right way of making seasonal corrections any more than there is a uniquely right way of constructing an index number; and just as index numbers have to be reweighted from time to time, so there may be a trend in the seasonal pattern that makes it necessary to change the pattern progressively through time.

Next, there is the fact that the available indicators are frequently inconsistent with one another just when they ought to tally. We can measure what is happening to production from the side of output, income or expenditure; and we know that the three methods of measurement ought to yield the same total. But in point of fact they rarely do. We can have years such as 1962 when on one indicator the national income increased and on another it fell. The quarterly expenditure figures for 1963 are impossible to reconcile with the output figures and, for that matter, with a great mass of other information. Nevertheless, it is to the expenditure data that we have to turn if we want to explain the changes taking place in production in terms of the forces operating through the different components of demand.

Forecasting and Extrapolation

Given all these difficulties in interpreting the statistics, we have to do the best we can with the information at our disposal. The simplest and most popular method of forecasting is undoubtedly extrapolation of past trends. There is a sense in which all forecasting reduces to this. When we forecast that the sun will rise tomorrow, we are extrapolating: there is no recorded case of the sun's not rising. Even if we call in a scientist who tells us why the sun is bound to rise tomorrow he, too, is extrapolating in the sense that he is predicting the continued existence of gravity or the characteristics of matter that give rise to gravity.

In this particular example, it makes very little difference whether we know the logical basis of the trend or not. But in economic forecasting it makes a great deal of difference. The trend in the death rate has been downwards for a very long time; but it would be rash to extrapolate unthinkingly unless we are prepared to end up with a negative death rate and see the dead gradually restored to life. I have the same difficulty with those more subtle forms of 'explanation' of economic variables that make use of variance analysis without first framing a self-consistent hypothesis and bringing together all the available evidence bearing on it, whether statistical or not. A trend can provide a firm basis for forecasting only where it measures the strength of one or more relatively constant forces, so that, if things go on as they are, the trend shows what will happen. In the absence of these forces, the trend is spurious, and without any significance. For example, it is meaningless to talk of a trend in unemployment except over a very short period in which the forces governing the demand for labour are operating fairly steadily in one direction. It would be absurd to predict the future level of unemployment by reference to this 'trend' and so take for granted the absence of any material change in the pressures in the labour market. The prediction is inseparable from a view as to the likelihood of a change in the demand for labour (or conceivably, in the supply).

The Econometric Approach

Once we advance beyond simple extrapolation, a variety of procedures is open to us. The first is to make use of a comprehensive model of the behaviour of the economy, seen as a set of interrelated behaviour equations with a large number of equations to express

132

the relationships between the selected variables. Prediction then becomes a matter of choosing the right variables, establishing from past data the mathematical equations governing their behaviour, and letting a computer do the rest. This is the econometric approach.

The trouble with this approach is that the relationships between economic magnitudes are not fixed. We are not dealing with a world in which the same forces are unalterably at work so that, once detected and measured, their operation can be recorded once and for all in the marble rigour of mathematics. There is no economic cycle, endlessly repeating itself; something new is always happening in a sense without counterpart in the physical world. The *dramatis personae* of an economic model – the coefficients, lags, functions and all the rest – are inevitably a travesty of the world we know, and perform too stiffly to fool us into taking them for the real thing.

Yet if nothing were fixed, forecasting would be absurd. Our power to predict the future rests on the continued operation of social forces and relationships that are relatively constant. We may hold strongly to the utility of econometric analysis of particular elements in the economic system without attaching equal value to predictions based on comprehensive models of the functioning of the system as a whole.

The Survey Approach

The second procedure goes to the opposite extreme. It does not purport to be at all systematic and may make no use of fixed relationships or even of a national income framework. Instead, it is essentially a 'go and ask' procedure, relying on what is being said by business men and government agencies about their intentions and expectations, on the Federation of British Industries' and similar surveys of industrial trends and the state of business opinion, on what seem to be significant and revealing straws in the wind; to put it succinctly, on the smell of the economy. This procedure obviously involves a large element of hunch and has the strength and weakness of good reporting unsupported by scientific analysis. It has the advantage of incorporating a great deal of non-statistical up-to-the-minute data about business conditions; but the data rarely fit themselves into a clear and consistent pattern and are likely to give an over-dramatic and partial view of the changes at work. It is also very dangerous to aggregate the forecasts of different persons or businesses or departments, however intimate their knowledge of their

133

own affairs. They are likely to be correspondingly ignorant of more general trends elsewhere in the economy and fail to see how these trends will in due course alter their own circumstances and eventually also their forecasts. Not that people, in forecasting their own affairs, pay no regard to what they think is happening to the economy. On the contrary, I have a strong suspicion that business men, when forecasting their own sales in foreign markets, allow their judgment to be heavily coloured by what they have been reading in the newspapers about export trends and performance. But this, unfortunately, makes their forecasts peculiarly difficult to interpret since one cannot be sure how far they reflect what has already happened and has found its way into the newspapers and how far they represent an independent assessment by each forecaster of his future prospects in export markets.

In spite of all these difficulties, there is no substitute for first-hand impressions, gathered over the widest possible area, of the business outlook: what I might call 'sniffery' as opposed to the 'niffery' of orthodox national income forecasting, It is foolish to base forecasts exclusively on impressions. On the other hand, unfashionable and unscientific as it may be to rely on anything that can be dismissed as hunch, there are also dangers about being too systematic, especially if this means giving precedence to published statistics over 'mere' impressions.

A Combined Approach

The third procedure is to assemble all the available information about the main economic aggregates such as investment, consumption, exports, etc., make a prediction about those of them that are governed mainly or exclusively by autonomous factors, and link in the others by making *ad hoc* assumptions about key relationships such as the savings ratio, the ratio of imports to gross national product and so on.

In making predictions for investment, exports and so on, this method makes extensive use of direct statistical indicators of the future, such as the state of order books, surveys of investment intentions carried out by the Board of Trade, the Federation of British Industries and other surveys of business opinion, and the government's own reviews and estimates of expenditure in the public sector. In this sense it has much in common with the second method in that the judgments expressed do not follow mechanically from a set of behaviour equations. On the other hand, it also has

134

much in common with the first method since, although not necessarily econometric in form, it does postulate a number of fixed relationships capable of mathematical expression. Its advantage over the first method is that one is not bound by mathematical formulae but can see what one is doing as one goes along and can vary the assumptions made in the light of all the available information.

When I first came in contact with organized short-term economic forecasting, I was astonished at the confidence with which precise forecasts were made. I had never myself got beyond the second rather impressionistic method of forecasting and recoiled instinctively from a purely econometric approach. But I was doubtful whether the third eclectic method, even if adroitly handled, could hope to give more than an approximate and very uncertain estimate of the future level of production unless all the major trends in the economy were strongly in one direction. It seemed to me that the big problem was to predict the turning-point in the two major exogenous variables, fixed investment and exports, and that on top of this came the intractable problem of predicting the movement of stocks. I still think that when it comes to predicting turning-points we have very little to go upon. It does not seem to me that an econometric model can be made to yield them. We really know remarkably little about the factors governing short-term changes in fixed investment or about the way in which the stock of fixed capital is likely to be adjusted to the level of output; and we should have the utmost difficulty to reduce the world economic system to an econometric model to yield a forecast of exports.

The Value of Forecasts

How far should one carry scepticism about economic forecasting? Is the whole business as hopeless as a recent letter to *The Times* suggested: 'Is it not the truth', said the writer, 'that forecasts, based on existing trends (in population), have turned out to be moonshine in the past, continue to be moonshine in the present and ought never to be made at all?'

It is no part of my purpose to lend support to so extreme a view. Forecasting is the stuff of life and we only escape from it when we die. Hardly anything we do is based on exact knowledge and every decision we take that is not a mere judgment on what has already happened implies a forecast. No business could survive for long without some form of forecasting and it is no use trying to forecast

135

if one insists on being right. The best one can do is to muster the relevant information systematically, analyse it so as to see in what direction it points, and then drew what deductions one can, with all the attendant risks of error.

The same is true in forecasting at the national level. Such forecasting has a practical purpose and is indispensable to efforts to manage the economy. In a country where total public expenditure exceeds 40 per cent gross national product, it is inconceivable that the government could go on from year to year paying no regard to the impact of this expenditure – which I need hardly remind you is not conspicuously stable – on the level of economic activity. Or, if you happen to think like some writers that the government is bound to get it wrong, why assume that the best way of forecasting is not to try?

When I hear judgments of this kind I take comfort from the derision that weather forecasts used to excite and the progress that has recently been made in that direction. During the war, bomber squadrons used to receive forecasts of cloud cover that had to be within limits finer than the available instruments could reliably predict. This did not prevent many notable successes, including some where the forecaster later discovered that the wrong information had been used and was astonished to be congratulated none the less on the accuracy of his prediction. There may well be some parallels here with economic forecasting.

Just as weather forecasts rarely tell us exactly what tomorrow or the next day will be like, so economic forecasts cannot hope to show exactly how the economy will develop. They are not at all like the forecasts made by racing tipsters or football correspondents.

Their object is not to get 'the right answer' with absolute precision. It is true that they are sometimes expressed in terms of a single set of figures and that many people treat these figures literally as *the* forecast. But the purpose of economic forecasting is to bring out the effective range of possibilities, to indicate the centre of the range and the probability distribution around this point, and to allow policy to be shaped in the light of the uncertainties and probabilities.

Although a forecast, therefore, may be expressed in the form of a self-consistent set of figures, its function is to allow one to judge how one should run one's risks. It should spotlight the uncertainties rather than give the impression that these can be compressed into a single set of figures.

136

The Margin of Error

The uncertainties and the margin of error corresponding to them are not objective facts but must be measured in relation to policy objectives. Every forecaster has to ask himself not only how likely it is that this or that part of his forecast may be wrong but how much it matters. If, for example, he is forecasting exports he may put down a figure that is at the centre of the range of probabilities. In some countries and at some times it may not matter a great deal if the actual and the forecast diverge by 5 per cent; in Britain in 1964 it would matter a great deal. Moreover, the consequences of an overestimate would normally be far more unwelcome than the consequences of an underestimate. This might seem to point to the desirability of erring on the side of prudence and making a lower forecast, but if the purpose of the forecast is to arrive at a view of the likely pressure of demand, this object would be defeated by such a procedure. One has to make a forecast before hedging one's best, not the other way round.

If one has to consider the inconveniences of error in relation to the individual components of demand, one has also to review the dangers involved in overestimating and underestimating the total; and here, in the modern world, a fresh problem arises. For, in a sense, one cannot afford to be far out in either direction given the danger of inflation and a balance of payments deficit if demand increases a little too fast and the equal danger of an unacceptable rise in unemployment if it increases a little too slowly; and yet, at the same time, one can hardly avoid being quite a long way out from time to time if the difficulties of economic forecasting are as real as I have suggested they are. At any rate, there seems to me a danger that unless public opinion is educated to a fuller understanding of those difficulties, it may ask for greater accuracy in forecasting than it is reasonable to expect.

The Possibilities of Improvement

But I do not want to end on a note of scepticism. Our methods of forecasting are not beyond improvement and we must do all we can to improve them. In particular, we should be able to learn from past mistakes by analysing systematically how they arose and whether they are liable to recur.

The amount of effort that has so far been put into economic forecasting is minute. The very concepts of modern economics are

137

astonishingly new – even index numbers do not go back beyond my father's lifetime – and the statistics and estimates on which we are now able to build did not exist as recently as 1939.

Quarterly national accounts have a history of less than ten years. It would be surprising if economists were already in a position to predict with confidence how much and how quickly the main determinants of economic activity will change. But we are enormously further on then twenty-five years ago: and if we take enough trouble in the next twenty-five years we may make just as much progress in improving our understanding of the functioning of the economic system and our power to forecast its behaviour.

8. Economic Forecasting: Further Reflections[1]

'If we could first know where we are and whither we are tending, we could better judge what to do and how to do it.'

Abraham Lincoln

A trend is a trend is a trend
But the question is, will it bend?
Will it alter its course
Through some unforeseen force
And come to a premature end?

Stein Age Forecaster

Forecasting occupies us all for much of our lives. It begins with the speculative wagging of heads over our cradles and continues until the prayers with which we are hopefully laid to rest. Sometimes it is an idle amusement, sometimes a matter of life and death, sometimes – and this is where the economist takes a hand – it carries rewards and punishments in the form of profit or loss.

There is nothing new, therefore, either about forecasting or about economic forecasting as such. Both are as old as human activity, of which economic activity has always been a prominent part. What is new is the kind of economic forecasting that is now carried on and the way in which it is organized. It is accepted as an integral and necessary part of policy-making at all levels of economic management, and tends to be undertaken systematically by a specialized group of experts recruited for this specific purpose. Whether it takes the form of market research, investment analysis or national-income forecasting, it has become a full-time occupation requiring preliminary training and is the subject of an expanding literature designed to assist such training.

I cannot discover any occasion on which the Royal Economic Society has ever discussed this new activity, in which an increasing

[1] Presidential address to the Royal Economic Society, 3 July, 1969.

139

number of economists are now engaged. I have thought it appropriate, therefore, to select this topic for a Presidential Address, all the more because I have myself been preoccupied with forecasting over the past few years to the almost complete exclusion of other aspects of economics. My preoccupation has been that of a consumer rather than a producer; but perhaps economists should be invited for once to swallow one of their own favourite prescriptions and have a look at the market before putting too much effort into production. In any event, I am not qualified to enter in detail into the technical issues involved in the preparation of forecasts. I shall also limit what I have to say to national-income forecasting, although I believe that a good deal of my argument has a wider application.

NATIONAL-INCOME FORECASTS

National-income forecasts are essentially forecasts of the behaviour of aggregate demand over a period which is usually between one and two years. Sometimes the forecast is expressed in the form of a year-on-year comparison, but in Britain it is almost always prepared so as to show the changes quarter by quarter, and the focus of interest is the situation predicted at the end of the period and the path by which it is reached rather than the average change in demand and output between one year and the next. National-income forecasts are usually coupled with balance-of-payments forecasts, and in these the absolute size of the expected surplus or deficit over the period is of interest equally with the changes that are predicted in the balance of payments from quarter to quarter.

Forecasts of this kind serve in principle important administrative purposes. First of all, they provide a frame of reference for policy decisions. So far as they express the best available judgment of future prospects, they allow the government to act incrementally on the economy: that is, to take for granted the changes already in progress and concentrate policy on reinforcing or modifying these changes. Instead of reacting to events as they occur, the government can frame its policies ahead of the events predicted in the forecasts.

Secondly, the forecasts form a channel of communication between those concerned with day-to-day administration and those who are involved in policy formulation. The preparation of a set of forecasts involves the first group, because their knowledge of what is going on currently ought to be consistent with the figures for the near future and the recent past; and it also involves the second group, because if the outcome of existing policies as revealed in the
140

forecast is unsatisfactory fresh policies will have to be introduced. The dissemination of official forecasts throughout Whitehall provides departments simultaneously with a common view of the current situation and a common view of what will happen unless something is done. Each can then react knowing what view of the future is held elsewhere and can either challenge that view or propose action based upon it.

Thirdly, the forecasts can serve a monitoring function and provide a basis against which to judge how policies are working out. Any serious divergence from forecasts rings an alarm bell and makes it easier to concentrate attention and effort on corrective action.

Although economic forecasts serve these purposes in principle, there are a number of practical difficulties that should not be overlooked. There are no doubt great advantages in using a single set of forecasts known to a large number of officials and ministers and accepted by them as a consistent basis for the management of the economy. But no ministers in any well-conducted government are likely to devolve completely on a small group of experts responsibility for formulating an authoritative view of future economic prospects; the risks of error are only too obvious whatever the auspices under which forecasts are prepared. Ministers (and officials) may well hesitate to commit themselves to a single set of forecasts to be appealed to in all contexts and for all purposes. It may also be far from self-evident to them that what emerges at the end of the day from a large-scale forecasting exercise by specialists drawn from each of the leading economic departments is necessarily a better basis for policy-making than the judgment of a single careful observer of current trends; statistical haggling has not always been the path to economic wisdom.

There are also great advantages in making official forecasts as widely available as possible. If it is helpful to involve the whole government machine in economic forecasting it would also seem helpful to involve the community at large. Since the forecasts underlie some at least of the decisions that ministers take, an explanation and defence of these decisions is incomplete without reference to the forecasts that form the background to them. But this is only half the story. The very size of the government machine creates problems in communication within it which are not overcome and may easily be aggravated by giving forecasts precise quantitative shape. As for the general public, any government has to give careful thought to the way in which it presents its policies and may scruple to blurt out its worst fears because they happen to be dig-

141

nified as economic forecasts. What one minister hesitates to reveal to another he is not likely to reveal to the press – although his colleague may for reasons of his own.

To some of these issues I shall return later. First, however, I propose to discuss some of the problems involved in forecasting.

The Basis of National Income Forecasts

A short-term economic forecast has to be based on two things: an informational system and an economic model. Some people lay the emphasis on one, and some on the other. For example, many economists who construct forecasting models take the availability of suitable data for granted or assume, usually mistakenly, that it does not matter in what form the data are fed into the model. Sometimes models are constructed from annual data, and so implicitly reject the contribution that can be obtained through access to the latest available information.

Just as some people feel in no need of recent data, others feel in no need of elaborate models. They find it sufficient to establish a trend and extrapolate. Or they conduct surveys of business expectations and build a forecast round the results. The origins of the trend may remain unexamined and shifts in expectations be treated as inherently unpredictable.

My own sympathies lie more with the unsophisticated second group, who at least have an ear to the ground, than with the often over-sophisticated first group, who take a bird's eye view of the situation. It is in practice quite possible to make forecasts of short-term prospects without a model; but it is impossible to make quantitative forecasts without quantitative data. Moreover, any model that is worth using has itself to be based on an analysis of such data. The system of relationships in the model may be derived partly from theoretical considerations, but it must also embody the results of empirical investigation of past experience in the values assigned to all the parameters. In a forecasting model, as distinct from an explanatory model, this dependence on statistical data is enhanced by the use of a large number of exogenous variables as forward indicators of investment, exports and so on.[1]

Forecasts based on economic models convey an illusion of continuity that can be highly dangerous. We may try to smooth the past

[1] For a fuller discussion of the issues involved see 'Short-term Economic Forecasting at the Treasury' (in *Models for Decision*, British Computer Society, 1964).

or crush it into a Procrustean bed of econometric relationships, but we know that it is made up like the future of a series of discontinuous and unique events. The economic outlook may be dominated by the likelihood of some specific event. such as a major war, an exchange crisis, an international agreement and so on, so that the only forecast that matters is whether and, if so, when that event will take place. In a state of crisis improvisation takes over from planning, uncertainties multiply and forecasting becomes a waste of time. The only thing to do is to react to a succession of emergencies, recognizing that it is impossible to be ahead of events that are inherently unpredictable. In the summer of 1940, for example, it would have been of little help in deciding what to do over the next few months to have a forecast of GNP extending into 1941.

The models may also mislead by implying a constancy in the pattern of economic events which experience belies. The same key variables may be present in successive cycles, and may operate on one another in much the same way: so far as this is so, ordinary economic theory can tell us what to expect. But the interactions are never *quite* the same, because the circumstances are different, the strength of the economic forces at work varies from one cycle to the next and the time for a given effect to show itself – a matter hardly touched upon in economic theory – is far from constant. In addition, the parameters are changing through time, so that in trying to establish them from the statistical record of the past we are analysing an economic system that has already ceased to exist. I would stress particularly our ignorance of the speed of response of economic variables, because any forecasting system that assumes this to be constant takes for granted what may well be one of the principal uncertainties that a forecast is intended to resolve.

CONSTRAINTS IMPOSED BY THE DATA

I do not propose to deal with the technical problems of model-building on which there is a considerable literature. I shall concentrate instead on the constraints imposed by the available data. These constraints may in due course be relaxed by improvements in the collection and processing of statistical information, but in my view they are largely inherent in the economic system itself, and should not be dismissed or ignored as a minor or transient affair. It is precisely because the variables are so numerous and complex and our information about them inevitably so imperfect that economics (and economic forecasting) is so much more difficult than it looks.

143

The ideal situation would be one in which all the data were bang up to date, completely reliable and mutually consistent. We should then be able to say with confidence what had been happening and where we were. Unfortunately this is hardly ever possible. The first thing we have to forecast is the past. So far from being easy, this is usually very difficult. In fact, it often makes more sense to project a forecast backwards as a guide to what the statistics should look like than to construct a forecast of the future on an uncritical acceptance of current figures. I have frequently had to confess that the best available guide to what was happening was the latest forecast of what was expected to happen.

Lags

First of all, the forecaster has to contend with the inevitable lag of statistics behind events. Sometimes this lag may be negligible: for example, we can keep track of the gold reserves from day to day. Sometimes it is extremely long: census data were collected until recently at intervals of ten years and published up to five years later, so that in 1966 the latest information might relate to 1951. Most of the data necessary for the construction of national-income estimates relate to a period at least one month ago, and often as much as three months ago. The quarterly figures, which give the most comprehensive picture of the economic situation, appear three months or more after the event. This means that when the February forecasts are being prepared in advance of the budget the latest available national accounts relate to the third quarter, i.e. to the quarter centred on August. Obviously a lot can happen in the seven months between August and April.

Unreliability

Next comes the issue of reliability. One index of this is the frequency with which the figures are subsequently amended, usually in the light of later information. An obvious example is the series for personal saving. The published statistics represent a residual, arrived at from figures of income on one side and figures of expenditure on the other. But until a few years ago there appeared to be a systematic tendency for new items of expenditure to be omitted, so that, in course of time as more and more of the omissions were identified, the figures of consumer spending crept up, and the residual was correspondingly narrowed.[1] In recent years the revisions have been comparatively

[1] National Institute of Economic and Social Research, *Economic Review*, May, 1963, p. 11.

small, but it would be rash to assume that the figures have greatly improved in reliability.

A second illustration is provided by the index of industrial production. In the first nine months of 1964 the index stayed obstinately level at a time when other signs pointed to increasing pressure of demand. Today the figures for the first three quarters read 126, 128, 129 – a very different picture. Similarly, the revised figures for 1962 indicate a much slower climb up to the third quarter of the year than the unrevised figures at the time of publication. I cite these examples not in order to point an accusing finger at British statistics (other countries, including the United States, amend their figures at least as often and as much) but because they relate to periods at which misinterpretation of the figures could have had serious consequences. Indeed, in 1964 press comment on the figures did contribute to the inertia of the government.

A more recent illustration has been provided by the discovery that exports have been consistently understated for nearly six years. Quite apart from the uncertainties introduced by this discovery, it has always seemed to me dangerous to treat the change in exports recorded in the trade returns from year to year (not just from month to month) as an entirely reliable guide to the actual change either in the value of work done on exports or in export proceeds or even in the flow of goods to foreign destinations.

One consequence of this unreliability is that one can never be sure whether a new trend for which there is no obvious explanation really exists. It is possible to build all kinds of interesting hypotheses around a series of figures until the bubble is pricked by an unpublicized amendment, and the theories lose their iridescence with a bang. Time and again in my experience, a disturbing but inexplicable change in the situation turns out to need no explanation, because it eventually proves that there has in fact been no such change. You can be just as wrong about the past as about the future.

Seasonal Adjustments

One particular source of unreliability that needs emphasis is the difficulty of making seasonal adjustments. It is easy to overlook this problem when the figures in regular use have been purged, nominally at least, of seasonal influences. But seasonal influences are neither invariable from year to year nor over longer periods. Walter Heller's remark that 'seasonally corrected, the weather in January was lousy' epitomizes part of the problem; and the shifting habits of car buyers points to another.

K

It is not possible in my judgment to dodge this problem by working out all the necessary econometric relations in terms of raw data and concealing the implicit seasonal adjustments from the sceptical eye. One might with equal justice exclude price changes and make all the calculations at current prices. On the other hand, there is no uniquely right way of making seasonal corrections, any more than there is a uniquely right way of constructing an index number.

The importance of making the right adjustments can best be illustrated by reference to the unemployment statistics. Broadly speaking, it is possible to apply a correction to these in one of two ways: either by making absolute adjustments to the figures, up or down, to remove the seasonal understatement or overstatement, or by using proportionate adjustments, on the assumption that the size of the seasonal correction is itself dependent on the current level of unemployment and not fixed independently of it. There are good reasons for thinking that part of the adjustment should be additive and part proportionate. But the two sets of adjustments can lead to very different results. In the early months of 1959, for example, the picture would have looked entirely different if the proportionate method had been used; and the difference would have been particularly striking at the very moment when the Chancellor of the Exchequer was looking for advice on how to frame his budget. In the six months between August 1958 and February 1959 the rise in unemployment on one basis was 70,000, while on the other it was no more than 20,000, and the peak had already been passed.

The unemployment statistics raise a further problem in reliability: the problem of comparing figures over time. Unemployment in 1969 is not the same phenomenon as in 1959, and other indices of pressure on the labour market may move in a quite different way. It is dangerous, therefore, to treat the recorded change in unemployment from one year to another as a reliable guide to the actual change in pressure. In Britain the various labour-market indices – unemployment, vacancies, hours of work, participation rates, migration flows, recruitment through the Labour Exchanges – did in fact agree remarkably well until a year or two ago, but in 1968 the unemployment figures diverged rather strikingly from the others. This posed a major problem, since the unemployment figures are usually the most up to date, reliable, unambiguous and significant of all the leading British indicators. It takes time to become alive to such an unaccustomed divergence, to make sure that it is not an aberration, to investigate its origins and decide how far to abandon
146

changes in unemployment as a guide to policy decisions.[1] Indeed, one of the greatest hazards in forecasting is that a statistical series which is generally highly reliable may suddenly and without warning prove quite unreliable.

Inconsistencies

As the unemployment figures show, the data may tell different stories. The fact that the statistical picture is inevitably full of inconsistencies is the most awkward problem of all. Even measures that in principle are equal to one another are often in flat contradiction. To take what may be an extreme example, between the first quarter of 1966 and the first quarter of 1967 the expenditure measure of GNP increased by 2 per cent, the income measure fell by $\frac{1}{2}$ per cent and the output measure was unchanged. Yet all these measure the same thing. Even when they all show the same direction of change, they often differ very perceptibly as to amount. By the second quarter of 1968, for example, one measure was 2 per cent above the level of 1966, another $5\frac{1}{2}$ per cent and the third 4 per cent.

How is one to reconcile evidence of this kind? Not surely by accepting implicitly the expenditure estimate because it happens to be the aggregate of the demand components of which forecasts are made up. Nor, in my view, by striking a simple average and treating the result as a firm estimate. One has to look at all the other evidence and judge what is most plausible.

OCCUPATIONAL DISEASES OF FORECASTING

Forecasters suffer from a number of occupational diseases of which I shall mention three. First there is what I should call the Jonah syndrome or Variant I. By this I mean the tendency to dwell on possible disasters ahead and to call for immediate action to avoid them. It is, of course, a powerful position to be in, since if disaster does occur the forecaster's reputation is made, while if it does not occur people will either be too relieved to call for the forecaster's head or will attribute the outcome to some action set on foot after

[1] In case anyone interprets this (like some readers of the Brookings Report on *Britain's Economic Prospects*) as implying that the British Government habitually overlooks the lag of unemployment behind output, let me hasten to point out that the Hopkin Loop illustrating this lag was part of Treasury lore by 1961 or earlier, and that the idea that the lag is a fixed one was abandoned long ago. (See J. R. Shepherd, 'Productive Potential and the Demand for Labour', *Economic Trends*, August 1968, p. xxvi.)

his predictions. When Nineveh was saved Jonah had no real need to go off and sulk; he could have taken credit by attributing Nineveh's good luck to his intercession with the Lord.

A more common disorder is the Overgrown Hedge or Variant II. The forecaster, instead of predicting a specific outcome, wisely takes refuge in quoting a range of figures, but sets the upper and lower limits so far apart that the policy-maker to whom the forecast is presented is no wiser than he was before. The forecaster suffering from Variant II may be led to claim that he has not suggested any outcome within the limits set as more probable than any other outcome within those limits. But if he is honest with himself he knows only too well that his forecast will be treated as implying that the most probable outcome lies mid-way between the upper and lower limits.

A third variant is what I would designate 'the phony average'. There was a time in the early fifties when the Royal Statistical Society used to invite its members in May to predict the average increase in GNP in the current year over the preceding year. It does not require much elementary arithmetic to show how valueless such a forecast would be to the policy-maker. By May two-thirds of the two-year period is already over; and if the available statistics showed a steady expansion up till March it would require a very large and sudden change of trend to move the expected outcome up or down by one percentage point. If, for example, production is rising every month from 100 by half a percentage point the increase in Year Two over Year One should work out at $8\frac{3}{4}$ per cent. To bring this down to 7 per cent would mean either that production had to stop increasing in April and remain flat until December or that a turning-point should be reached later, with production falling towards the end of the year – a change of trend far more violent than the layman would deduce from a wobble in the forecast by one percentage point.

None of these variants lacks for professional support. I have heard Variant III stoutly defended by the head of the forecasting staff of a continental country whose practices are held up to our admiration by British journalists. It is true that year-on-year forecasts are usually made about November rather than in the following May. But this still means that the forecast is made nearly half-way through the period to which it relates and is subject to a very wide margin of error as an indication of the situation at the end of the period. For purposes of economic management in Britain such a forecast would be largely valueless if not highly misleading.

Variant II has also many respectable and eminent defenders who argue that the uncertainties behind any forecast can be adequately conveyed only if the forecast is expressed in terms of a range of possible outcomes. The difficulty is that in practice it is at least as hard to state precise limits to the range as it is to plump for some central outcome. The unsophisticated user is inclined either to pooh-pooh the forecast or simply strike an average, while the sophisticated user is usually well aware that any figure is subject to a wide margin of error and wants not a measure of the timidity of the forecaster but detailed information about the vulnerability of the forecast to specific alternative assumptions.

As to the Jonah syndrome, which you may think a rather attractive form of disorder, it may be true that those afflicted with it could usefully have bitten British policy-makers more severely during the sixties. But if so this is not because it would be right to erect into a principle that one should always forecast the worst possible outcome, but because in the circumstances of the last decade or two it would probably have been appropriate to err more strongly on the side of caution.

ERRORS IN FORECASTING

This brings us to the interesting question of errors in forecasting. These are of various kinds.

First of all, the forecast may rest on bad theory. The model used may be wrong in the sense that it either selects the wrong variables or specifies wrong relationships between them. As to what I mean by 'bad' theory or 'wrong' relationships, let it suffice that one characteristic of what is 'bad' or 'wrong' is that it could be superseded with advantage by something which would give a more satisfactory and consistent account of the inner logic of the observed phenomena. For example, the forecast may rest on a model which excludes from the parameters monetary influences such as the rate of interest or the money supply when it is clear that economic activity does respond to changes in monetary conditions. Or it may introduce monetary influences as if they operated mainly on business investment rather than on, say, housing, when better results can be obtained from a model connecting monetary factors and house-building more closely.

On the whole, I doubt whether bad theory has played a major part in forecasting errors in this country over the past decade or two. It is conceivable, to take the example I have given, that the model has allowed too little influence on the economy to monetary

149

factors. For what it is worth, this is not my own impression. There have been a number of occasions – notably the introduction of SET in 1966, with the consequent forced loan to the government, and the import deposits scheme of 1968/96 – when it might have been reasonable to allow a good deal for the reflection of financial restriction on business outlays. But on these occasions it has proved difficult if not impossible to trace such effects – in marked contrast to the clear reflection of hire-purchase restrictions on consumer spending.

The next source of error is a change in some variable outside the model. This covers everything that the model assumes to remain constant, and hence everything assumed to have no systematic relationship with the rest of the model. But this obviously covers a great deal of what does in practice determine the movement of economic activity: strikes, assassinations, elections, chance events like the closing of the Suez Canal, and so on. Some of these things are capable of being included in the model, and others can to some extent be allowed for. But the economy is never

'A creature that moves
In determinate grooves'

so that even in principle there is no reason to expect economic forecasting to become an exact science. The difficulty is to decide whether, when an error occurs, the forecaster's alibi is sound because the error springs from the unfathomable complexity of the real world and the inherent randomness of events.

These sources of error apart, mistakes can arise out of misinterpretation of the statistical data. First of all, it is very easy to get the starting-point wrong, especially as the data for the past three months or even the past year are necessarily highly uncertain. Anyone conducting a post mortem on a forecast has to face an almost invariable discrepancy between the current level (e.g. of GNP) assumed at the time when the forecast was made and as seen retrospectively when the post mortem is undertaken. He has then to ask himself whether the forecast was related to the level x months away or to the increase in the level over x months. But at this point it almost always emerges that the two things are part and parcel of the same forecast: had a different starting-point been taken for the forecast, both the eventual level and the rate of increase to that level would have been altered. Sometimes this reflects technical factors: for example, if GNP is put at a higher initial level this alters the stock–output ratio, and so the amount of stock-building required in order to restore equilibrium. Sometimes what is involved is the changed

150

view of future prospects that is occasioned by a changed view of the recent past. If it became clear that an upswing in business investment was in progress instead of the level trend previously assumed this would automatically change the forecast, perhaps quite radically. The forecaster might claim that the only satisfactory way of testing his accuracy would be to allow him to repeat the forecast in the light of the newly available information about the past. But here, as over other errors, the recipient of the original forecast might view the matter less sympathetically and ask in all innocence whether there were no other ways of checking on the starting-point.

The data may give rise to other kinds of misinterpretation. Any forecasting model has to use a large number of equational relationships, complete with coefficients and lags which are bound to be of uncertain magnitude, if only because the relationships have to be based on a limited number of observations, and these extend over a period in which the whole system of relationships is itself likely to have been changing. No one can be very confident, however successful his curve-fitting, that he has found the unique explanation of past experience. Anyone who has watched econometrics applied to short-term forecasting knows that a wide selection of equations can be generated with highly impressive R^2s from the same set of past observations, and that there tends to be a distressing scatter in the predictions yielded by these same equations when they are projected into the future. I believe that the Board of Trade have used over twenty equations, all with impeccable credentials, to forecast imports, but without any means of deciding which is right.

There is, of course, no reason why an equation which is intended to represent some underlying relationship should hold in the special circumstances of any single year. But it is a more serious matter if one cannot be sure that the underlying relationship will reassert itself or re-emerge after a wobble as a quite different relationship. Take, for example, the familiar story of consumer spending in 1968. Many people, observing the spending spree at the beginning of this year, were inclined to conclude that personal saving would remain negligible for the rest of the year and that the imposition of higher taxation would have a very limited effect in checking consumption. It became an article of faith in some quarters that there had been a fundamental change in saving habits and that fiscal methods of regulating demand were ineffective. All this was idle talk and showed little appreciation of what goes to make up personal savings. But there *might* have been a continuing shift in propensities: we don't know for sure that there wasn't.

151

It is often assumed that forecasting errors would be reduced if use were made of a computable model rather than the less elaborate forecasting models usually employed. I see nothing inevitable about this.[1] Indeed, there is a serious danger that computable models will yield less reliable results, particularly if they are fed with statistics in a very raw state. At least half the problem lies in the need to refine the data and ensure self-consistency. This requires detailed inspection of the kind which the methods hitherto used in Britain are calculated to provide. What is undoubtedly true is that computers are indispensable to forecasting for the analysis of specific equational relationships, for exploring alternative hypotheses and for providing rather quicker results by dispensing with iterative processes. They do not necessarily reduce the risk of error.

Anyone engaged in forecasting has always to be jogging back to see what went wrong. But this is not as easy as it sounds. If the government took action in the light of the forecast that in itself would give rise to a change in the forecast. But how big a change it is impossible to say without resort to the very model and system of equations on which the original forecast rested. So in assessing forecasting errors it may be necessary to take for granted the very apparatus that is being tested.

Much the same applies in allowing for random events outside the model. Both in the forecast and in the post mortem it is necessary to assign to such events a precise value for their impact in the economy – something which the average administrator would rarely make bold to do and which he may never imagine going on all the time in a different area of government. There may be no way of testing whether the allowance made is correct except by methods that are themselves of the nature of a forecast. Once again a post mortem may involve forecasting backwards.

When we come to errors that clearly originate within the equational system and connot be explained away in terms of a wrong starting-point, external events or a change of policy, the trouble usually lies in the speed or violence of reaction, on the one hand, or in a shift in the underlying relationships, on the other. Either of these may be associated with a change in mood or attitude which can originate outside economic events altogether or have as much to do with the way in which policy is presented as with policy itself. Whatever the source, it is not easy to predict accurately how quickly smoke will give way to flame so that all the normal interactions are

[1] See 'Short Term forecasting at the Treasury', in *Models for Decision*. This essay, although attributed to me, is almost entirely the work of Mr A. D. Roy.

speeded up. Even when one is on one's guard for the evidence of acceleration after an obvious turning-point, it may first be extraordinarily slow to appear and then exceed expectations in the most disconcerting way. Both in 1959–60 and in 1964–65 these cumulative effects seem to have been inadequately foreseen in the forecasts of GNP and still more of the balance of payments. It is always a little sinister when the forecasts begin to be revised uniformly in one direction.

Revision of Forecasts

Given the obvious need to revise forecasts, how often should this be done? The answer inevitably depends on the frequency with which policy adjustments can be contemplated: in this sense a fresh forecast should be available at any time. Yet something must also be allowed for the logistics of forecasting. Where this involves extensive consultation with other departments, the preparation of a new set of forecasts may stretch over weeks and can rarely be undertaken at short notice. The normal practice in the Treasury is to engage in three major forecasting exercises every year: in January/February before the budget; in June/July after the budget; and in October/November to allow a preliminary view of the budget to be taken. But, of course, other less elaborate forecasts are made more or less monthly, and the forecasting staff is also called upon to predict the effect of particular acts of policy. My personal impression is that the less elaborate forecasts are subject to a wider margin of error than the others. The reason for this in my view is that it is usually only when the major exercises are undertaken that the situation is radically re-examined and a fresh view taken of current trends. It is much easier in a month-by-month approach to persist in discounting evidence of a change in the underlying situation and preserving the basis of earlier forecasts unchanged.

THE USE OF FORECASTS

I come, finally, to the way in which forecasts are used. How should one look at a forecast, and how ought one to frame advice on it?

It is important to make clear at the start that policy is not governed exclusively by economic forecasts. A government, being a government, cannot isolate economic policy and decide what to do or when to do it on economic grounds alone. It may wish quite properly to defer action or draw up plans undeterred by the latest forecast in

153

order to strengthen its political position at home or for reasons of defence or foreign policy. It has also to weigh up different objectives of economic policy, and when these are in conflict no forecast can by itself resolve the conflict. Short-term considerations may point one way, long-term considerations the other; domestic and external pressures may be opposed to one another; the particular interests that would benefit from one kind of policy may have to be balanced against other interests that would suffer. No Chancellor ever feels, therefore, that the forecasts as such tell him what to do.

Secondly, it is important not to treat forecasts as gospel truth. It may seem odd to insist on this view of the fallibility of economic forecasters. But the world is full of people who are only too willing to treat a forecast with excessive reverence (or in revulsion dismiss all forecasts as mumbo-jumbo). There are no more dangerous men in government than those who take figures literally, and this applies both to statistics of the past and to forecasts of the future. Such readers appal the righteous forecaster, who regards the figures he sets down as no more than the beginning, not the end of the story. For he knows that the essential function of a forecast is to help ministers in deciding what risks they are running and how they should run them; and although the figures summarize the most probable outcome as the forecaster sees it, they are far from conveying all that is in his mind. They do not reveal the conviction with which he regards his own forecast; the margin that separates it from other quite plausible outcomes; its vulnerability to a change of assumptions at critical points; the direction in which departures from forecast seem most likely. All this may be elaborated in the text accompanying the forecast, but cannot be incorporated in the forecast itself.

Thirdly, the forecaster has to ask himself, not: 'Is the forecast likely to be right?' – it is better to assume that all forecasts are *ipso facto* wrong – but: 'How wrong might the forecast be? How seriously would it matter if it were that much out? What action would I then recommend which I would not recommend on the basis of the forecast?' In other words, the forecast has to be judged in terms of the policy advice to which it leads, not in terms of the accuracy of the forecast itself.

This may seem strange doctrine to those who want to be shown the basis of policy and imagine that it would be revealed in its nakedness if only all official forecasts were made public. But as I have argued above, policy rests on an assessment of risks taken in a state of ignorance and uncertainty; and advice consists fundamentally in
154

emphasizing particular risks and indicating how those that are least acceptable could be reduced or avoided. Forecasting is one stage in this process of assessing and coping with risks; but it is one stage only, and not always the most important.

If forecasts are published this introduces a further element into the calculations of the forecasters. For they may find it necessary to forecast public reactions to the forecast itself. These reactions will form part of the economic system, and may affect the balance of payments, domestic investment, labour attitudes and so on. In ordinary circumstances one might disregard such repercussions as of secondary importance. But if business confidence is low, the external situation is precarious and official forecasts are believed, the release of a gloomy balance-of-payments forecast could have major consequences.

The forecaster may have to concern himself with other consumer reactions. If he is trying to take a view of the future honestly he may have to ask himself whether it is reasonable to start from the assumption that official policy will remain unchanged. Later, in framing policy advice, he cannot escape raising from time to time the question whether ministers will persist resolutely in their policies and whether therefore it is wise to encourage them to set out on a course from which they may yet have to beat a retreat. Forecasting what ministers will yet do may be a necessary preliminary to analysing the choices open to them now, and assessing the risks to which the various alternatives expose them.

PUBLICATION OF OFFICIAL FORECASTS

I have raised rather obliquely the issue of publication of official forecasts, and perhaps I might conclude by commenting on this at more length.

It seems to me that the reasons why ministers have been reluctant to publish forecasts have little or nothing to do with the accuracy of the forecasts. Of course, it is always embarrassing to be wrong; but the average man knows enough about forecasts from his study of form or his weekly flutter on the pools to recognize that error is human (even if he does not couple this with forgiveness). Error is not the main hostage that a Chancellor thinks he is giving to his political opponents. It is rather that an official forecast becomes in the act of publication a plan. As soon as the figures are released they imply that the government is content that events should be in accord with forecast. This exposes the government to immediate criticism not for

155

what it has done but for what it has not done. Some people are bound to be dissatisfied with the prospects summarized in the forecast; they will agitate for a change of plan where previously they found no fault in the actual policies of the government. On the other hand, if things fall out differently from forecasts the government will be asked what it proposes to do where there might otherwise be no presumption at all that policies were in need of change.

On top of this must be put the reluctance of any government to give publicity to a situation plainly calling for action when it has still to decide what to do. This means that while a government may publish a forecast after the budget (i.e. after it has taken all the action it thinks necessary), it will be reluctant to publish forecasts at set times throughout the year. Governments hate issuing bad news at any time; but they like it still less if they have not had time to couple it with mitigating announcements outlining how they propose to improve matters.

There is also a real risk that government will insist on cooking the forecasts rather than reveal how awful the situation is. If things are worse than is commonly believed the government may well hesitate to give a jolt to opinion, especially if it has reason to expect an early improvement. Forecasts are, in fact, no different from other pieces of information which governments would like to withold: a government which jibs at revealing the state of its reserves of foreign exchange or its short-term foreign debts is hardly likely to want to parade the side of the external deficit that it expects. Similarly, where government thinking on other matters is shrouded in secrecy it would be surprising if there were full and regular disclosure of official economic forecasts. But there are, I admit, some paradoxes. In the United States, where in other respects government is more open than in the United Kingdom, there is no appreciable difference in public access to official forecasts. And in the United Kingdom governments that were unwilling to issue forecasts covering the next twelve months have been known to issue plans covering the next four or five years.

I am not, of course, seeking to argue against publication of forecasts. I am merely emphasizing some of the inconveniences from the ministerial point of view in putting official forecasts in front of an unsophisticated public. Publication exposes them to pressure, and the pressure may be misguided. They may be less free to decide what to do or forced into acting at the wrong time and in the wrong way. But it is axiomatic that ministers are always under pressure and that they may be no less misguided than their critics. It is arguable that they should not have the freedom of manoeuvre that they derive from non-disclosure and that if publication were on a regular footing ministers would be at more pains to avoid situations in which publication would be a serious embarrassment.

My own view is that the issue is not nearly as important as it appears. There is no particular reason to publish official forecasts if outside forecasts are as reliable. The government has no monopoly of forecasting, and the more competition there is the better. Non-official forecasters may lack the resources at the disposal of the government,[1] and there is always some secret information to which they do not have access. But there is no reason why they need stand at any great disadvantage. It should be an aim of government to put them on as equal a footing as possible in respect of access to information: not just current economic information but the analysis and research that goes on in government into how the economy is actually working. The official forecasters on their side have much to learn from the weight of research that is carried on outside the government machine, particularly if it can be focused more clearly on the specific problems encountered in forecasting. Econometric analysis of specific relationships should be the subject of a joint programme of research, and these relationships should be kept under continuous review.

The Limitations of Forecasting

What is needed most is a deeper appreciation of the purposes of economic forecasting and of its limitations. At best, forecasting amounts to no more than a full and systematic review of the evidence in the light of the best available understanding of the way in which the economic system works. This calls for a considerable staff of high quality, which up till now has been hard to recruit: too few first-class economists have been willing to dedicate themselves to this kind of work. Moreover, although techniques have greatly improved and methods have grown enormously in sophistication in the last twenty years, the margins of error in the forecasts themselves, even when small in relation to the magnitudes involved, remain large in relation to policy objectives and to the reserves held against contingencies. This seems to me to imply not that forecasting is a waste of time but that the policy objectives have been in the circum-

[1] Particularly in Britain. I know of no more appalling fact about British industry than that it subscribes less than £30,000 annually to the National Institute for Economic and Social Research.

157

stances too ambitious. It is not possible to run an economy without some fluctuations in economic activity and unwise to try to run it without considerable fluctuations in the balance of payments. If fluctuations are avoided we ought not to give all the credit to the forecasters and policy-makers: luck plays its part too. But if fluctuations do occur – as they will – let us not blame the forecaster too hastily for failing to predict them in time.

9. Economic Planning: the Short Term and the Long[1]

On 10 January, 1956, the Economic Development Institute was launched, quite literally, with a splash. The previous evening, one of the participants in the first course at the Institute arrived late, rather tired, and decided to have a bath and go to bed. Unfortunately, he forgot to turn off the bath water, which in due course found its way through the ceiling on to the beautiful new carpet that had been laid for the opening ceremony.

Dampening though this was, it did not delay the proceedings. But it was not only the bath water that dripped through. A large invited audience arrived in instalments throughout the delivery of the inaugural address by the Director because it happened to be one of those winter days in Washington when a little ice here and there throws the traffic into utter confusion. Thus, although it was heartening to see the audience grow rather than melt away, it was impossible not to reflect, as newcomers dropped in all the way to the final paragraph, on the obstacles to development – in this case the development of a theme – that persist even in advanced societies and on how much, momentarily at least, the Institute had in common with a cinema.

Apart from the need for a continuous performance when there is a message to be got across, the events of the morning pointed a number of salutary morals. One was that interest in economic development tends to increase rather then to decline. Then there was the obvious fact that plans are apt to go awry and that one must exercise constant vigilance to adapt them to new circumstances. But above all, the cold water poured on the Institute by one of its own participants prompted the reflection that it might not be a bad way of studying economic growth to look at it in the light of the Institute's

[1] Tenth Anniversary Lecture to the Economic Development Institute, Washington, 6 January. 1966.

159

own experience, the impulses that made it grow and the obstacles that it had to overcome in doing so.

From this point of view the last ten years have been immensely encouraging. The Institute is now firmly established and its activities have developed in many different directions. All over the world one meets Fellows of the Institute who carry increasing responsibility in the administration of their countries. The collective knowledge and experience of those who have studied or taught at the Institute must by now be enormous and should make it easier not only to carry out the practical tasks of development but to investigate the outstanding characteristics of the process of development itself.

In the presence of that accumulated knowledge and experience I feel rather like a first-year undergraduate called upon to address the Faculty. It would be possible for me, in the brash way that undergraduates have, to prescribe for all and sundry, and propound the lines along which the Institute ought to develop over, say, the next ten years. But it has been borne in on me before now that there is a limit to the advice that can be usefully offered from outside, that the ideas with which one starts off are progressively modified through contact with the hard facts governing the growth of institutions (just as much as economies), and that to trace the inner logic of that growth and fathom the real alternatives of policy needs very careful study of past experience, current resources and future opportunities. Living at a distance of several thousand miles from the Institute and absorbed by other duties, I am not equipped to speculate on its future and am happy to content myself with a tribute to its past. On this anniversary to celebrate its emergence from infancy, I am delighted to have been summoned back from outer darkness although I should have preferred, in my capacity of Chief Ghost, to have confined my share in the proceedings to a walking-on part.

MARRYING SHORT-TERM AND LONG-TERM PLANNING

The first thing that those who attended courses at the Economic Development Institute ten years ago wanted to hear about was how to set about preparing a development programme. Their interest lay not in economic theory nor even in specific problems in applied economics, but in an area of discussion where there are few good textbooks – the administration of economic policy. I thought, therefore, that I might select for my theme today a topic falling with-
160

in this area. What I propose to do is to consider the relationship between the short term and the long in economic planning. I shall deal with a number of problems that are posed by this relationship. For example, what limitations on long-term planning does the need to make short-term adjustments impose? And, conversely, what limitations on short-term policy are necessary in order to take account of long-term trends and plans? What administrative machinery is calculated to secure the right balance between long-term and short-term considerations? What division of responsibility between departments is desirable in order to marry short-term and long-term planning effectively?

Let me begin by reminding you that the idea of planning an economy, irrespective of motive and time-horizon, is of comparatively recent origin. Short-term economic planning to maintain full employment and prevent fluctuations in the level of activity is largely a post-war development. This kind of planning has been associated with the use of budgetary and monetary weapons and the time-horizon rarely extends beyond about one year. The budget, which in most countries is the principal instrument employed, was not originally a tool of economic management at all but rather a means of keeping public receipts and outgoings in an appropriate relationship to one another judged by exclusively financial criteria. Long-term plans prepared by governments with the object of bringing about a systematic transformation of an economy by changes in its economic structure, and with an eye to speeding up the rate of growth of output, are also a post-war development (leaving the special case of the USSR out of account).

But it ought not to be necessary for me to remind you here in Washington that every administration has to weigh up short-term and long-term considerations, and that it is not infrequent for one agency to be entrusted with responsibilities centring on the preservation of equilibrium while another agency is charged with responsibilities for promoting development over time. The most obvious example on the international plane is the existence of the International Monetary Fund alongside the International Bank for Reconstruction and Development. But in many other countries the same dichotomy exists in a different form, with the Ministry of Finance co-ordinating policy on a short-term basis while long-term policy is co-ordinated through a Planning Commission or a Ministry of Planning.

Ten years ago there was no doubt that in the less-developed countries long-term planning was in the forefront, while in the more

L   161 industrialized countries what I have described as short-term economic planning dominated policy. Why was this? and why is it that there have been shifts in both sets of countries towards a more balanced approach?

The answer seems to me to lie in the state of economic theory, the nature of the planning process, itself, the peculiarities of the less-developed contries, and the respective dividends that the two sets of countries expected to enjoy from improvements in planning of one kind or the other. Let me take these in turn.

THE THEORETICAL FOUNDATIONS OF POLICY

Economists devoted a great deal of time before the war to the analysis of economic disequilibrium and had developed concepts and policy prescriptions appropriate to coping with disequilibrating forces. It is true that they did not visualize the persistence of inflationary disequilibrium and were thinking more in terms of conspicuous and sustained departures from full employment. But as soon as economic stability was accepted as a definite aim to which short-term policy should be directed, a whole apparatus of thought was ready to hand to guide policy in the selection and use of stabilizing techniques.

Long-term planning was in an entirely different situation. The purpose of long-term planning was obscure and it was rarely thought of as promoting faster growth. On the contrary, it was usually associated with the use of dictatorial powers in the USSR or in Germany without much regard to consumer welfare, or with war-time controls that no one wished to perpetuate, or (at best) with programmes of recovery designed to ensure that moneys advanced or borrowed from abroad would be used to good advantage. Even when the ideas of planning and growth became firmly associated with one another there was no theory of economic growth on which development planning could rest. Ten years ago almost the only contribution to development planning that economists had made was the popular doctrine that faster growth required higher investment and that planning ought, therefore, to concentrate on raising the level of investment. If anything, the doctrine is even more popular today. But it is doubtful doctrine and far from an adequate theory for policy purposes. If you make higher investment your watchword – even higher 'productive' investment, whatever that is – you may do little to accelerate growth and may even slow it down; and if you want
162

higher investment, planning is not necessarily the best way of getting it.

Thus, whereas short-term policy rested on a definite aim, developed concepts and familiar techniques, long-term policy had no such firm foundation. The idea of growth was slow in acquiring a central importance and the role of the government in promoting growth remains a matter of controversy. Although the preparation of growth models became itself something of a growth industry, economists did not develop a coherent theory of growth capable of translation into policy measures, nor did they provide an intelligible account (except in terms of higher investment) of the role of planning in the formulation of such measures. The preparation of development plans was accepted as natural in countries incurring foreign debt or receiving foreign aid but was not usually justified in terms of faster growth. This in itself meant that planning fell out of favour in industrial countries when the Marshall Plan came to an end but that it continued in favour in the less-developed countries to which foreign aid flowed on an increasing scale.

THE BUDGET AS A PLANNING INSTRUMENT

There is, secondly, the simple fact that the people who plan most successfully are not necessarily the people who issue most plans. Industrial countries all engage in some form of short-term planning: but how many of them issue short-term plans setting out how they expect demand and output to develop over, say the next year? Many of them profess not to engage in long-term planning: but they all issue budgets in which may be concealed commitments stretching over several years and an effort to plan ahead indistinguishable from that underlying many published plans. Budgets bring into existence an elaborate planning machine that is kept constantly in play because fresh decisions about expenditure and revenue have to be made more or less continuously throughout the year.

Budgets also happen to be an almost ideal instrument for co-ordinating short-term and long-term policy. The value of the budget as a short-term regulator has been increasingly recognized in industrial countries and its importance in this role has grown the more they have abandoned the use of administrative controls or become sceptical of the effectiveness of monetary policy by itself to counter inflation. But although the budget has traditionally a rather short-term orientation it is also capable of being used to promote long-term growth, and public expenditure in particular has to be

163

viewed against a fairly long time-horizon. The existence of a highly developed budgetary apparatus and its evolution into an instrument of long-term planning has been one of the most powerful reasons why industrial countries have been slow to create separate machinery for the preparation of long-term plans.

In the less-developed countries the budget normally plays a subsidiary role in planning both short-term and long-term and the administrative machine is less well adapted to successful short-term economic co-ordination involving frequent changes of policy. Very often the necessary information is simply not available for assessing the state of the economy at frequent intervals and deciding what to do. Long-term plans are much easier to prepare because the process can be spread over a longer period of time, and because the intervals at which long-term plans are likely to be altered are almost certain to exceed the intervals between short-term adjustments.

One could, of course, put forward a rather different explanation of the emphasis on long-term plans, although I am in no position to judge what foundation in fact it may have. For young mandarins who have recently returned from the universities of the west, initiated into the abracadabra of input-output analysis, linear programming and other mysteries, the preparation of long-term plans is a very beguiling operation, and one full of intellectual challenge even when the practical outcome may be highly obscure. On the other hand, the short-term management of an economy that is subject to rapid changes in circumstances offers harsher and more restricted choices with little scope for subtlety. Economists have spent a great deal of time analysing the long-term inter-relations between different parts of an economy and given far less thought to short-term relationships whose operation in many economies escapes statistical measurement and in all economies had to be guessed at until comparatively recently. The preparation of a long-term plan, viewed as a kind of statistical massage rather than as a way of ensuring co-ordinated action, is also a much safer occupation than short-term ecomomic planning because there is plenty of time for the plan to be changed or for the public to forget before the calculations and forecasts in the plan are put to the test.

THE PECULIARITIES OF THE LESS-DEVELOPED COUNTRIES

There are, thirdly, differences springing from the special circumstances of most of the less-developed countries. They are highly vulnerable to forces that they cannot control in the short term: agricultural output, which forms a large part of their national income, is subject to wide fluctuations because of weather conditions on the one hand and changes in world prices on the other. Whether one looks at the balance of payments, at the instruments of monetary policy, at rationing and other controls, or even at the budget itself, one has to recognize again and again that large changes may occur which the governments of these countries cannot effectively counter in a short period of time.

On the other hand, the importance of government action designed to promote long-term growth is bound to seem far greater to such countries. They are conscious of the need to make large structural adjustments such as seem to them unlikely to arise as the result of the unaided workings of market forces. They recognize that their economy is in need of a major transformation and that it makes sense to try to visualize the different elements in this transformation in relation to one another by drawing up a development plan. The more industrialized countries, however much they may feel in need of modernization, rarely feel so strongly the compulsion to bring about major structural changes within a comparatively limited period of time.

Largely for this reason the less-developed countries have a strong incentive to concentrate on long-term development plans. The dividends that they expect from such plans – and certainly from economic growth, however secured – are bound to seem large in relation to the dividends from any greater degree of economic stability that they could secure through their own efforts. The industrialized countries, by contrast, have been conscious throughout most of the past half century of the enormous loss that might be inflicted on them through failure to maintain short-term economic stability. Their attention, therefore, has been drawn to the problems that this raises and to the ways in which such losses could be avoided by better short-term economic management. It is only as the dangers of economic instability have receded that attention has begun to be focused on economic growth and on the possibility that government policy might be able to accelerate it. An extra 1 per cent per annum may be hardly worth bothering about when the national income is liable to fall by 5 or 10 per cent in a single year; but if variations in the national income can be kept down to 3 or 4 per cent per annum (in relation to trend) it is no longer possible to treat a cumulative gain of 1 per cent every year as a subsidiary matter.

165

THE GROWING INFLUENCE OF CENTRAL GOVERNMENT

I doubt, however, whether this is the main reason for the renewed interest of the industrialized countries in planning. A more powerful factor has been the expansion of the public sector and of the influence of the central government on the whole economy. The more public expenditure grows, the more necessary it becomes to look at it, not year by year but in relation to longer-term trends, and not item by item, but as part of an aggregate for which the government has to raise the money. It is also necessary to foresee what will be involved in financing this aggregate over a period of years and how far the private sector is likely to be able to keep in step. Public expenditure has to be planned over a period of years, first in order to get the make-up 'right' in relation to social priorities and then in order to get the total 'right' in relation to the parallel growth in GNP. There are also a whole series of interconnections between the constituent parts that it is important to establish and preserve: for example, in order to ensure that there are new schools to match the growth in the school population, teachers for the schools when they are built, colleges in which to train the teachers, and so on. The motives for planning public expenditure must be at least as strong as the motives of any large firm in planning for expansion.

But in fact they are much stronger. The interconnections are not all within the public sector but between it and the private sector. For one thing, the private sector has to provide a great deal of the money. For another, the private sector cannot engage in forward planning without making assumptions about the evolution of government policy and developments in the public sector. Similarly, it is difficult for the government to avoid making some long-range forecast of the way the private sector will grow and natural to go on to frame policies for the whole economy on the basis of this long-term assessment. These policies are already a plan in embryo.

On top of all this comes the strong tendency in the modern state towards centralization. The more pervasive the influence of the central government, the greater the urge to give coherence to that influence in some form of planning. Where central planning has a bad name it is all too often because centralization of power and influence has a bad name. The central government may be disinclined to use its influence to the full because it is conscious of the dangers. But its scruples have generally been overridden by desperation – the desperation of war, or depression, or, nowadays, disappointingly slow growth. In the industrial countries, the vogue for planning is greatest where there is a combination of strong central government and a deep anxiety to grow faster. It is hardly necessary to add that both of these are also characteristic of many under-developed countries.

THE NEED TO IMPROVE SHORT-TERM PLANNING

If the industrialized countries have become more aware of the possibilities of long-term planning it is perhaps time for the less-developed countries to consider whether a more deliberate attempt might not be made to improve short-term planning. They cannot and certainly do not escape sudden pressures that take them unawares and force on them decisions only dimly related to their long-term plans. These decisions are taken by different agencies and departments, sometimes in a remarkably uncoordinated way. The departments in charge of expenditure programmes, foreign aid, taxation, import controls, exchange restrictions, monetary policy, regional policy (if there is one) and all the other aspects of general economic and financial policy, often give the impression of being at sixes and sevens, taking defensive action or fresh initiatives without any apparent regard to the line of policy still pursued elsewhere. Apart altogether from what might be done to bring such action into closer relationship with long-term development plans, there is need for a more wholehearted effort of planning current policy-making. This means putting more administrative time and energy into short-term forecasting, improving the information on which it is based, devising machinery for proper consultation between the key agencies elsewhere in grappling with the problem of economic co-ordination, and devoting to the whole business a larger share of the administrative talent and skilled economic advice at the disposal of the government.

THE TIME-HORIZON

I should now like to turn to the first of the questions which I undertook to discuss. What are the mutual limitations imposed on long- and short-term planning when they have to be carried on simultaneously?

Although this is how I originally formulated the question in preparing this address, it is not how I was inclined to put it once I had drafted it. It now seems to me that it is not the length of the time-horizon that distinguishes one kind of planning from the other.

167

All planning for the future must extend over a period relevant to the problems to be solved; and how short-term and long-term considerations are reconciled within that period depends on the specific problem under discussion rather than on rules of general application. If one is planning transport or power or educational facilities there is no escape from a very long time-horizon although at any point in time one must make the best of the facilities that exist. On the other hand, if one is planning the future level of employment one has to take a short time-horizon although at any point in time one may want to know the underlying trend in the size of the working population. It is the fact that these time-horizons are different that gives rise to the conflict between short-term and long-term planning. The measures taken to preserve a steady level of employment are only too likely to conflict with measures to give effect to a long-term plan for the development of the transport system, power supplies or education.

DEMAND MANAGEMENT AND STRUCTURAL CHANGE

The really critical distinction, as I now see it, is between planning approached as a matter of demand management and planning that takes the form of an effort to influence supply directly. The first focuses on the regulation of demand within the framework of an existing set of supply responses while the second is concerned with structural changes in the social and economic framework itself. The distinction between the two broadly corresponds to the economic distinction between the short period and the long. In the short period demand is subject to much larger fluctuations than supply and, within the limits set by full employment, governs supply. In the long period, the growth of the economy, except in conditions of chronic depression, is governed by the capacity to produce or, in other words, by supply.

The objectives of the two forms of planning coincide roughly with the classical aims of stability (of demand) and growth (of productive capacity), and it is the conflict between those objectives that underlies the conflict between the short term and the long. In an economy where governmental planning was confined to demand management and no effort was made to influence supply except through the regulation of demand, there would be no fundamental difference between short-term and long-term planning. The same kind of calculations would fall to be made in each, the same kind of staff could undertake both, and the co-ordination of economic policy would rest unmistakably with a single governmental agency, presumably the Ministry of Finance. On the equally extreme assumption that planning was directed solely to bringing about structural changes in supply conditions (for example, mobilization for war, or organizing for rapid industrialization) and that demand could be neglected or forced into line by shortages, inflation, or – at a pinch – higher taxes, the co-ordination of economic policy would again be greatly simplified and could be entrusted to a single agency on the model of Gosplan. I am not suggesting that there would be no conflicts between the short run and the long, for this would be absurd. The point is rather that there would be none of the special obstacles to effective co-ordination that arise from the need to consider demand and supply relationships simultaneously – usually in separate departments of government.

The Conflict between Stability and Growth

The conflict between short-run and long-run considerations is essentially a conflict of aims. In plans for a short period such as a year the principal aim is to see to it that no more is undertaken than can be carried out, or alternatively, that enough is put in hand to make the fullest possible use of available resources. Where a long period is taken – four years or more – the principal aim is different: it is to add to available resources and increase the productive potential of the economy by a stated amount and to bring about various 'structural' changes calculated to sustain further growth. The contrast, to repeat, is between planning the use of existing capacity and planning the enlargement of that capacity, with stability the principal aim of the first and growth the object of the second.

I am not concerned, of course, with the extent to which these aims are achieved. There are plenty of sceptics who think that national economic planning makes for less stability not more, and slower growth not faster; and there are others who are enthusiastic about short-term and hostile to long-term planning – or, sometimes, the other way round. My concern is with the aims themselves and the extent to which they are compatible with one another.

Now they are obviously not entirely incompatible. On the contrary, economic stability is a powerful contribution to economic growth and it is conceivable that success in accelerating growth might make for greater stability. Many things can obviously be done to improve one without doing injury to the other.

On the other hand, a full reconciliation of long-term and short-

169

term objectives is far from easy. To accomplish such a reconciliation in a world free from unexpected setbacks it would be necessary to aim at a rate of growth over the short term that it seemed possible in the light of experience to sustain in the long run; and conversely to aim at a rate of long-term growth that was not out of accord with what could be hoped for in the immediate future. In addition, since life is full of unexpected setbacks, provision would have to be made both in long-term and short-term plans for unforeseen contingencies either by setting aside adequate reserves or by refraining from firm commitments for at least some proportion of available resources.

These may seem modest conditions. Most countries, however, have not found them so. How is a country to decide what long-term rate of growth it can sustain even if the balance of payments imposes no external constraint? It is only in recent years that advanced countries have begun to examine the underlying trend already achieved and to recognize the intricacies of the conceptual and measurement problems involved. Nearly all the published estimates cover limited periods of time without any adjustment for changes in capacity utilization, participation rates, occupational structure and so on. One need not go as far as Professor Morgenstern in order to entertain considerable doubt as to their reliability. What then of less-advanced countries with less-advanced statistical services? And even if they are confident that they know how productivity has been growing or (by some miracle) accelerating how are they to translate the policies for faster growth that they propose to adopt into fairly precise estimates of the outcome of these policies? If they start off blindly at what seems to them a reasonable rate of expansion how can they avoid having to change their minds long before they reach their goals because the pace proves to be hotter or slower than they can stand or, still worse, because they begin to have doubts whether they misjudged the situation at the outset?

THE CHANGING SITUATION AND MODIFICATIONS OF PLAN

Equally, every country that issues a plan has to ask itself whether it is consistent with what is currently happening and with the succession of events and decisions that seem likely along the line before the plan is realized. If the plan implies a different course of events and a different set of decisions, whether by government or by private industry, it becomes not only incredible but inappropriate as a basis for further decision-taking, and in the strict sense, not a plan at all.

This may seem a very elementary point; but it cannot have struck those who still think of a plan as something one set of people prepare while another set get on with the job of handling the current situation. The current situation usually changes pretty violently every year or so and a plan that looked reasonable at the beginning of the year may well look near-impossible at the end. Should one then still try to steer towards the original objectives and leave the long-term programme untouched? Or should one alter course at once and try to effect some fresh reconciliation between short-term and long-term objectives? Reason may suggest the latter; but planning is not in practice the rational process that it may be in principle and few countries, if any, make a practice of engaging in continuous modification of development plans except in minor respects.

A clash between short-term and long-term objectives can be softened by the use of reserves to screen the long-term plan from disruption or by the avoidance of completely fixed long-term programmes.

The first alternative is most familiar in terms of reserves of foreign exchange and the line of thought is already familiar in the recent literature on compensatory finance. Because of the perennial shortage of foreign exchange in the less-developed countries they run a constant risk of under-insuring against disruption of their plans and there is a strong case for channelling some aid to them so as to increase the insurance on which they can draw. The second alternative involves giving only provisional sanction to some programmes and parts of others, with the power to impose cuts up to stated limits or to make additions of the same order of magnitude in the later years of the plan. Essentially this means the power to defer or bring forward some parts of the total programme if required so that although the bulk of the plan is firm a contingency element remains. There is no doubt as to the utility of arrangements of this kind as a means of dealing with the uncertainties of the real world. But planning to provide for contingencies is the antithesis of what is popularly thought of as planning: it means either refusing to allocate resources at all or refusing to allocate them firmly and leaving over decisions until it is known how things will turn out.

Suppose that something happens to throw existing plans out of gear. The key question then arises: how is the shock to be taken?

There are some countries where it may not be necessary to do anything at all. A country like, say, Saudi Arabia has large external reserves to cushion any change affecting its foreign trade or the

171

inflow of capital. Its revenue is drawn so much from one commodity, oil, or from customs tariffs that are changed very infrequently, that fiscal policy is of no help in the short run. Public expenditure may be limited almost exclusively by the difficulty of getting work carried out. In those circumstances the only way in which the short-term situation is likely to impinge on the development programme is through the need for some (possibly) informal building control or the use of credit restriction if inflation seems to be getting too much of a grip.

There are other countries where there are almost literally no instruments of short-term policy; for example, in an economy of primary producers with no administrative controls and fixed rates of taxation. In such economies the only protection against short-term dislocation of long-term plans is the use of reserves, either of domestic savings or of external reserves, or foreign borrowing and aid.

But in most countries, there is a need to act and there are policy instruments to use. The danger is that action will be deferred so that when it does come it will be more violent and on a larger scale than if the process of adjustment had begun earlier. The longer the delay, the stronger the government's eventual preference for something that is quick-acting even at the expense of something that would do less harm in the long run.

The preservation of equilibrium, at whatever level of activity, is an object of policy likely to require much less detailed government intervention than faster growth – at any rate if the means to faster growth is taken to be central economic planning. By the same token, action to preserve equilibrium will tend to cut across some of the specific elements in a plan for faster growth because it is likely to include the use of general weapons to check or stimulate demand rather than the specific weapons of expenditure control that usually figure prominently in plans for long-term development. Even when this type of conflict is absent, efforts to cope with short-term dangers to stability are likely to involve some sacrifice of long-term growth.

THE BURDEN OF ADJUSTMENT

Broadly speaking, the government has a choice between action to put the burden of adjustment on the current standard of living (e.g. through higher taxation) or on the means to future growth (e.g. by cutting investment). The choice is not an absolute one since any

172

downward adjustment is bound to have some repercussions on expectations of future trends: investment may suffer indirectly if consumption is cut directly. But there is a choice: and the choice ultimately relates to the price of growth.

The way this choice is made will obviously differ from one country to another. In an authoritarian régime, the government may pitch the claims of the future high not only in the plan it puts into operation but in the obstinacy with which it pursues the objectives of the plan through thick and thin. In more democratic regimes there is usually less readiness to sacrifice the present standard of living on the altar of the future. This affects the shape of democratic plans. But it also affects their immunity to short-term changes. Governments with a limited expectation of life and dependent on popular favour, discount future income fairly heavily and are more alive to current dangers than future risks. This is not the only reason why they are more willing to let a short-term crisis affect investment. All governments have a strong tendency to meet disequilibrium where it arises rather than take offsetting action that will operate indirectly on some other part of the economy. If they have difficulty in maintaining the planned level of investment, therefore, they may well cut it instead of trying to make more room for it. But in any event the problem facing a government is often not which to cut, consumption or investment, but how to reduce the total pressure on resources and this means that consumption, as the largest element in final demand, can hardly fail to take part of the knock.

In practice the range of possibilities is usually limited, and the points at which the plan is threatened also form a familiar list. We all know by now the post-war cycle of ambitious investment plans, balance of payments deficits, exchange control and appeals for more foreign aid, with the inelasticity and variability of agricultural earnings and the shortage of skilled labour as the steady accompaniment.

THE MACHINERY OF PLANNING

I turn from these rather general considerations to more concrete issues about the machinery needed to give them effect. This machinery must obviously differ widely from one country to another so that the scope for valid generalization is limited. One country is governed by a personal dictator, a second by a military junta. One has a President who happens to be extremely interested in economic affairs, in another they are left to technical experts, and in a third

173

the Minister of Finance is himself both a professional economist and an influential political figure. Different administrative solutions are inevitable in these very different situations. I wish I knew more about the solutions that have been adopted in practice: and perhaps it would have been more sensible of me to find out before presuming to address you on the subject. But from long experience of lecturing on subjects about which I know next to nothing, I recognize that ignorance not only emboldens a speaker when knowledge would inhibit but also allows his audience the gratification of correcting his errors. So at the risk of encouraging you in over-indulgence, I propose to go on describing a wood that I have rarely been in and drawing your attention to one or two trees in it that may bear only a coincidental resemblance to the real ones.

THE ROLE OF THE MINISTRY OF FINANCE

It will not surprise you if I say that, as a Treasury official, my main interest in the machinery of planning is in the role assigned to the Ministry of Finance. There are, of course, countries where the Ministry of Finance takes no part whatever in the key decisions. In the Soviet Union, for example, this has been so since the first Five Year Plan; I have never once seen a reference in the western press to the Soviet Minister of Finance. On the other hand, there are countries – of which the United Kingdom until 1964 was one – where the Minister of Finance is entrusted with full responsibility under the Cabinet for the co-ordination of economic policy both short term and long. To some extent this contrast reflects the distinction that I drew earlier between a régime under which co-ordination takes place on the side of supply and one under which it takes place on the side of demand. But it would be misleading to describe the Soviet and British systems in such terms since there is, after all, a Soviet budget which is not presumably just a piece of accountancy, and there is in Britain a large public sector under the direct control of the authorities as well as a variety of ways of influencing or controlling what goes on in the private sector.

Even where economic co-ordination is the responsibility of a single minister this leaves a good many other administrative problems unresolved. Policy is many-sided: economic and other considerations (defence, foreign policy, social justice and so on) have still to be weighed against one another and co-ordinated on some inter-departmental basis. Again, policy-making cannot always be divorced from the execution of policy: if one department is charged with
174

co-ordinating duties its responsibilities are liable to grow the more it scrutinizes and controls the projects and decisions which it co-ordinates. It may become too large to do its job efficiently. Finally, the mere fact that various co-ordinating roles are all united within the ambit of one department does not dispose of the conflicts between those various roles. In particular, long-run and short-run considerations have still to be reconciled; and the reconciliation achieved on an intradepartmental footing is not necessarily more satisfactory than one arrived at through interdepartmental conflict.

INTERDEPARTMENTAL CO-ORDINATION

However co-ordination takes place, a number of different departments control one or other of the key instruments of economic policy. One department may deal with commercial policy, a second with taxation, a third with control over public expenditure, a fourth (usually the central bank, which may retain a good deal of independence) with monetary policy, a fifth with foreign aid, a sixth with relations with subordinate authorities whether state, provincial or local, and so on. Traditionally, the major role in co-ordination is taken by the Ministry of Finance; but the degree to which this department itself operates any of the instruments of co-ordination varies a great deal, partly because of historical circumstances and partly because the size and complexity of the fiscal or monetary system, the importance of the public sector, relationships with subordinate authorities, and so on, differ from one country to another.

The traditional supremacy of the Ministry of Finance in economic affairs has also come under attack for a variety of reasons of which the growing importance of long-term planning is the most obvious. In the first place the objectives of policy are nowadays less exclusively financial: the management of the economy calls for an entirely different approach from the balancing of the budget. Co-ordination is no longer the comparatively simple matter of making next year's expenditures add up to a given total but the much more complex one of trying to maintain domestic and external balance and simultaneously promoting economic growth by government intervention over a wide front. The instruments of policy, as an immediate consequence of this, are also less exclusively financial: the government is far more intimately involved in the affairs of the private sector, quite apart from its own direct responsibilities within the public sector. It has other ways of influencing the economy than making

175

use of monetary or fiscal weapons and these other ways are often more appropriate and effective. Above all, the staff engaged in co-ordinating policy now requires a training extending far beyond finance. However this staff may be distributed between departments, its functions are less concerned with specific areas of policy than with the links between policies, and this applies whether the policies themselves relate to the immediate future or to the long-term development of the economy. What is needed is a grasp of the economic interconnections that lie beneath the surface and are not always apparent to the ordinary administrator or even to the financial expert reared in the ways of Treasury control.

THE MINISTRY OF FINANCE AND THE PLANNING COMMISSION

Now there is no reason why the staff of the Ministry of Finance, given the right training, should be less capable of acquiring this grasp than a staff recruited to some other department and charged with the duty of planning the economy. Indeed, the creation of a separate staff of this kind can lead to unfortunate conflicts which are, perhaps, more observable in the less-developed countries than elsewhere but are by no means confined to them. It is all too easy, for example, for two centres of co-ordination to come into existence, one dealing with day-to-day decisions in the Ministry of Finance while a second, in the Planning Commission, has the benefit of a strong staff of economic experts and may also enjoy the authority that comes from having the Prime Minister or President in the chair. Such an arrangement, with its polarization of long term and short, may easily militate against a proper balancing of the different aspects of policy and leave what I may call the operational departments of government between the upper and the nether millstones. Whatever instruments of policy a department uses it cannot avoid seeking to balance long-term and short-term considerations, however imperfectly or unwisely it may do so. What is usually needs is help in visualizing the consequences, especially the long-term consequences, of alternative policies and in taking due account of the probable state of the economy throughout the period involved. It is not helped if it finds itself under pressure from the Ministry of Finance to take action of one kind to meet an immediate crisis and from the Planning Commission to move in the opposite direction in order to carry out a long-term plan.

The existence of two – or more – central departments is not by itself fatal to good administration. There are more important things in government than consistency; and to aim at perfection in the co-ordination of decisions is not only to pursue a will o' the wisp (since one man cannot decide everything) but to invite the evils of over-centralization. What is indispensable is that there should be machinery for resolving differences and that it should be clearly understood who has the last word. What is impossible is that the machinery should resolve all differences or that whoever has the right to the last word should exercise his right very often.

Let me make this a little more concrete. If differences are to be resolved there has to be provision for consultation. This may seem platitudinous. But it is striking how haphazard, if not indeed nebulous, interdepartmental consultation often turns out to be. I can think of countries where the economic co-ordinators in different departments rarely if ever meet. An economic development plan may be prepared almost in secret and without the participation – perhaps even without the knowledge – of the Ministry of Finance, only to be rejected on completion by those who had no hand in it. Or the central bank may decide to expand credit just when the Ministry of Commerce is about to reduce import quotas. None of the economic departments may be represented in the Cabinet. In other countries there is consultation at the top but the staffs pursue their ways in ignorance of one another's reasoning or diagnosis. Some banker friend of the President may convert him at a week-end party to the expectation of a foreign exchange crisis and the idea may percolate from echelon to echelon without prompting any organized attempt to devise counter-measures. There are countries where the leading economic co-ordinators are hardly on speaking terms with one another; and others where, although on speaking terms, they speak what are practically different languages, the planners talking to a baffled Ministry of Finance in the higher mathematics of capital-output ratios, inverted matrices, and shadow prices only to be answered in classical turkey. Even where the language is the same, the creed may be different: crude believers in the quantity theory cross swords with heretics who are opposed to the use of monetary weapons of any kind.

THE NEED FOR AN ECONOMIC GENERAL STAFF

Consultation, always time-consuming, is likely to be fruitful only if it is based on an agreed view of the state of the economy and the forces at work in it. I attach importance for this reason to the role

M   177 of an economic intelligence staff, centrally located and working closely and continuously with similar staffs in the other main economic departments. The function of such a staff cannot, in my view, be confined to the assembly of statistical data or the preparation of a long-term plan. Its main function should be to analyse and interpret the trends at work in the economy, both short term and long. For this purpose it must have ready access to the latest available economic information from all sources and fashion from that information the best and most up-to-date picture it can of the changes in progress. If the picture changes rapidly, the work of such a staff is bound to be heavily concentrated on short-term changes. But it can never neglect the need to analyse and re-analyse the relationships to which these changes conform. This alone brings constantly before it some of the underlying trends that are equally important to satisfactory long-term planning; and where such a staff exists it can either be enlarged to prepare the outline of a long-term plan or co-operate with a similar staff concentrating on that task.

The duties of such a staff as I have described them relate mainly to the analysis of demand relationships. The natural place to locate it, therefore, is in the Ministry of Finance provided it is the Minister of Finance who takes the key decisions on demand management. But in countries where it is the President in person who takes those decisions the staff would be attached to his office. Where long-term planning is little more than a matter of demand management, and consists essentially of the projection over a period of several years of the main economic aggregates, the variables and calculations do not differ from those entering into short-term planning so that no separate staff is needed. But the more an analysis of supply relationships is involved because planning extends beyond control over expenditure and the regulation of demand into direct intervention by the government, the more will be the need for a rather different staff with more experience of industry and trade. Where planning involves extensive intervention designed to bring about structural changes in the economy, a separate department with a separate staff is likely to be necessary. Either a Ministry of Planning or Planning Commission will be set up, or the existing departments responsible for industrial and commercial affairs will be reorganized so as to co-ordinate the longer-range aspects of their activities.

Such a development creates an obvious danger of duplication. So far as it is activities within the public sector that are planned, the duplication is with the agency or agencies responsible for the control of public expenditure. So far as it is activities within the

178

private sector, the duplication is with the individual departments regulating those activities. Let me take these in turn.

THE PLANNING OF PUBLIC EXPENDITURE

There is rarely any overwhelming need to create new machinery for the purpose of planning the public sector. Indeed, in countries that lack experienced administrators and economists it might well make more sense to concentrate them in the existing agency controlling public expenditure – usually the Ministry of Finance – and build up at least one competent co-ordinating unit. Control over public expenditure already presupposes some rudimentary form of long-term planning. It is true that it can be exercised against a time-horizon of one year and many governments still carry on as if they were entirely free to exercise such control. But everybody knows that decisions taken today – especially decisions to make cuts – have often little effect over the next six or twelve months and that, if genuine control is intended (not just approval of individual projects), it has to be over a longer stretch of time. Commitments to spend public money, whatever parliaments may think or the legal position may be, are not very flexible for several years ahead (except when the commitments take the form of transfer payments); and they do not allow much room for manoeuvre in re-assessing priorities from year to year. Governments have, therefore, a strong incentive to relate their spending programmes to a long-term view of economic prospects whether they draw up a formal plan for the whole economy or not.

It is sometimes argued that people who control spending develop an anti-spending psychology, and that the habit of scrutinizing expenditure programmes causes too little weight to be attached to the growth that such expenditure generates. On these grounds, the programmes need to be championed against their critics by a central department, headed by a major political figure and staffed by a specially selected team of administrators and economists.

If there is any truth in this, it does not rest on the psychology of those who control public expenditure. In my experience there are few pressure groups ranged against the use of any control more powerful than those who administer the control itself. Those who administer import controls are usually the most sceptical of their value; the monetary authorities heartily dislike tight money and take the first opportunity of insisting that the right thing to do is to cut government expenditure; similarly, the controllers of public

179

expenditure easily persuade themselves that there are few or no short-term advantages to be gained from attempts to reduce it in a crisis.

What is more debatable is whether public expenditure can be satisfactorily controlled in the absence of a long-term plan. It is one thing to examine each project thoroughly and make sure that it is well conceived and calculated to do what it purports to do; this, after all is not usually the job of a central co-ordinating department or Planning Commission (although, I need hardly add, they often make it their job). It is a quite different thing to examine projects and programmes in relation to one another in order to make sure that they are manageable in total and so composed as to reflect the priorities decided upon by the government and yield the right balance between one kind of expenditure and another; this is a budgetary operation that is, or might be, carried on in a Ministry of Finance or Bureau of the Budget in much the same way as in a Planning Commission. Whether it is or is not depends mainly on the level of economic sophistication in the Ministry of Finance and on the extent to which the totality of public expenditure is planned on the basis of a view of the probable future development of the economy as a whole.

But there is a further consideration. If public expenditure decisions are taken, or even reviewed, by a Planning Commission, this is likely to engage the Planning Commission in their defence against attempts to revise them on short-term grounds; and this in turn will force the Ministry of Finance (or whatever department is concerned with short-term co-ordination) to rely more exclusively on other instruments of economic stabilization. The Planning Commission, in other words, is more likely to act as a pressure group in favour of fixed (and perhaps also high) expenditure programmes than a department more closely involved in day-to day decisions and policy adjustments.

Expenditure is, of course, only one side of the balance sheet. Annual revenue is far easier to change – at least from the technical point of view. Decisions to alter the level of taxation, social insurance contributions and so on not only take effect more quickly: they are also more straightforward since individual decisions may involve very large absolute amounts of revenue. But this very adaptability (which does not extend, of course, to the system of taxation) makes it unnecessary to plan revenue far ahead, except in a rather tentative way; and it also makes changes in the level of taxation, social insurance contributions, and the price of public services a useful if not indispensable instrument in the short-term

180

regulation of the economy. Whatever department has responsibility for such regulation is unlikely, therefore, to be willing to forego control over taxation; or if it does, the effects are not likely to be very happy.

PLANNING AND THE PRIVATE SECTOR

Let me turn next to the private sector. It has always struck me as odd that most long-term plans should lay so much emphasis on the private sector (which, by definition, is not directly under government control) and so little on the public sector (which they and they alone can control). It is hard to look on public expenditure as something engaged in solely or mainly because of its impact on the private sector, or to imagine that the plans that are published for the development of the private sector are intended merely to help in settling public expenditure programmes. Development plans, except in so far as they are statistical dreams or political fanfares, are guides to action by government departments and, in intention at least, private industry. But the action taken within the private sector is inherently uncoordinated, although there is plenty of scope for co-operation, i.e. voluntary co-ordination, if the government encourages it.

Just as it is practically impossible to segregate short-term and long-term considerations in the control of public expenditure, so it seems to me impracticable to divide the work of departments in contact with the private sector so that it falls into two separate sections, one of a long-term and the other of a short-term character. Every decision has short-term and long-term consequences and every decision is subject to revision in the light of changes from day to day. Hence no such clear-cut division of function is possible. If the work is to be co-ordinated by a single department rather than by ministerial committees, then the department cannot escape interesting itself in current problems as well as those of longer range. It would be possible, for example, to have a Minister for the Private Sector working alongside a Minister for the Public Sector who might simultaneously be Minister of Finance. The work of the two ministers might be co-ordinated with the help of a relatively small planning staff attached either to the Prime Minister or to some senior minister who acted as Chairman of the Cabinet Committee on economic policy and worked in close association with the Prime Minister. In countries with a Planning Commission the two might

181

act as Chairman and Vice-Chairman respectively, the latter taking charge of the detailed working out of the Plan.

MINISTERIAL RESPONSIBILITIES IN PLANNING

As you can see, my bias is in favour of strengthening the hand of the Minister of Finance and equipping him to look further ahead and take more account of producer relationships. But you may reasonably ask whether it is realistic to regard him as a kind of Chief Planner and whether this would put him in too powerful a position in relation to his colleagues. The President or Prime Minister, particularly in a less-developed country, is bound to attach great importance to economic policy and is unlikely to entrust any other minister with full responsibility for it. He will not be content to limit his interest to those issues of policy that become so much the subject of ministerial disagreement that they cannot be settled without his personal intervention. Yet he cannot himself assume responsibility for the whole of economic policy. He may act as Chairman of the Planning Commission, or at least occupy the chair occasionally without presiding over the detailed work of the commission. But it is practically unknown for him to act as his own Finance Minister. The nearest a President is likely to get to personal control over economic co-ordination is when he appoints technicians to head the Ministry of Finance and the Planning Commission. But this does not seem a very satisfactory solution. The more able the technicians are, the more inclined they will be to settle things between themselves without calling in the President at all: this may mean that compromises are struck that reflect, not political will and popular support, but personality and departmental convenience. On the other hand, the less capable the President's nominees the more they may shirk taking decisions or warning him of the dangers ahead so that by the time the issues are brought into the open they have already been decided by events. Not that this need prevent lengthy and earnest debate on what is to be done or solemn amendments to the plan in order to make it seem that the course of events is conforming to government decree rather than the other way round. Whatever the calibre of the heads of the two departments, there is bound to be a tendency for the two to drift apart in mutual distrust, one department limiting its field of view to the immediate future while the other occupies itself with plans for the spending of public money, with only an imperfect grasp of its powers to implement them.

The case for having two central departments, one directed towards the short run and one towards the long, does not seem to me to rest on the reluctance of the head of the government to entrust any member of his Cabinet with responsibility for both aspects of economic policy. If he can find somebody capable of doing such a difficult job well he is unlikely to improve matters by cutting it in half; and he need lose little sleep over the danger that he may build up a rival and successor.

THE NEED TO SURVIVE THE SHORT-TERM

What seems to me unhealthy, and this is the essence of what I have to say, is to think of economic co-ordination exclusively in long-run terms, and still more to think of it as satisfactorily discharged through the periodic preparation of a document called a Plan. Co-ordination means trying continuously to get consistency and this is impossible if there is no consciousness of the need for consistency: if the Central Bank, the Import Licensing Board, the Tariff Control Board, the nationalized industries, and all the departments of government go their several ways without regular consultation and exchange of information. Of course, long-run development is highly important. Economists to whom the long run is meat and drink (even if it is the death of them) are only too well aware of its importance. But to get to the long run you have to survive the short.

10. The Work of an Economic Adviser[1]

It is one of the paradoxes of the world we live in that there always seems to be an abundance of economic advice but a chronic shortage of economic advisers. We all need economic advice because we are so much preoccupied with economic affairs – our own or the affairs of the country or of the world at large. But we never lack for it from those who seek no payment for their services. It is only if you try to hire a professional economic adviser that you have difficulty in finding one. At home wife and children are sure to take a keen interest in such matters as the allocation of resources and the distribution of income. In the press there are plenty of public-spirited characters who are moved to write to the editor from entirely non-economic motives, as well as those equally high-principled commentators who are unremitting in their priestly zeal for the public good. From Monday to Saturday and *always* on Sundays the air resounds with economic advice, especially in Britain where economics was invented and faith in economic policy has displaced older forms of religion.

THE CHANGING ECONOMIC ROLE OF GOVERNMENT

It is in part this concern over economic policy that accounts for the emergence of the profession of economic adviser. Both things reflect a more fundamental change over the past fifty years: the development of a managed economy. When the economy was supposed to manage itself and the government did not profess to control it, there was little need to employ professional economists, because there was little scope for economic policy. This is not to say that economic issues were unimportant: one need only think of

[1] Lecture to the Royal Institute of Public Administration, on 6 November, 1967.

184

the controversies over the Corn Laws, statutory limitation of hours of labour, or trade union legislation, to recall that economic policy remained the subject of active parliamentary debate. But these were issues that occupied Parliament rather than the administrative machine; and when advice was sought it was through royal commissions and advisory councils rather than through the full-time employment of professional economists – of whom, in any event, there were very few.

Similarly in business it was enough for employers to fasten their attention on obvious market indicators without much thought of the way in which the economy functioned or the steps that the government might take to influence its behaviour. It was more important to know what your competitor might do than what the government was up to.

In the last fifty years, however, the role of the government has been transformed. It is now held responsible by public opinion for the standard of economic performance in all directions. Not only does it set out to achieve macro-economic objectives such as a satisfactory rate of growth, full employment, and stable prices, but it is expected to intervene in detail for all sorts of reasons: to limit the rundown in the coal industry; to encourage exports; to promote the reorganization of the machine tool industry; to decide whether makers of artificial limbs are entitled to a retrospective increase in pay; and so on. Whatever happens in the economy the government must be ready to say what it thinks about it and what it proposes to do about it: in speeches, answers to parliamentary questions, White Papers, television interviews, press conferences with attribution and without attribution. Economic policy, from being general and limited in scope, has now become specific and all-embracing.

The business of government has thus become much more extensive, more complex, and hence more in need of specialist advice. The administrative machine is much larger and has now more in common with large-scale business organization. The task of co-ordinating policy and ensuring that it proceeds on common assumptions and in accordance with common rules and priorities has become at once more difficult and more necessary.

It is not only that there are more decisions to be taken and that the economic element in them is more predominant. It is also that the decisions, like business decisions, are more and more quantitative. Where it was once enough to show the direction that things would take, it is now necessary to be more precise and specify the path

185

that they will follow, how fast they will change and how big the change will be. We live in an age not so much of planning as of programmes, budgets, balances; in which the past has to be reconstrued as trends and the future is faced as a series of projections. It is an age in which everything has to be expressed in statistical terms. And since nothing – not even the past – is certain, the statistics are never as hard as they seem and reality presents itself as a vast stochastic process.

In these conditions, economic management gives rise to an increasing need for statistical data and to a continuous flow of such data into and between departments. The government, because it is asked to take responsibility for so much more, has to know much more. It can no longer be content with information reaching it as a by-product of other administrative functions, but has to go out and collect what it needs for purposes of economic management. It has to plague us all, but particularly the business man, with surveys, censuses and statistical returns. It has then to ensure that all the information at its disposal is adequately processed, analysed and assessed.

Both the change in the character of economic policy and the rising tide of statistics create a need for economic advice on a continuing footing. This is as true in business as in government and indeed the employment of trained economists at the working level in business antedates their employment in a similar capacity in government. The growth of the business economist – an animal not unlike the economic adviser but considerably more numerous – is traceable to much the same forces as have given rise to the need for economic advice in government: except that the more economic advisers the government employs the greater seems to be the need to employ economists in business so as to fathom what the government is trying to do or is likely to do next.

The government's need for economists does not arise solely because of its dealings with the private sector. It arises also from its role as manager of the public sector: although when I entered the Treasury in 1961 I doubt if there was a single professional economist anywhere in Whitehall who was engaged on a full-time basis in analysing the problems posed by the need to manage the public sector. I need not remind you that one man in four is now employed in the public sector and that the cash flow through all the agencies of government, central and local, including the capital spending of the nationalized industries, is not far short of half the national income.

The growing importance of the public sector and its implications for economic analysis are far from being fully appreciated even by economists. If a survey were to be conducted of academic research in progress it would be bound to show a heavy concentration on work on the problems of the private sector, or public policy towards the private sector, rather than work on the problems of the public sector. No doubt many economists regard the problems of the public sector as largely organizational – as if economic organization was not itself a prime subject for economic analysis – or as involving no more than the application of cost-benefit analysis – and perhaps, therefore, intellectually unrewarding. I believe all this to be profoundly mistaken. There are plenty of interesting economic problems involved in housing, health, defence, crime, education, pensions and so on, to say nothing of the problems of the nationalized industries. But I doubt whether those economists with no experience of work in Whitehall would be able to perceive the problems that would most repay study. They would probably be unable to make headway with many problems which even those in Whitehall have had to neglect. For example, although the Inland Revenue is one of the largest financial organizations in the country, we know remarkably little about the financial flows to which it gives rise or about their effects on the availability of funds in the private sector. There is practically no literature on the macro-economic effects of different types of government expenditure either in the short run or in the long. Very little has been written on a comparative basis about the management of the public sector in different countries. All these are subjects more likely to be discussed fruitfully, and indeed more likely to be pursued at all, by economists with first-hand experience of government operations.

ECONOMISTS AND ADMINISTRATORS

It follows from what I have been saying that in the modern world a much larger part of the whole administrative machine is concerned with economic policy and that it becomes increasingly difficult to be a successful administrator without some understanding of economics. It is not possible to secure effective economic administration merely by tacking on a few economic advisers: what is needed is a higher level of understanding of economics throughout the administration. Economic advisers can contribute to this by providing the administrators with an education on the job in the economics of public policy; no one who has been in touch with the Treasury over the past thirty years would under-rate the importance of this contribution. It is also important that administrators should have had an opportunity to study basic economic concepts such as is provided by their training at the Centre for Administrative Studies; a great deal of what matters in economics is first-year stuff and well within the grasp of young assistant principals. At least a sprinkling of administrators whose first degree was in economics is indispensable. But it is not necessary to turn every administrator into a professionally trained economist. Whatever the merits of professional economists, they are at best amateur administrators and there will always be many jobs to be done where a little economics goes a long way and administrative ability takes undoubted precedence.

When economists are employed alongside administrators (or, for that matter, business men) there is sometimes a clear distinction in their role: the economists are advisory while the administrators or businessmen are the operators and make the decisions. But very often, particularly in government, the distinction is not so clear: administrators and economists are both functioning as advisers on issues of economic policy and the final decision rests with the minister. In such cases the administrators, whatever they are called, have to be economists of sorts and the economists are rarely able to rest their advice on purely economic considerations. More weight will attach to what the economist has to say the more predominant the economic aspect of the issue to be decided and the more complex the economic considerations entering into it. But the collaboration will be more fruitful if the administrators have a working knowledge of economic concepts and theory and if the economists have some experience of administrative practices and procedures.

A further consequence of the managerial character of modern government is that economic advice has to take account of public reactions, not just of mathematical relationships. Policy takes shape in a climate of opinion; and without the support of public opinion cannot be persevered in. Opinion may be, and frequently is, perverse, ill-informed and confused. But it is largely beyond the reach of economic advisers who are rarely seen or heard and could not, in any event, express views contrary to government policy. They must, therefore, make what forecasts they can of the acceptability of current policies and frame their advice with some regard to what can be sold, not just to ministers, but to the public by ministers. There is a marketing aspect to advising as well as a production aspect.

THE WORK OF ECONOMIC ADVISERS

I turn now to what economic advisers actually do. It is possible to distinguish five (or possibly six) different roles apart from a number of odd jobs like writing speeches, attending international conferences, coping with other economic advisers and trying to recruit more economic advisers.

First of all, they may deal with economic intelligence. This requires them to be experts on the available information of interest to their colleagues and to assess the current situation in the light of the latest statistics as they come to hand. They may also be able to contribute to the handling of current problems by drawing attention to the existence of information or analysis familiar to them from their training as economists but unfamiliar to their colleagues in their more limited field of interest.

The earliest employment on any scale of professional economists appears to have been in this role. The banks and other financial institutions were particularly prominent in setting up economic intelligence departments, because the wide scope of their activities made it necessary for them to systematize available economic statistics and form views on this basis of the likely course of economic activity.

Coupled with this function is that of economic forecasting. This is perhaps the most important operational role in which economists are used, and one in which they are more nearly deciding than advising since they produce the forecasts and do not merely contribute to their production.

The employment of economists in this way is an indication that there is presumably some scientific content to economics since it is increasingly accepted that in some kinds of forecasting at least economists are more likely to be right than non-economists. The most important forecasts prepared within the government are those prepared under the leadership of the Economic Section of the Treasury for the main economic aggregates including GDP and the balance of payments. These forecasts guide the Chancellor in the preparation of his budget and in the management of demand throughout the year. The preparation of these forecasts demands a special skill and flair which are, unfortunately, very rare and neither the National Institute of Economic and Social Research nor the Treasury has found it at all easy to maintain even a minimum staff to carry out this work over the past ten years. Indeed, the advancement of this work within the government over the past decade has

189

rested on a handful of distinguished economists who remain largely unknown to their colleagues outside.

Economic forecasting extends well beyond the forecasting of the national income and the balance of payments. It embraces market research in its more sophisticated forms, manpower forecasting, and the preparation of a host of specific forecasts both in financial and in real terms. Moreover, in addition to short-term forecasting there is plenty of scope for economists in medium- and longer-term forecasting and in planning activities of all kinds. The limitations of economic forecasting should not blind us to the positive contributions which it can make.

Economic forecasting leads on to economic co-ordination, since co-ordination has to be based on as accurate a view as possible of the constraints on policy and of the direction that events are taking. Wherever there is a budget, for example, or a programme, it has to be based on a forecast and it probably requires examination by an economist who can interpret the forecast and bring it to bear on the budget or programme. Especially at the national level, and hence especially in government, it is increasingly important to see the way in which different elements in the economy interact and hence to form a judgment of the risks to which any programme is exposed and of the damage that its non-fulfilment might involve.

Another way in which government economists are used is in economic research. But this rarely involves setting aside a staff segregated from other economists and occupied solely in undertaking research in the form of a series of reports. Such a staff, if competent, tends to be drawn sooner or later into the analysis of urgent problems and so bit-by-bit into work on economic intelligence and advice. On the other hand, some of this work itself generates a need for continuous research. Economic planning and forecasting, for example, rest on observed relationships which alter through time so that the research necessary in order to keep the parameters up-to-date is an integral part of the forecasting function. Very often it is possible to make use of university economists to carry on research in which the government is interested. But this is not always easy to organize satisfactorily and in addition there may be difficulties over the confidentiality of the statistical and other material. In any event, the government will always require the services of some economists to undertake research within government or to follow, interpret and promote research work outside government.

Lastly, economists are used as advisers on policy. This can be taken to include economic co-ordination, although from some points of view this goes more closely with the forecasting function. Advice on policy may be limited to a specific area (e.g. housing), or it may cover a wider field such as development assistance or investment policy, or it can be at the most general level of all and include advice on all the instruments of policy open to the government.

ECONOMISTS IN GOVERNMENT

So far as the government is concerned these functions are performed in Britain by a comparatively small number of people. In the government Economic Service there are about 120 economists scattered over different departments. This is not a very high proportion either of the stock of economists or even of the current output. The universities alone employ over 1,300 economists and are producing every year 700–800 graduates in economics with firsts, upper seconds or undivided seconds. Comparatively few of the members of the Government Economic Service – less than one in three – are established civil servants. A number of others are on five-year contracts but regard themselves as government economists and are likely to remain throughout most of their career in government. About a dozen have been seconded from various universities. The majority are young economists, still in their twenties or early thirties, and employed on a temporary footing.

In addition to the members of the Government Economic Service there are a large number of other economists in government service including, for example, the agricultural economists in the Ministry of Agriculture and a large number of economists in the Research Office and other classes. There are also over 300 members of the Administrative Class with degrees in economics, including at least twenty-five with post-graduate degrees.

Apart from those who work full-time in government departments, there are a number of economists who undertake work for the government on a part-time footing as consultants or as members of a Departmental Committee, or in other ways.

The economists (in the sense of members of the Government Economic Service) work alongside members of the Administrative Class of whom there are about twenty times as many. The Administrative Class includes among its number many who took their first degrees in economics (often with distinction) and this is particularly true of the economic departments. It also includes men who have

191

been handling economic problems for many years and are a good deal more familiar with these problems than most of the economists who lecture on them in academic life. It would be a mistake, therefore, to assume that the relationship is one of professional and amateur, or that the economists occupy themselves with the less urgent but longer range issues of policy while the administrators merely make day-to-day decisions and show little interest in the longer term aspects of the problems with which they are dealing.

What tends to happen is that a division of labour develops between the economists and the administrators, with the economists taking over the more technical side of the problems under consideration and playing a particularly important role where general issues of policy are involved.

Inevitably, when economists enter government service their interest tends to be concentrated on policy decisions rather than on the way they are taken. Administrators, on the other hand, are often more interested in the process of getting decisions taken and implemented. Perhaps their training disposes them to seek a consensus rather than develop a conviction about what is 'right'; perhaps they are less willing to usurp what they regard as a ministerial function; or perhaps they have been longer at the game and are less sure that anybody – economist or not – has the 'right' answer. It is, at any rate, not infrequent for the economist to feel that the administrator doesn't even understand the question and is too willing to blur it by considerations of procedure, while the administrator in his turn has to cope with economists who are unaware that the question has already been studied times without number, that their views are irreconcilable with those of the responsible department, or that what they are urging is in flagrant contradiction with some recent ministerial pronouncement.

But I would not want to make too much of all this, at least once economists and administrators have had time to learn one another's ways. I am speaking more of their immediate impact on one another as I recall it in the war and have observed it on occasion since. Nowadays economists and administrators are not always easy to distinguish in those committee meetings where so much of the business of government is done and the meetings themselves often approximate to economic seminars.

Collaboration between economists and administrators imposes obligations on both. The administrator has to learn how to use an economist – not easy for someone completely ignorant of the subject and sometimes unaware of his ignorance. The economist has to

192

learn that a degree in economics does not necessarily give him an advantage over the administrator who may not only have a far more thorough knowledge of the subject under advice but may turn out to have taken a degree in economics himself. What the economist aims to do is to make a contribution which the administrator, through ignorance, uncertainty or pressure of time, would not be able to make for himself. He has also to be able to communicate and put forward his comments as an economist with lucidity. He has to work as a member of a team and be ready to recognize the importance of considerations other than those in which he is expert.

THE TRAINING OF AN ECONOMIC ADVISER

Young economists, with no previous experience of government, are likely to be better employed in association with other economists than on their own. This is not just a matter of inexperience or diffidence. If they are on their own in a department which has never previously employed an economist they will find it difficult to hitch on to the administrative process and are very liable to be by-passed. They may be unable to learn their job because they are given no job to do and have no idea how to find themselves one. Even more important is the need for discussion and debate with someone who has undergone the same training and speaks the same language. Economists need to develop judgment at least as much as professional competence, and judgment is not easily formed and strengthened in isolation. For this reason it is always desirable that young economists should begin their training as members of an economic staff rather than by themselves without adequate direction.

An economist entering government service usually does not take long to recognize the limitations of his own intellectual preparation for work as an economic adviser. First of all it becomes clear to him that economic logic by itself does not take him very far. There are very few issues where nothing of importance except economic theory is involved. Wicksell put the point vividly enough when he said, 'I would be quite nonplussed if I were to be asked to find an economic proposition other than of merely formal significance which might be adduced as a scientific result recognized by everyone.' The logic has to get to grips with the facts and here the trouble begins, both because there are so many of them and because one can never be quite sure whether they are facts or not.

A new adviser usually finds that he has to begin by gorging himself with statistics. He has to learn how to handle data, not through

N   193 the application of mathematical techniques, but by steeping himself in the figures so as to learn when and how far to trust them. He has then to be educated in the real nature of decision-taking and management as distinct from the simplified versions of maximization procedures that figure in economic theory. He has to acquire the ability to judge a situation from limited and uncertain evidence just like any other administrator (or business man).

In this sense the economist is always in a very different position from other scientists. In the natural sciences there is always *an* answer to a given question although that answer may from time to time be superseded and replaced by a new one. But in economics there is usually a variety of answers which different people would give to a given question and it is not possible to demonstrate that one is right and the other wrong. Even when someone who is not an economist uses arguments that the economist knows to be mistaken to defend a particular line of policy or course of action he is not necessarily on that account wrong. It is not enough to show that somebody's view rests on muddled thinking although it rightly excites some distrust. The older one gets the more conscious one is of the wide range of possible outcomes and unforeseen factors that may enter.

An economic adviser has to arm himself, therefore, with a certain humility, realizing that neither he nor anyone else may know the answer to the major decisions which ministers have to take. This does not imply, however, a need to suspend judgment and decline to offer advice or a willingness to accept that others are necessarily better placed to make the judgment. The conviction and assurance with which the advice is offered – the tone of voice, if you like – has to vary with the state of economic theory on the subject under discussion, with the reliability of the available information, with the adviser's own familiarity with the theory on the one hand and the evidence on the other, and with his degree of confidence in his own insight into all the factors involved.

From this point of view it is a great advantage to an economic adviser to have handled a variety of problems and acquired firsthand experience in a number of quite different situations. Anyone wishing to be an economic adviser would probably do well to alternate between academic life and government service and would be likely to gain from moving between different departments and organizations from time to time. I am inclined to doubt, however, whether there is really any very fundamental distinction here between economic advisers and other administrators. It might be
194

healthy for both, for example, if they had more opportunity of a spell with one of the nationalized industries. My own experience is that I gained more insight into economic administration through spending three and a half years in the planning of aircraft production than from anything I learned in academic life.

There is some danger that the young economic adviser may become infatuated with technique to the exclusion of matters of more importance. It is true that one of the advantages which he enjoys over administrators is often his mathematical training in the handling of statistical data. I should not wish to underrate the importance of this. But pure economics – at any rate in its more mathematical and model-building forms – is rather like gin: it is no doubt highly potent in its pure form but it needs to be mixed with something else. In economics, as in many other subjects, a little first-hand observation is worth a lot of theoretical refinement, although it is equally true that first-hand observation is often not worth very much without an adequate theoretical preparation. Economists need a training in mathematics to give them the necessary rigour and a training in history to give them a sense of process and a more empirical temper. An overdose of either is likely to be damaging. Too much history can operate like opium and lull the mind; too much mathematics can operate like arsenic and instead of stimulating, destroy all sense of perspective.

CONCLUSION

A great many of the economists of my generation served in the government during or after the war and all of them, I think, would agree that this enriched their understanding of their own subject and led them into new fields of enquiry. It has surprised me that so few of the academic economists of this generation show any anxiety to profit from this experience by seeking employment for a year or two as economic advisers in government, in business, or with one of the international organizations. Economic theory has to deal with the economy as it exists; and in a managed economy this means that much of what economists are analysing relates to the activities of government either in the public sector which it manages directly or in the private sector over which it exercises a different form of control. It would seem to me almost inevitable that analysis of governmental activity would profit from immediate experience of the way in which policy takes shape within government. Yet this is an ex-

195

perience which too few young academic economists show any particular anxiety to acquire.

There is, secondly, some danger of a divorce between economic theory and practice if more provision is not made for mobility of economists between academic life and practical affairs. It would be a pity if a division grew up between the 'ins' and the 'outs' and it continued to be true that discussion of the major issues of policy tended to be left largely to the journalists.

Finally, there must always be a need not only for circulation of the economic élite but for personal contact between those who are engaged in advising the government and those who remain in academic life. This contact would be much more fruitful if there were scattered through the universities more economists with experience of government. Their contribution to economic debate would be more constructive and, what is at least as important, they could be more useful critics of current policies.

11. Economists in Government[1]

As a general rule those who act in advisory capacities have had a bad Press. The serpent in the Garden of Eden; the prophets who told Ahab to go up to Ramothgilead; the courtiers of King Canute – they have all been pilloried for giving advice which appears in retrospect to have been unsound. Since we do not know their side of the story they may all be victims of gross injustice ... It is possible that the serpent was really an enthusiast for the higher education of women. The prophets may have warned Ahab to take special precautions against arrows. Perhaps the courtiers decided that it was high time that Canute washed his feet. But the damage has been done. The accepted versions have been so widely publicized that it is probably too late for even modern American research to remove the stigmas.—Sir Dingle Foot, *The Observer*, 11 September 1960.

No modern government could get along satisfactorily without the services of professional economists. Economic policy is too important and too complex for ministers to dispense with their advice. But there is still ample room for debate on their appropriate role. What constitutes an 'economist'? Where and how should they be employed? What should be their relations with other administrators and with ministers? What influence do they or should they have on policy? What changes should be made in present arrangements for their employment in the British government?

GROWTH OF THE ECONOMIC SERVICE

It may be useful to begin by summarizing the existing situation. Throughout this century there have always been at least one or two distinguished economists in government service. Even before 1914 one can point to Giffen and Llewellyn Smith at the Board of Trade, Keynes at the India Office, Hawtrey at the Treasury, Stamp at the

[1] From *Lloyds Bank Review*, January 1970.

Board of Inland Revenue and Beveridge at work on unemployment insurance. (None of these, so far as I know, ever sat a university examination in economics.)

It was not until the Second World War, however, that academic economists entered government departments in groups that came to exercise a profound influence on economic policy-making and co-ordination that had no precedent in British history. Most of these economists left government service at the end of the war or soon afterwards but a few joined the civil service as administrators. The most influential group – the Economic Section of the Cabinet Office – remained in being, although it had to be largely reconstituted when the older members returned to their universities. The Economic Section was moved to the Treasury in 1953 and has remained there ever since. At no time have there been more than a score or so of economists in the Economic Section and the main burden of work has usually rested (as it had done in the war) on a few of the more senior members. In departments other than the Treasury, until 1964, there were few, if any, economists of equal standing. A large number of economists were employed, however, in research and similar capacities in the Ministry of Agriculture, the Ministry of Defence, the Board of Trade and elsewhere. By the mid-sixties there were also over 300 members of the Administrative Class with degrees in economics and a small proportion of these had post-graduate degrees.

In 1964 the incoming Labour government established a Government Economic Service in place of the Treasury Departmental Class and the public was left with the impression that, for the first time since the war, large numbers of professional economists were entering government service. To some extent, this was an illusion: the total number of economists of any seniority remained small. A number of the main departments, however, including the Department of Economic Affairs, the Ministry of Transport and the Ministry of Overseas Development, acquired teams of economists under high-level direction. In the early stages, it was probably more accurate to regard these teams as private 'armies' than as members of a single Economic Service, since many would have been reluctant to move from the department which they entered to any other department, and nearly all were on a temporary footing. Few of the economists who came to Whitehall in 1964 regarded their work there as of a continuing character or expected to pass the main part of their career in government service.

For a long time before 1964 there had been a demand for more

198

economists by the main economic departments but it had proved impossible to meet this demand by attracting enough senior professional economists from academic work. One or two joined the Treasury each year on secondment from their universities for a two-year spell but this left nothing in hand for other departments. By comparison, there were literally hundreds of economists in academic life and the number was mounting rapidly all through the sixties. There was, therefore, very little foundation for the view that the universities were being drained of economists by the government. In the two years between 1964 and 1966 the number of economists increased from about twenty-five in the Treasury Departmental Class to about one-hundred in the Government Economic Service; but a substantial part of this increase could be accounted for by the entry into the DEA of the economists who had previously been recruited as the staff of the National Economic Development Office. What happened in 1964 was, essentially, that the entry of a small group of senior economists into government service made it possible to set up economic sections in a few departments that had previously lacked them, and provided direction within those sections for an increasing number of young economists with no previous experience of government. Coupled with this was the arrival on the scene of a handful of politically committed economic advisers whose role clearly overlapped with that of the Economic Section of the Treasury. All of these have now left government service and the DEA no longer exists; to that extent, things are back to where they were in 1964. But in other respects things have moved on. A far larger number of economists have now had a spell in the Government Economic Service and well over one-hundred still remain in Whitehall, scattered over a wide range of departments.

NEED FOR ECONOMISTS IN WHITEHALL

The first question which I should like to discuss is why one needs professional economists *within* government. They could, after all, be consulted from time to time if they remained in academic life and some of them do exercise considerable influence on policy without occupying official posts. So far as policy reflects ideas rather than pressures, these ideas are highly unlikely to reach ministers exclusively through their officials, and the officials in turn are bound to be influenced by ideas originating elsewhere. The formulation of advice takes place in a climate shaped by prevailing orthodoxies, newspaper comment, lunch-table debate, and all that goes to make up

199

current controversy. What is said inside does not necessarily carry more weight than what is said outside.

But there are a number of ways in which ministers are highly dependent on their official advisers. They are, above all, short of time and cannot sift all the suggestions pressed on them from every direction or decide at leisure the innumerable issues confronting them. They need, in particular, a clear assessment of what is going on and what is likely to happen; and it is no accident that economic intelligence has generally been among the earliest and most important of the responsibilities falling on economic advisers. These are not responsibilities that can be discharged on an intermittent or part-time basis. The latest information has to be quickly and continuously assimilated and its bearing on policy brought at once to the attention of other officials and ministers. Most policy issues, moreover, are embedded in history and reveal fresh facets with the passage of time, so that it is difficult to submit them in isolation for expert judgment without lengthy explanation and constant updating. Even when this is possible, the need for consistency creates a bias in favour of relying on the same group of inside advisers who can exert themselves to keep policy within an agreed framework, rather than turning episodically to an outside expert who may have only an imperfect understanding of the complex of considerations affecting interrelated decisions.

Whatever the position *vis-à-vis* ministers, experience shows that, in dealing with other officials, even advisers who work part-time within a department are at a disadvantage compared with those who are prepared to work full-time. If they are not on hand when something has to be discussed, they are unlikely to be consulted about it later; and it is an easy step from finding that they are not available then to assuming that they will not be available when the next occasion for consulting them arises. There are, of course, ways in which professional economists *can* be used fruitfully on a part-time footing: for example, if they can serve as members of some official committee and join regularly in its discussions or if they can advise on some limited issues of importance rather than urgency. But no amount of part-time advice of this kind removes the need for full-time advisers; indeed, they are often all the more necessary in order to organize part-time advice and make sure that it is offered in the most effective way.

Apart from all this, there is the simple fact that the work of government has a large economic component and that most of it cannot be subcontracted to outsiders, however expert. The formulation of policy is something that goes on all the time and requires a full-time staff, capable of understanding the technical issues involved. In domestic negotiations, international consultations, drafting of speeches, analysis of confidential data, forecasting and so on, a high level of economic competence is imperative in order to deal with the economic aspects of policy. The question, therefore, is not whether it would be sufficient to make intermittent use of outside economists but how to make sure that there is a satisfactory blend of economists and administrators within the government.

ECONOMISTS AND ADMINISTRATORS

This brings me to the relationship between economists and administrators. It is common for professional economists, when they first come in contact with administrators, to feel that the administrator is grossly ignorant of elementary economics. Sometimes this is justified; but it is equally true that the professional economist may be grossly ignorant of administration. There is no need to debate whether it is easier to turn an administrator into an adequate economist or the average professional economist into an adequate administrator. Given the shortage of competent economic administrators, the right thing to do is to try both: to aim at improving the level of understanding of economics among administrators and, at the same time, at ensuring that as many economists as possible are given some experience of administration at an early stage in their career.

It is not as if administrators *have* to be hopeless economists. Far from it. A number of them were trained in economics as undergraduates and a few even hold a higher degree. As time goes on these men become increasingly proficient in those areas of applied economics into which they are carried by their professional duties. There are others whose undergraduate training was not in economics but who are by now thoroughly familiar with the views of economists on the subjects with which they deal – sometimes perhaps too familiar – and who are quite capable of holding their own in argument on the economic aspects of those subjects. In due course, all the senior administrators will have been through the new Staff College or the Centre for Administrative Studies and become familiar with at least the basic concepts and elementary principles of economics. In departments like the Treasury, where there has been a whole procession of economists engaging in day-to-day debates on policy issues with the administrators for the past thirty years, it is inconceivable that some of the economists' expertise could have failed to rub off on the administrators. Men who have been dealing with economic issues for the better part of a life-time may be perfectly capable of appreciating the theoretical niceties, even if they did not include economics in their university curriculum.

Equally, there is no reason why an economist should be thought incapable of learning to have regard to administrative necessities if he is willing to take the trouble. What is needed in the central economic departments is a mixture of administrative competence and economic insight; and too sharp a line of demarcation between economists and administrators does not help to secure this mixture. There ought to be a gradual shading of specific jobs, from those which make heavy demands on skill in economic analysis at one end to those in which the primary requirements are administrative.

It also seems to me misleading to distinguish the work of a professional economist in government from that of any other administrator dealing with economic policy, in terms of the purely advisory functions of the expert as against the operational role of the administrator. Where matters of high policy are in debate this distinction is largely meaningless. The administrator may marshall the advice and decide how and when it is to be presented to ministers. But, in the end, what counts is what is said to ministers, what policy or course of action is recommended to them (if indeed ministers ask for a recommendation) and who drafts any public explanation or defence of the decision taken. On all these matters, when advice is tendered – for it can be no more than advice – the administrator is in exactly the same position as the economist, in the sense that he is bringing his own specialized knowledge and experience to bear on the issues in dispute. Not that the work done by administrators and economists is, in fact, the same. There is usually a fairly clear distinction in role between the two; in some matters, such as economic forecasting, the economist is in the lead, while in others it is the administrator.

Administrators have to learn to call on economists to help them. They may be able to do most of their job without technical advice because most of the issues in debate do not involve very profound economic analysis. But there are times when the economic considerations that arise are not all simple; and nearly all the time the professional economist will have a different perspective and be conscious of different economic interactions from his administrative colleagues.

Twenty-five years ago Lionel Robbins, then Director of the Economic Section, put the point this way:
202

'Economics, at any rate that branch of economics which is most applicable in practice, is not a difficult subject in the sense in which, say, mathematical physics is difficult. The most useful economic principles, when stated in their most general form, seem often mere banalities, almost an anti-climax after the formidable controversies amid which they have evolved. Yet experience seems to show that, without systematic training in the application of such platitudes, the most acute minds are liable to go astray; the economist, if he is humble, is heir to perpetual surprises, as he witnesses the incredible muddles which continually emerge from lay discussions of these matters.'

This is part of the truth, but part only. For one has to admit that the laymen who might be led astray by intellectual muddle are not necessarily much better off if they are marched in bold logic by the priestly up the garden path. Economists may avoid muddle only to fall into other traps baited to catch the theoretician: excessive abstraction, disregard for inconvenient facts, unwarranted assumptions. I should be inclined to cite, by way of example, some of the current controversy over monetary policy, which is hardly calculated to alert the layman to the full inconvenience, in seeking to manage the economy, of relying heavily on sharp fluctuations in interest rates, short and (more particularly) long.

The case for increasing the number of senior economists in government service is not assisted by representing economists as supermen able to transform the economy by technical wizardry and rendering administrators and ministers alike redundant. Anyone who talks in these terms has never been present at the kind of discussion between economists, administrators and ministers at which it is by no means uncommon for the economist to talk politics, the administrators to talk economics, and ministers to discuss administrative complications. An outsider might have great difficulty in deciding who, among those present, was a professional economist and would be very unlikely to conclude that an economist, as such, was in a particularly powerful position in debating most issues of economic policy.

In the last resort, economic advice must be tendered by experts because neither economic analysis nor economic problems stand still. The framework of thought within which professional economists work does not stay constant. There are advances in theory; and, as we found in wartime, circumstances may change so drastically that it is necessary to bring new principles to bear on economic problems and most unsafe to go on relying on analytic conventions

203

that were framed to deal with a different order of things. It circumstances change abruptly, a smattering of the current orthodoxy is no longer sufficient and it becomes doubly important to have that firmer grasp of economic logic that comes from a thorough professional training.

When it is suggested, therefore, that the government has too few economists this apparently straightforward and incontestable proposition lends itself to different interpretations. It may mean that the level of economic sophistication of the average administrator is too low; or that too few of the top administrative posts are held by economists; or that the administrators do not take advantage of the economic advice to which they have access and do not rate sufficiently highly the importance of adding economists to the staff of their department. If all these interpretations held good, one might still ask whether Whitehall is any different in these respects from other areas of management either in the public or in the private sector of the economy and whether, if the government has too few economists some other sphere of activity – the Universities, for example – has too many. So far as my own experience goes, I can only record that from the moment I returned to Whitehall in 1961 there were always a large number of unfilled vacancies for economists which I was under pressure to fill and that there was no lack of awareness in most departments of the need for easier access to economic advice. The posts remained unfilled largely because the sixties were a period of unprecedented expansion of the universities. Chair after chair in Economics was created without much regard to the competing claims of government; but it is fair to add that these claims were not vigorously asserted at the political level and supported by a drastic revaluation of the terms of recruitment until the arrival of the Labour government in 1964.

RELATIONS WITH MINISTERS

What, next, of relations with ministers? Many people, I suppose, have an image of the chief economic adviser, whoever he may be, closeted with his minister every working day, pouring out new proposals, briefing him for debates in Cabinet or Parliament, rebutting press criticism, and more or less monopolizing the unfortunate man's time and attention.

Different ministers have, of course, different habits. But, in my experience, anything of this kind is rare. For days, weeks, even months, an economic adviser may hardly set eyes on his minister and, when he does, it is likely to be in a meeting of some size, along with several other officials, to discuss some specific issue of policy. The man who is most likely to see the minister alone at frequent intervals is his chief adviser, the permanent head of the department. The normal situation, therefore, is that the economic adviser keeps in close touch with the permanent secretary and makes sure that his views are known to him, leaving it to a large extent to the judgment of the permanent secretary how these views are further discussed within the department and how and when they are presented to the minister.

The fact is that an economic adviser, to be effective, has to work within the administrative machine, not as a kind of hanger-on of the minister or *éminence grise* who can get his way single-handed. He is advising the administrators far more than he is advising the minister. In the Treasury, the Director of the Economic Section is *ipso facto* himself an administrator, since he has to organize and circulate economic intelligence, including the preparation of economic forecasts, and is responsible for advising on the general direction that fiscal and monetary policy should take. The staff of the section are also an important part of the whole machine, working alongside other officials on a host of problems in which their influence is exerted almost exclusively in the form of expert advice to their colleagues.

Economic advisers usually maintain contact with ministers on paper far more than in the flesh. The time of ministers tends to be fully taken up with urgent immediate issues and it may be only when they get back home with their papers that they have time to reflect on more general trends and policy problems. What is put down on paper and gets into their despatch box may make a more lasting impression than a few random comments in a meeting. Under modern conditions, at any rate, advice is normally offered either in minutes or memoranda or at the meetings where a decision has to be taken.

It might be supposed that relationships are somewhat different with advisers of the minister's own political persuasion. This is not always so. Ministers resent being asked to accept political judgments which they feel to be not only within their competence but within their province; and they resent it still more when these judgments are passed off as economic advice. They want to have the alternatives presented to them as clearly and objectively as possible and do not want to listen to economists who are plainly riding a hobby-horse or straying into fields in which they have no claim to be expert. Of

205

course, ministers may deceive themselves. They may be in more need of political than of economic advice, poor judges of public opinion, or unskilled in handling it; but that will not make them any the more disposed to be put right by economic advisers or handed a ready-made political programme by them.

It is also difficult for an adviser who seeks to work through the minister and without regard to the administrative machine to make any great impact unless he is in a department of low competence and little cohesion. However much a new arrival may think that he is the professional and the permanent civil servants are amateurs, he soon finds that, unless he has an extraordinary mastery of detail, the boot is usually on the other foot. His knowledge and experience are necessarily limited in comparison with the combined weight of the top civil servants, if he insists on ranging them against him. There may be exceptions when someone of outstanding ability, personality and drive is introduced into a sluggish department; and no one would question that it takes only two or three first-rate men working together to revolutionize a department. But in an efficient department with heavy responsibilities teamwork is indispensable; the much-derided committees provide a filter that separates sense from nonsense in a way few individuals can hope to do; and an able adviser soon learns that he must argue things out with his official colleagues, not appeal constantly over their heads to the minister.

A COUNCIL OF ECONOMIC ADVISERS?

It is sometimes suggested that it would be desirable to set up in Britain a body comparable to the American Council of Economic Advisers. No doubt there are people who imagine that such a Council has existed in Whitehall from 1964 onwards.

Where there are a large number of senior economists in the central economic departments it is obviously desirable that they should take counsel of one another. When they were scattered over the Treasury, the Department of Economic Affairs and the Cabinet Office, as in 1964–8, it was inevitable that some provision should be made for them to meet and discuss the major issues calling for expert advice, and that from time to time other senior economists in Whitehall should be associated with them when the affairs of their departments were involved. But there is no analogy here with the Council of Economic Advisers. The Chairman of the Council (Mr McCracken, for example), is more than a professional adviser of the President. He is a political figure like the Secretary of the Treasury and is expected to expound and defend government views in public in a manner more in keeping with ministerial office than with purely official responsibilities. He is, at the same time, the head of a group of economists, all of whom hold office during the tenure of the party in power in the United States and are liable to lose office simultaneously with a change of administration.

It would be possible to run the Government Economic Service on this principle; but if that were done it would distinguish the economists in government service from the administrators in a very sharp and undesirable way. It seems highly unlikely that, if the appointment of economists were on a political footing, the appointment of administrators could continue unchanged on a non-political footing.

If the idea is that there should be a number of senior economists in the main economic department (i.e. the Treasury) and that they should be jointly responsible for advising the Chancellor of the Exchequer and the government, then that is exactly the situation that obtained in Britain until 1964 – and to some extent since 1964. If, on the other hand, the idea is that the economists in different departments should meet and discuss problems arising out of the policies pursued by these different departments – that is, if what is suggested is an interdepartmental committee of senior economists – then this has nothing in common with the Council of Economic Advisers in the United States. The existence of the Council in no way diminishes the need for interdepartmental machinery. Although a very influential body, it is by no means the only source of economic advice available to the President of the United States and he has usually found it necessary to set up co-ordinating machinery between the Council, on the one hand, and the Treasury, the Bureau of the Budget and the Federal Reserve Board, on the other, often with the help of a personal economic adviser, such as Mr Gabriel Hauge or Professor Arthur Burns. In Britain, the counterparts of all of these agencies except the last already form part of the Treasury, so that formal machinery for co-ordination is unnecessary.

The idea of a Council of Economic Advisers seems to me to hark back to the situation in the 1930s, when the Economic Advisory Council was set up with no executive responsibilities and as a purely advisory body. We have surely got beyond that stage and need to have a more intimate relationship between professional economists and those who are framing and carrying out policy in Whitehall.

One innovation that might be tried in Britain would be to find a way of associating the economic advisers to the government with

207

economists in industry and in the universities. The economists in government service need to be able to exchange ideas with their professional colleagues and with the economists advising the leading business and trade unions organizations. I do not, of course, want to imply that no contacts of this kind take place now. The Treasury is able to take soundings at least once a year of the views of the leading forecasters on the economic outlook; and it sometimes organizes a small conference of academic economists on specific topics. Government economists are not conspicuously absent from the succession of university and other conferences that take place throughout the year. But there are no standing arrangements that bring government and non-government economists together to debate current policy.

The record of the CEA highlights one weakness of arrangements in Britain. The CEA has made very full use of the means at its disposal for educating the public: through speeches, testimony and publications it provides a running commentary on the general economic situation that has a major impact both on the general public and on professional economists. The Annual Report of the Council, for example, is on a level of analysis not approached by any reports published in this country. By contrast, Treasury economists in Britain have had practically no channel of publication. There have been plenty of efforts to release more information, especially in *Economic Trends*, and there is now a short monthly assessment of the economic situation. But the primary responsibility for explaining policy rests with ministers. It is idle to expect that officials will ever enjoy complete freedom to publish their views on how policy is working out if this means freedom to be critical (even by implication) of ministerial acts and professions. All that can be hoped for in the immediate future is that there should be greater openness on matters on which public debate is desirable and the technical considerations involved need full exposition. Public expenditure should provide a useful touchstone of the government's attitude.

ADVISING THE CABINET

A second, rather different, idea is that there should be a chief economic adviser in the Cabinet Office to advise the Cabinet as a whole (and brief the Prime Minister), on the analogy of the Chief Scientific Adviser. The Economic Section of the Treasury started life in the Cabinet Office, so there is nothing unthinkable about rebuilding a staff of economists there. It can be argued that, although the

Chancellor must usually take the lead in economic policy, he is bound to look at any issue of policy from a rather special angle and that other ministers will see things differently. Are they not entitled to look for advice from a more impartial source than the Chancellor's own staff? And is the Prime Minister to form a judgment on economic issues without any expert guidance or entirely in the light of such exchanges as arise out of interdepartmental disagreement?

The answer to both of these questions is, I think, no. But this does not imply either the creation of a large economic staff in the Cabinet Office or (what is by no means the same thing) the designation of a group of economists within the Cabinet Office to serve on the personal staff of the Prime Minister. It is axiomatic in Whitehall that expert staffs should go with operational responsibilities and that it is dangerous to try to build up a policy-making staff that is answerable to no minister and duplicates the work of a staff that is. The Economic Section in the war acted as the staff of the Lord President (not as advisers in some undefined way of the entire Cabinet). The Lord President was chairman of the main economic committee of the Cabinet and in practice was co-ordinator of economic policy (for a time the Chancellor was not even a member of the Cabinet). Now that co-ordination is unmistakably the function of the Chancellor it is inevitable that the main stronghold of economic advice should be the Treasury and, within the Treasury, the Economic Section. If the Section were moved back to the Cabinet Office the only result would be the growth of a new, rival Economic Section in the Treasury and the gradual fading away of the old for lack of sufficiently powerful backers.

This does not mean that the existing situation is a satisfactory one. Other economic ministers do need more adequate economic advice: not, however, from a staff in the Cabinet Office but from advisers in their own department. If their responsibilities make them take a different view of economic problems, this will be far more adequately reflected in the advice they get if it comes from men who have day-to-day experience of these responsibilities. In particular, if it is felt that the Treasury sees things too much in financial terms or without sufficient understanding of industrial affairs (and I am far from convinced that this need be so), then there is all the more need for a powerful staff of economists in the ministries that are in immediate touch with industry: in particular, in the Ministry of Technology. I should have a great deal more confidence that the recent changes in the machinery of government will work out satisfactorily if I thought that the Ministry of Technology had a staff of economists to match the Economic Section of the Treasury.[1]

It also seems to me unsatisfactory that the Prime Minister should have no professional economists in his staff. Without seeking to do the work of his ministers for them, he has to keep himself informed on what they are doing and not doing, and he may need expert comment and briefing, particularly if he is not himself an economist. The natural way to secure this would be to assign a senior economist of good sense and tact to Sir Burke Trend, to work under his direction alongside other civil servants on the Prime Minister's staff.

INFLUENCE OF ECONOMISTS ON POLICY

I come next to the impact of economists on policy. This is not a matter on which it is easy to be specific, for it is often very hard even for those at close quarters with policy-making to know what does in the end shape the decisions that ministers take – or, still more, do not take. Many decisions reflect no more than the force of events and all that an economist can claim in respect of those is that he may be more alive than others to underlying trends and so better able to prepare the ground for the decisions to which they point. Where the issue is in dispute, who except the minister (or even including the minister) knows what clinched the matter? It is very rarely that one can say with confidence that the decision would have been different if x had not been there. The people who think they know and say so may, in fact, be ill-qualified to judge.

It might be thought that, at least, one can trace the influence of economists in those major acts of policy, such as devaluation in 1967 or the decision in 1964 not to devalue, that presumably follow consultations between ministers and their professional advisers. But, here again, one can take too much for granted. Without access to the documents (and perhaps even then) it is impossible to know for sure what attitude was taken by this adviser or that, how and when any individual adviser was consulted, and what weight was attached to his advice. If political considerations took precedence over economic, the collective influence of government economists might well be nil. What one can say is that there is no reason to assume that the comparatively elementary considerations urged upon the government between 1964 and 1967 by economists and commentators in the press were unfamiliar to the government's

[1] The Ministry of Technology has disappeared since this was written. But similar remarks might apply to the Department of Trade and Industry.

advisers, whatever conclusions they drew as to the appropriate policy to recommend.

Whenever I have read in the press that 'the Treasury thinks this or that' the statements have not only been untrue most of the time but quite often the reverse of the truth (that is, as far as the official Treasury could be said to have a view, rather than a collection of conflicting opinions). So it would be a great mistake for any member of the public to assume that this measure or that can be ascribed with confidence on the basis of press comment to advice from government economists.

There are, of course, well-known examples of the influence of government economists, notably Professor Kaldor, on specific acts of policy. But even those examples are not always quite as well-established as is popularly supposed. It has become common form to make Professor Kaldor a kind of economic bogeyman and to saddle him with responsibility not only for SET, but for every new tax introduced over the past five years and a lot more besides. So far as corporation tax and capital gains tax are concerned, it is obvious that these taxes would have been introduced whether Professor Kaldor had entered government service or not.

There can be no doubt, however, that economists have exerted very considerable influence on government policy. Some of this influence comes from the academic community and the climate of thinking which radiates from there either by influencing the views of ministers or by changing the ideology of the public. The influence of economists within the government has been more at the technical level. It is most conspicuous in what is called nowadays 'demand management' (i.e. the regulation of purchasing power so as to maintain a steady pressure of demand on the economy). But there have been many other areas of policy where the economists have had a field-day: international and domestic finance, for example, the enunciation of criteria for public investment and the pricing policy of the nationalized industries, regional and transport policy and so on.

I am not, of course, arguing that the influence of economists has been always to the good. I can imagine one of my more cynical professional colleagues suggesting that the net effect of demand management has been to make the economy not more but *less* stable, that, whatever purpose the Treasury forecasts may have served, what ultimately moved the government to act was almost invariably the balance of payments or an unacceptable level of unemployment, and that the forecasts themselves were usually not

211

much (if at all) better than a straight trend projection. Even when it came to judging how big a package was necessary to stabilize demand, what devaluation would do to the balance of payments, or how investment would respond to higher interest rates, economists inside and outside government, he might continue, have been hopelessly wrong.

I do not myself share these views but I recognize some element of justice in them. So far as the management of the economy reflects the capabilities of economists and the limitations of their power to forecast, it is bound to be imperfect. Economics is still a very imprecise science: as Jacob Viner remarked some years ago, 'the list of handicaps of the economic theorist as a participant in the formulation of public policy is discouragingly long'. But anyone who feels too defensive about the uses of economics has only to enter a department where no economists are employed to have his faith in the subject restored. The fact that doctors make mistakes does not prove that it is best to reject medical advice.

RECRUITMENT PROBLEMS

There is not much point in arguing about the role of professional economists in government if professional economists themselves keep out. There will probably always be difficulty in attracting enough top-rank economists to the departments where they are most needed. They show no great reluctance to join the Treasury, provided they do not lose financially (and this is not a minor reservation for an economist who has to move to London for a couple of years or so). But they are often more difficult to persuade to enter other departments, where there may be more exacting specifications because of the larger administrative duties falling to heads of the economic sections in these departments. There are inevitable difficulties in matching candidates with the views of departments on the kind of man they will accept. It has happened more than once that nothing less than a direct approach by the minister overcomes the hesitations of a suitable candidate or brings home to the department that he really is suitable.

A special problem in the past has been lack of previous experience of government work. This is obviously desirable, although not indispensable, in a man who is chosen to set about building up an economic staff in a department that previously lacked one. A remarkably high proportion of the leading applied economists in this country, or of those holding university chairs in economics,
212

have had experience of government service, usually in the Treasury. But few of them have been prepared to give up their chair in order to return to a full-time government post. Perhaps this would not have applied had really large salaries been offered, without regard to relativities. Since it was not possible to disregard relativities the matter was never put to the test; but even if it had been, there would almost certainly have been a continuing shortage of candidates for the top posts.

A further problem is that of obsolescence. Professional economists are liable to find their stock of intellectual capital depreciating over time, and need to be given opportunities of renewing it. This can best be done for those who enter government service either by releasing them for further study and research or by bringing in academic economists for limited periods of service. Keynes, in a war-time comment, foresaw both possibilities:

'It will not be easy to bring in academic economists for brief periods except possibly quite early on in their careers. But . . . I should have thought that there might be a great deal of movement between the academic world and the Civil Service, not by way of a sabbatical year but for longer periods . . . An economist would be in government service for a number of years together. But he would not necessarily come in at the beginning of his career, nor remain there until the end. I am sure that some arrangement of this kind is essential wherever up-to-date technical qualifications are required: as, for example, in scientific work.'

Whatever the need to encourage movement in and out there is also a need for continuity. The small group of economists who have made their career in Whitehall, while others came and went, have received little public recognition of the burdens which they have carried or the pioneering work which they have done. When comparisons are made with the US, for example, they are never mentioned. Yet, it would be difficult to find in Washington a group of career civil servants of the standing and originality as economists of Christopher Dow, Jack Downie, Bryan Hopkin, Fred Atkinson and Wynne Godley, to name only five.

On the whole, recruitment arrangements for junior members of the service are working well. Successful recruitment calls for contact with the universities to make known how the service works. Such contact may take the form of an occasional talk to students, a visit to establish what research work is in progress, or participation in a conference between government and academic economists. The service has to sell itself both to the young graduate and to the junior member of staff, and get across to them what they have to do if they want a spell of government service. The recent trend towards direct advertising by departments where there is a vacancy is a step in the right direction.

Nowhere is the change in the attitude of the Civil Service to the employment of young economists more apparent than in the matter of training. New entrants with no more than a first degree (or even with a master's degree) soon feel the need for further training if they are to be looked upon as experts by their contemporaries among the administrators. They also become conscious of the need for greater familiarity with econometrics and statistical analysis. Some of this training may be given 'on the job'. But, for the more systematic training that a professional economist must ultimately draw upon, a further period of academic study and research is highly desirable, if not indeed indispensable. Facilities for such study have generally been provided. After a few years an entrant can be released to take a one-year M.Sc. degree at government expense. Indeed, he can do so without actually being established or binding himself to spend the whole of his career in Whitehall. There has also been provision for many years for older economists to take approved employment outside the Civil Service, and several have taken advantage of this and worked at the National Institute of Economic and Social Research or elsewhere for several years before returning to their department.

Because their greatest strength lies in so-called 'macro-economics', it is natural that economists should be concentrated in the central economic departments, where the operation of economic forces over the whole of the economy has to be foreseen as well as possible. It is no accident that it was in the Treasury that a small group of high-level economists survived after the war or that it should have been the Treasury, DEA and the Cabinet Office that attracted the most distinguished among the influx of senior economists in 1964. Indeed, it is arguable that too many economists flocked to the central departments and too few to those which had no staff of economists at all. So long as there was only a handful of economists in Whitehall it made sense to hold them together in the Treasury, with no more than a few secondments to departments badly in need of help. But, with the increase in numbers, it is now highly desirable to set about building up an adequate team in other economic departments.

It seems to be easier to attract economists of high calibre to deal with general problems of the economy than to get them to give time to industrial problems. The three departments outside the Treasury best supplied with economists are those dealing with transport. regional problems and overseas development. But there are whole tracts of government where economists are very poorly represented. One need only think of the enormous sums represented by defence, health, pensions, the police, etc., to reflect how little is written by economists on the problems involved. This is no doubt partly because there are few lectureships or courses of study in the universities devoted to these subjects, while the economics of transport (or education), by contrast, engages the attention of large numbers of economists. Perhaps the government should seek to endow lectureships in those areas of study where it feels the need for academic enquiry. The same kind of problem arises in connection with the nationalized industries. There is plenty of interest in fuel problems, while hardly anyone works on electronics and the problems of the Post Office: this at a time when the capital expenditure of the Post Office is higher than in any other industry (including electric power).

Above all, there is a need to support a broader attack on the problems of modern government and to make more systematic use of research for this purpose. The economic sections that are being built up could be extended to include representatives of other disciplines and should, in particular, interest themselves in problems of organization as well as other instruments of policy (for organization *is* a policy instrument). The duties of these sections rarely allow them adequate time for research. But, even if they did engage in more research, this would not dispense with the need for academic study of the same wide range of problems. We know far too little about the success of different forms of organization inside and outside government; about the interconnection between economic and administrative factors, for example in relation to problems of decentralization; about the interaction of economic and social forces.

More research into these problems might in future be undertaken within the government. But the problems of government in the large need also more academic study. It is time that we had in this country some place of research akin to the Brookings Institution in the United States. (The Canadians have already come to a similar conclusion about their own country.) There are various places where this might be done. The American analogy points to London, and to

215

an institute familiar with applied economic problems, like the National Institute. But the location is less important than action to put more weight behind research into economic problems as they present themselves to government.

Index

217

GEORGE ALLEN & UNWIN LTD

Head office:
40 Museum Street, London, W.C.1
Telephone: 01–405 8577

Sales, Distribution and Accounts Departments
Park Lane, Hemel Hempstead, Herts.
Telephone: 0442 3244

Athens: 7 Stadiou Street, Athens 125
Barbados: Rockley New Road, St. Lawerence 4
Bombay: 103|5 Fort Street, Bombay 1
Calcutta: 285J Bepin Behari Ganguli Street, Calcutta 12
Dacca: Alico Building, 18 Motijheel, Dacca 2
Hornsby, N.S.W.: Cnr. Bridge Road and Jersey Street, 2077
Ibadan: P.O. Box 62
Johannesburg: P.O. Box 23134, Joubert Park
Karachi: Karachi Chambers, McLeod Road, Karachi 2
Lahore: 22 Falettis' Hotel, Egerton Road
Madras: 2|18 Mount Road, Madras 2
Manila: P.O. Box 157, Quezon City, D-502
Mexico: Serapio Rendon 125, Mexico 4, D.F.
Nairobi: P.O. Box 30583
New Delhi: 4|21–22B Asaf Ali Road, New Delhi 1
Ontario, 2330 Midland Avenue, Agincourt
Singapore: 248C–6 Orchard Road, Singapore 9
Tokyo: C.P.O. Box 1728, Tokyo 100–91
Wellington: P.O. Box 1467, Wellington

FACTORS IN ECONOMIC DEVELOPMENT

SIR ALEC CAIRNCROSS

This is a most valuable compendium of the lessons Sir Alec has drawn from his wide and varied experience and is of interest as an insight into the outlook on this subject of the Economic Adviser to the Government.

'. . . *extremely wide ranging and refreshingly unparochial . . . The author has his feet firmly on the ground, and everywhere he is fair-minded, humane and sceptical.'* The Observer

'*As one would expect, the treatment is distinguished . . . The whole discussion of these broad issues is well done. It has the great merit that the difficult, delicate and often highly frustrating impediments to any theory of growth are not assumed out of the way . . .'*
The Financial Times

'*Cairncross expounds his views on these issues of economic development with a wealth of illustrative material, all of it used with great skill and wisdom.'* The Guardian

BRITAIN'S ECONOMIC GROWTH 1920-1966

A. J. YOUNGSON
Professor of Economic Science, University of Edinburgh

What is wrong with Britain? Why do we have recurrent balance of payment crises? Are we really much less efficient than the Germans? Why does our share of international trade go on declining? Are the trade unions an obstacle to progress?

Such questions as these are frequently asked. Answers are all too often based on a review of the situation at the moment, perhaps with a word about changes in the preceding twelve months. Such answers are unlikely to be of much use. An economy, like an airliner, cannot suddenly change its course; it is subject to persistent forces and tendencies; it is powerfully affected by what has happened in the recent and sometimes in the not so recent past. Therefore to understand the problems of today we must know something about how persistent they are, and about what solutions have already been tried.

'*The book bears the hall mark of erudite scholarship, will be invaluable for reference purposes, and has the dual merit of being lucidly written and eminently readable.'* The Scotsman

BRITAIN'S ECONOMIC PROSPECTS

RICHARD E. CAVES and ASSOCIATES

'. . . the most up to date, comprehensive and penetrating study of our economy, its problems and prospects, to appear between the covers of one volume. A distinguished group, mainly of the younger generation of American economists, under the leadership of Professor Caves, the chairman of the Economics Department at Harvard was got together by that eminent body, the Brookings Institution, to provide this invaluable analysis.'　　　　　SIR ERIC ROLL in The Times

'. . . the best single volume on the British economy since the war. . . . This is the most scholarly and practical study which exists of our economic problems.'　　PROFESSOR ALAN DAY in The Observer

'. . . much the best single volume analysis of the British economy to have appeared.'　　SAMUEL BRITTAN in The Financial Times

The first paperback reprint of this celebrated book. As is shown by these brief extracts from the massive reviews which greeted its appearance, there is no other comparable source of information and analysis. The American team has put together the whole of the available information in a way which has not been done before. But this is not only the best guide to our present position and future prospects. Historically too it will remain an outstanding study of the British economy in the 1960s. And beyond that, it is an instructive example of economic analysis, an exercise in method for future generations. As Sir Eric Roll commented: 'The authors bring to their difficult task . . . a splendid technical equipment.'

The Brookings Institution

BRITAIN'S ECONOMIC PROSPECTS RECONSIDERED

SIR ALEC CAIRNCROSS (EDITOR)

This book is a sequel to *Britain's Economic Prospects*. Two years later, just after the British General Election, six of the American economists who prepared the Brookings Report met with a number of other leading economists from Britain and the United States, at a weekend conference to review the findings of the Report.

Britain's Economic Prospects Reconsidered is neither a detailed critique of the Brookings Report nor a rejoinder to it, but rather an attempt to reassess British performance and policies in the light of experience since devaluation. Its central concern is the question of why economic growth in Britian since the War has been slower than in other countries. It will command the same attention as the original Report.

THE BRITISH ECONOMY: PROBLEMS AND PROSPECTS

JOHN AND A-M. HACKETT

With a Foreword by Professor Brian Tew

The seriousness of the present crisis in Britain calls for a reconsideration of the aims and methods of economic policy. This book provides a detailed survey of economic events from the early 1950's to the present day. It therefore provides a unique source of reference on economic policy issues, and will also be invaluable as a textbook of recent economic history.

BRITISH BUDGETS IN PEACE AND WAR 1932-1945

B. E. V. SABINE

As the *Daily Telegraph* put it, B. E. V. Sabine scored a redoubtable first with his *History of Income Tax*. He now follows this with the study, in depth, of a shorter period. The period is 1932 to 1945, from the depression through the limited recovery of the late thirties to World War II and its ending, examined from an unusual angle, and told in relation to the Budgets of the period.

By ingenious cutting and scrupulous editing, he presents each Budget as the participants, from the Chancellor to the backbencher, saw it and debated it. Only at the end of each summary does he draw his own conclusions and encourage the reader to do the same from the evidence available. The four Chancellors, Chamberlain, Simon, Wood and Anderson, emerge, incidentally, with a good deal of credit.

'It is a rare gift to be able to write as Mr Sabine does, lucidly and humorously on such a subject.'   The Economist

'will be invaluable for economic and political historians of the period.'

Daily Telegraph

'well written . . . amusing . . . essential reading.'   The Spectator

LONDON · GEORGE ALLEN & UNWIN LTD